Studien und Texte zur Geschichte der Architekturtheorie,
herausgegeben von Werner Oechslin

John Ruskin
Werk und Wirkung

50. Goldau.

«Goldau», Taf. 50 in: John Ruskin, *Modern Painters*, vol. IV, London 1856

Internationales Kolloquium
Stiftung Bibliothek Werner Oechslin, Einsiedeln
24.–27. August 2000

John Ruskin
Werk und Wirkung

gta Verlag, Zürich • Gebr. Mann Verlag, Berlin

Studien und Texte zur Geschichte der Architekturtheorie,
herausgegeben von Werner Oechslin

Akten des Internationalen Kolloquiums
«John Ruskin. Werk und Wirkung»,
herausgegeben von der Stiftung Bibliothek Werner Oechslin

Redaktion
Elisabeth Sladek

Gestaltung
Philippe Mouthon (Konzept)
Angelika Wey-Bomhard (Satz und Layout)

Scans und Bildbearbeitung
Reproatelier E. Höhn, Oberhasli

Druck
Grafisches Centrum Cuno, Calbe

ISBN 3-85676-110-1 (für die Schweiz)
ISBN 3-7861-2452-3 (für die übrigen Länder)

Die Deutsche Bibliothek – CIP-Einheitsaufnahme
Ein Titeldatensatz für diese Publikation ist bei
der Deutschen Bibliothek erhältlich.

John Ruskin on himself and things in general, Liverpool 1893, Einband

Werner Oechslin

Zur Einführung

> «Ruskin hat unser Zutrauen zu dem Wirken der Apostel wieder wach gerufen und zu den Möglichkeiten und Vorteilen, die darin liegen könnten, die Gefühle der Masse anzurufen; aber man kann sich nicht verhehlen, daß die Bewegung, die er hervorrief, stark gefärbt war von einem zeitgemäßen romantischen Enthusiasmus, welcher die Massen der Eroberung der Schönheit entgegendrängte, wie im Mittelalter die religiöse Schwärmerei die bewaffneten Scharen zur Eroberung des Gelobten Landes trieb.»
>
> Henry van de Velde, «Kulturpolitik»,
> in: *Insel-Almanach auf das Jahr 1912*, Leipzig 1912

Der Anlass zur Publikation der hier vorgelegten Arbeiten, Ruskins hundertster Todestag, ist wie immer bei solchen Gelegenheiten 'rein zufällig'. Die Beschäftigung mit Ruskin im nicht angelsächsischen Kulturraum jedoch ist in höchstem Masse überfällig. Das deutschsprachige Schrifttum zu Ruskin bleibt dünn. Wolfgang Kemps 1983 erstmals erschienene Darstellung *John Ruskin. Leben und Werk* steht weiterhin ziemlich alleine da. Er selbst hatte schon damals das krasse Missverhältnis eines umfassenden englischen Schrifttums und nur spärlicher deutscher Zeugnisse kritisch vermerkt.[1] Er musste bis auf Charlotte Broicher, die 1899 Ruskin noch besucht hatte, zurückgreifen, um festzustellen, dass es einmal anders war. Damals hatte der Leipziger Verleger Eugen Diederichs Ruskin – angefangen bei der biographischen Darstellung Charlotte Broichers – in sein umfassendes Buchprogramm aufgenommen und ihm eine Verbreitung gesichert, die trotz umfassender Übersetzung der kunst- und architekturkritischen Werke in erster Linie dem Schriftsteller oder gar dem Propheten galt. «Der Schriftsteller hat etwas zu sagen», so steht es in *Die Kunst zu lesen*, «was er für wahr und nützlich oder für schön empfunden hält».[2] So ausufernd breit war die Rolle des Schreibenden definiert und dementsprechend akzeptiert. Ruskins Schrifttum bot sich als nie versiegende Quelle solcher – 'sozialethischer' – Zeugnisse an. Johanna Severin liess 1907 in dieser Absicht der Übersetzung *Über Mädchenerziehung* diejenige zu *Die Kunst zu lesen. Arbeit* folgen. Und so wie hier beliebig Texte verbunden und zum passenden Thema zusammengeschnürt wurden, so bediente man sich – durchaus dem Zeitgeist folgend – der Ruskinschen Texte als eines Steinbruchs. Mit ausdrücklicher Genehmigung Diederichs' publizierte Carl Hagemann so 1906 die *Worte Ruskins*

1 Vgl. Kemp 1983, S. 453.
2 Vgl. Ruskin 1907, S. 9.

und fügte sie ein in die Reihe der *Breviere ausländischer Denker und Dichter*. Ruskin – zerlegt – in Aphorismen, wie sich dies für einen Propheten geziemt. Das lag damals im Trend. Und Charlotte Broicher, die 1902 feststellte, Nietzsche komme «in seiner Genealogie der Moral zuweilen zu denselben Ergebnissen wie Ruskin», um dann aber doch den Unterschied festzustellen, fasste das in die Worte: «Denn wo Nietzsche negativ ist, ist Ruskin positiv».[3] Ruskin eignet sich bestens zur Hebung der Moral und zur Stützung bürgerlicher Tugenden. Dem sollte wohl auch in erster Linie der ganze Bildungshintergrund zugeführt werden. Die Kultur bricht sich in moralischen Maximen. «Unter symbolischer Schönheit verstehe ich alles, was an materiellen Dingen zur Erweckung der Vorstellung immaterieller Dinge charakteristisch ist».[4] So ein Zitat aus *Modern Painters* in der Herausstellung jenes Ruskin-Breviers Hagemanns. Und wie diese, moralisch so hochzielende Aussage, wieder angenehm in den kulturellen Hausgebrauch zurückgebogen wird, kann man gleich dem nächstfolgenden der *Worte Ruskins* entnehmen: «Ich halte dafür, dass das allerhöchste Schönheitsbewusstsein übertragen wird durch eine leise, durchsichtige, sanfte, aber nicht glänzende Fläche von Weiss und blassem aber warmen Rot, das von dem reinsten und zartesten Grau gedämpft ist – wie in den schöneren Teilen des menschlichen Anlitzes, in schneebedeckten Gipfeln und weissem Vogelgefieder unter rosigem Licht».[5] So lässt sich der Prophet und Moralapostel Ruskin auch von der Kammerzofe anfassen!

Breviere
ausländischer Denker und Dichter

Herausgegeben von

Carl Hagemann und Edgar Alfred Regener

Band III

Worte Ruskins

J. C. C. Bruns' Verlag
Herzogl. Sächs. u. Fürstl. Sch.-Lipp. Hof-Verlagsbuchhandlung
Minden i. Westf.

John Ruskin on himself and things in general, Liverpool 1893, Titelblatt und Porträt

C. Hagemann, Worte Ruskins, Band III in: Carl Hagemann, Edgar Alfred Regener (Hg.), *Breviere ausländischer Denker und Dichter*, Minden 1906, Titelblatt

Die künstlerische und architektonische Moderne hat kaum übertriebenes Interesse gezeigt, Ruskin von diesem Modergeruch zu befreien. Daran hat die frühe Liebe Le Corbusiers für Ruskins Schriften nichts nachhaltig verändert. Das Verdikt gegen das gehasste oder eben zumindest zweigeteilte neunzehnte Jahrhundert (pro oder contra Maschine, Glas und Stahl!) hat eine offenere Diskussion im Keim erstickt. Jene Ruskinbegeisterung im ersten Jahrzehnt des zwanzigsten Jahrhunderts passte zwar zu den Idealen und Vorstellungen des Deutschen Werkbundes und der sie umgebenden Gebrauchskultur, aber sie blieb darin auch häufig genug stecken. Dabei war schon bei der Publikation des ersten Bandes (1900) der Werke Ruskins bei Diederichs die eine oder andere Einschränkung deutlich hervorgehoben. «Wir Deutschen schwanken noch zwischen Anglomanie und Anglophobie haltlos hin und her», schrieb damals Wilhelm Schoelermann. Und dem ging die Warnung voraus, ja nicht «auf Ruskin als den unfehlbaren Orakelmann zu schwören». Schliesslich wäre es jetzt Zeit, «uns auf uns selbst (zu) besinnen».[6] «Ruskin war seinem Volke ein Erzieher; uns kann er das nicht sein».[7] Deutschland, so muss man beifügen, hatte längst von Schiller und Fichte bis zum Rembrandtdeutschen seine

3 Vgl. Broicher 1902, S. 227.
4 Vgl. Hagemann 1906, S. 86.
5 Ebd.
6 Vgl. Wilhelm Schoelermann, «Zur Einführung», in: Ruskin 1900, S. 2.
7 Ebd.

JOHN RUSKIN
AUSGEWÄHLTE WERKE IN
VOLLSTÄNDIGER ÜBERSETZUNG

BAND I

BUCHSCHMUCK VON J. V. CISSARZ-DRESDEN
UMSCHLAGZEICHNUNG VON O. ECKMANN-BERLIN

JOHN RUSKIN
DIE SIEBEN LEUCHTER
DER BAUKUNST

AUS DEM ENGLISCHEN VON
WILHELM SCHOELERMANN
MIT VIERZEHN TAFELN

VERLEGT BEI EUGEN DIEDERICHS, LEIPZIG 1900

eigenen 'Erzieher' gewählt und Verleger wie Diederichs stellten diesem Thema ganze Buchreihen zur Verfügung.[8]

Gleichwohl stand das Publikum damals in Deutschland – wie auch in Frankreich – unter dem Eindruck des 'späten', 'prophetischen' Ruskin. Sein Kunstwissen mochte noch so weitverbreitet sein und in Handbücher in der Art des *Hand-Book of Art Culture* auftauchen, wie es der Rev. W.H. Platt «for the use of Schools and Colleges» schon 1877 in New York durch John Wiley & Sons verbreiten liess, es war in erster Linie der Moralapostel und Prophet und der religiöse Schriftsteller, der die Gemüter bewegte. Schliesslich waren auch noch die von J. Howard Whitehouse zum Zentenar von 1919 herausgegebenen Studien «Ruskin The Prophet» gewidmet. Dort definierte C.F.G. Masterman als «Prophetical Books» jene späteren, um die *Fors Clavigera* versammelten Schriften. Masterman gestand damals ein: «I find some difficulty in going back to the old artistic writings».[9] Der Kunstschriftsteller scheint hinter dem Propheten zu verschwinden, so wie ja eben auch seine vielschichtigen Analysen und Argumentationsweisen in scheinbar so 'klare' und 'eindeutige' Aphorismen längst zerlegt und aufgelöst wurden.

Denkt man an das Schicksal eines anderen Grossen des 19. Jahrhunderts zu Beginn der Moderne, an Gottfried Semper, dem Alois Riegl mechanistische Denkweisen

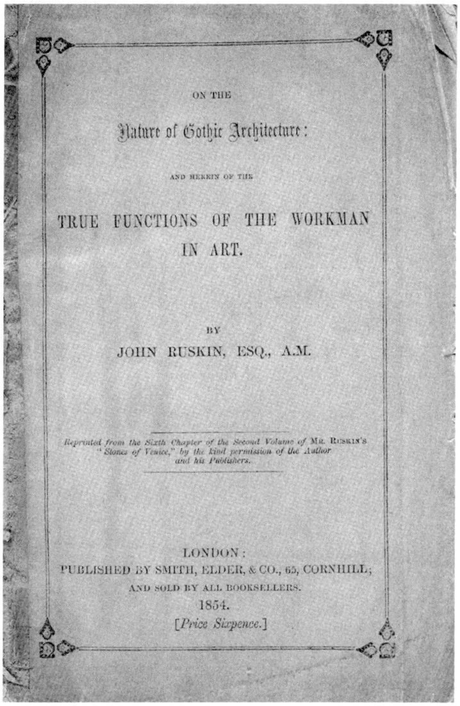
ON THE

Nature of Gothic Architecture:

AND HEREIN OF THE

TRUE FUNCTIONS OF THE WORKMAN IN ART.

BY

JOHN RUSKIN, ESQ., A.M.

Reprinted from the Sixth Chapter of the Second Volume of MR. RUSKIN'S "*Stones of Venice,*" *by the kind permission of the Author and his Publishers.*

LONDON:
PUBLISHED BY SMITH, ELDER, & CO., 65, CORNHILL;
AND SOLD BY ALL BOOKSELLERS.
1854.
[*Price Sixpence.*]

John Ruskin, Die sieben Leuchter der Baukunst. Aus dem Englischen von Wilhelm Schoelermann, in: *John Ruskin. Ausgewählte Werke in vollständiger Übersetzung*, Band I, Leipzig 1900, Titelblatt

John Ruskin, *On the Nature of Gothic Architecture: and herein of the true functions of the workman in art*, London 1854, Einband

unterschob, was dann Peter Behrens dazu veranlasste, zur Überwindung Sempers aufzurufen, so ist es umso erstaunlicher, dass – im Zuge des erwiesenen bedeutenden englischen Einflusses auf die Anfänge der modernen Architektur – John Ruskin durchaus in positiver Weise neu erscheint. Nikolaus Pevsner war es zwar mehr als geläufig, dass Ruskin ein Maschinenhasser war («[he] hated the machine and consequently the new steel and glass architecture»),[10] doch fand er gleichwohl 'dank Ruskin' zu einer in sich geschlossenen und abgerundeten Vorstellung der kurz zuvor aus der Taufe gehobenen 'modernen Architektur': «Gropius», so Pevsner in seinem einflussreichen, erstmals 1936 in London publizierten Buch Pioneers of the Modern Movement, «regards himself as a follower of Ruskin and Morris, of van de Velde and of the Werkbund. So our circle is complete».[11] Diese Formulierung zu einer in sich abgeschlossenen modernen Kunstepoche ist in mancher Hinsicht äusserst bemerkenswert. Natürlich ist die damit neuangesetzte, 'moderne' Bedeutung Ruskins von der weitherum beanspruchten sozialen Programmatik des Neuen Bauens nicht zu lösen. Pevsner hatte zwar Ruskins Bedeutung als «of a primarily aesthetic nature» bezeichnet und Morris den sozialen Part zugewiesen. Aber

8 Vgl. Oechslin 1999, S. 117ff.
9 Vgl. Charles F.G. Masterman, «Ruskin the Prophet», in: Whitehouse 1920, S. 45ff., insbes. S. 47.
10 Vgl. Pevsner 1936, S. 136.
11 Ebd., S. 42.

man konnte ja schon in so klassischen Darstellungen wie den *Philosophischen und Sociologischen Grundlagen des Marxismus* von Tomáš G. Masaryk, damals noch Professor an der böhmischen Universität Prag, eine entsprechende Wertung lesen: «Eine sociale, ja bereits eine socialistische Aesthetik entwickelt sich in England. Ruskin's Einfluss ist an der englischen Kunst zu merken, und seine socialistischen Schüler sind noch weiter vorgeschritten. Von Morris und Bax besitzen wir schon eine ganze Geschichte und Theorie der Kunst vom socialistischen Standpunkt aus».[12] Da wird es also, 1899, beschworen: «L'art pour l'art ist das Grab der Kunst».[13] Und man erkennt, wie weit man mittelbar eben doch von Ruskins früheren Untersuchungen, in denen jemand radikal der Kunst und nur der Kunst und immer wieder der Kunst in ihren verborgensten kapillaren Gefässen und Verwicklungen mit der Natur und dem Leben nachspüren wollte, gemeinhin weggerückt war.

Anlässe und Bedürfnisse gab es also zuhauf, um vom 24.–27. August 2000 in Einsiedeln ein von der Stiftung Bibliothek Werner Oechslin organisiertes internationales Kolloquium zu «John Ruskin. Werk und Wirkung» durchzuführen. Die Ergebnisse dieser Tagung, an deren Vorbereitung Robin Middleton wesentlich mitgewirkt hatte, liegen nun vor.

12 Vgl. Masaryk 1899, S. 506.
13 Ebd., S. 507.

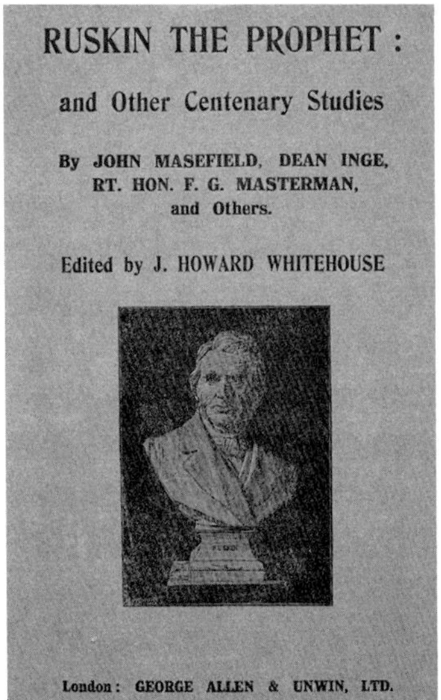

John Masefield, Dean Inge, Charles F. G. Masterman,
Ruskin the Prophet and Other Centenary Studies,
hg. von J. Howard Whitehouse, London 1920, Einband

«Lake, Land and Cloud (near Como)», Frontispiz in: John Ruskin, *Modern Painters*, vol. III part IV, London 1856

John Dixon Hunt

Ruskin and the poetry of landscape architecture

I.

Between November 1837 and December 1838, while still an undergraduate at Oxford, John Ruskin, under the pseudonym «Kata Phusin» (According to Nature), contributed a series of essays to *The Architecture Review*, edited by John Claudius Loudon. The series, entitled *The Poetry of Architecture*, was never concluded, and the essays were not gathered into book form until first a pirated American edition of 1873 (John Wiley & Son) and then an authorized English edition by Ruskin's own publisher, George Unwin in 1893.

Since these were Ruskin's earliest writings on architecture, they have largely been studied by his commentators as prolegomena to later work,[1] as promissory notes for the full scale studies of modern painting and architecture that were to preoccupy him for twenty years from the early 1840s in *Modern Painters*, its sequel into *The Seven Lamps of Architecture*, then into *The Stones of Venice* and back to *Modern Painters* via *The Political Economy of Art*. Ruskin himself certainly endorses this proleptic analysis by constantly explaining his current work by its debts to earlier – the most famous example of which, perhaps, is his claim that «All *Modern Painters* together will be the explanation of a parenthesis in *The Stones of Venice*» (10.xlvii). And beginning *Praeterita* in 1886 he looked back to the writing of *The Poetry of Architecture* in 1837 and asserted that «I find myself in nothing whatsoever changed» (cited I.xliii).

A few critics have attempted to read *The Poetry of Architecture* for its own sake rather than as anticipations of later pronouncements, yet their tendency is still to engage in proleptic analysis, reading the essays as immature stumblings toward both a viable subject matter and a personal voice and agenda.[2] But what his critics forget is that throughout the next twenty years of writing on painting, architecture and cultural production, Ruskin himself still scarcely knew in advance where he was going or to whom he was talking or about what: in 1846 his father shrewdly observed that John's search for «real knowledge» will «neither take the shape of picture nor poetry» (8.xxiii). So, instead of looking at *The Poetry of Architecture* as a seed-bank of

1 Shapiro 1971, pp. 70–83.

2 See in particular Dougherty 1982, pp. 16–31; Stein 1985, pp. 328–341.

later ideas (which only with hindsight could we or Ruskin himself identify), I want on this occasion to ask how it enabled Ruskin to recapitulate and formulate his learning and experience up to that point. My project here is, so to speak, to read backwards from *The Poetry of Architecture*, as if (momentarily) ignorant of his later œuvre.[3]

I want in fact to argue that these essays contributed to Loudon's *Architectural Review* concerned, not in fact architecture, but more properly landscape architecture. Further, that Ruskin's approach exactly mirrors the state of thinking about that topic at the time he was writing – that is to say his handling of his subject falls between the usage of «landscape architecture» that then customarily referred to the depiction of buildings within landscape paintings and the usage of the phrase to which we are now accustomed, designating the layout and embellishment of grounds. Given the picturesque underpinning of much of *The Poetry of Architecture*, it is of course wholly apt that one meaning for Ruskin of the term «landscape architecture» would have meant the representation by painters of buildings in their landscape settings: such is the thrust of a book that Ruskin might even have known, G.L.Meason's *On the Landscape Architecture of the Great Painters of Italy*, printed at «Hullmandel's Lithographic Establishment» and published in 1828. Yet just two years after Loudon stopped publication of *The Architectural Review* and so abruptly terminated Ruskin's series of essays, he issued the complete writings of the landscape gardener, Humphry Repton, under the title *The Landscape Gardening and Landscape Architecture* ... 1840 was thus the first time the phrase was used as we would understand it today. Furthermore, Ruskin even contributed a long footnote to Loudon's edition of Repton's writings, an essay significantly entitled «On the Proper Shapes of Pictures and Engravings».[4] It seems likely then that Ruskin could have not only heard the term 'landscape architecture' from Loudon, but have gathered something of his mentor's enthusiasm for landscape gardening in which Loudon had been trained. Loudon was, after all, what Ruskin would later call his «first literary patron» (I.xxxvi) and a somewhat uncritical promoter of the young writer. The closest Ruskin comes to designating the field of landscape architecture as we understand it today is in his phrase «garden architecture», which is (he notes) «utterly useless unless it be assisted by the botanical effect» (I.158). But, as will be shown later, Ruskin shows many indications of having read and absorbed some of Repton's writings, presumably as a result of Loudon's direction.[5]

Ruskin may seem to stumble about for his theme(s), for that is how we are likely to read *The Poetry of Architecture* in the light of Ruskin's many later indirections, contradictions and digressions (this latter being the standard reproach leveled against his writings by critics from his mother onwards). But perhaps it is also possible to read the essays as Ruskin's formulation of landscape architectural theory in the light of his own experiences of visiting landscaped sites during the family's extensive summer tours[6] and of other discussions and readings on this topic of which we have no direct record. If we attend to *The Poetry of Architecture*, then, for what it actually does as opposed to either what it occasionally promises but never delivers or what we think, because of his later writings, Ruskin would have been concerned to write about at the start of his career, we may be surprised at how much the agenda coincides with the standard repertoire of conceptual writings on landscape architecture at that time. This repertoire shares at least four central topics with Ruskin's essays: the siting of buildings in the landscape; the 'character' of such sites; the picturesque constituents of both built work and visitor's responses to it; and the national identity that was either articulated by design or readable into it.

Ruskin himself and the editors of his collected works, Cook and Wedderburn, were so wedded to the notion of the genius-as-autodidact that they omitted to investigate debts that did not simply illuminate Ruskin's own self-education and learning; the editorial annotations to the text of *The Poetry of Architecture* in their Library Edition, for instance, are almost entirely devoted to subsequent writings by Ruskin; they make, astonishingly, no attempt to reference the considerable literature on landscape architecture that had been accumulated during the half century of so before Ruskin went up to Oxford. I am not, however, engaged in tracking down Ruskin's sources; but rather in suggesting how *The Poetry of Architecture* takes its shape and direction from a topic, that until 1840 did not get its current label of landscape architecture, but that had nonetheless a fully established literature and even tradition, into which the young writer could tap to provide Loudon with these essays. I shall then, of course, need to consider why it was that Ruskin did not seem to be further interested in a landscape architectural direction for his work.

3 The only study that directs its attention wholly to Ruskin's debts is Paul Quinn Beeching's unpublished MA thesis at Saint Louis University (Beeching 1956). The author kindly made a manuscript copy available to me during the final stages of drafting this paper, and I am most grateful to him for his time and trouble and for its confirmation of many of my own lines of enquiry.

4 In the modern facsimile reprint of Loudon's 1840 volume Ruskin's contribution is the long note: Loudon 1840, pp. 32–38.

5 This point is made well by Beeching 1956 as well as in passing by myself elsewhere (see note 28). By the time Ruskin got to know Loudon, the latter had begun his move towards an appreciation of Repton, having earlier been highly critical of it.

6 The family took foreign tours in 1825, 1833 and 1835; they made excursions to Scotland in 1824, 1826 and 1827, to Wales in 1831, to the West of England in 1828, to Derbyshire in 1829, and to the Lakes in 1824, 1826, 1830, 1837 and 1837. All the British excursions were through prime picturesque country, made famous by writings such as those of William Gilpin.

II.

Unsurprisingly, given both Ruskin's temperament and the status of the term 'landscape architecture', Ruskin vacillates between two approaches, uncertain which to privilege: one focuses upon buildings in the landscape; the other he refers to as «embellishing, as it is called, fine natural scenery» (I.138), where it is the landscape itself and not the buildings that seems primary. Whereas he can never free himself from the stated commitment to explore a series of building types in different national contexts, he veers more and more into considerations of the landscapes in which he has experienced buildings; in doing so, often in lengthy asides, he begins his career-long habit of invoking footnotes that then usurp the main text.[7] Even when it is buildings that he addresses, they are not solely the major types of cottage or villa, but smaller insertions («fabriques») into landscaped sites.[8] Furthermore his architectural interest is almost exclusively on the outward forms of the structures, often as they merge with the site.[9] At best, we might say his concern is with the threshold between building and field, between the outer walls of the house and its relationship with the larger spaces it commands. Even here his tendency is to regard the architectural siting from the viewer's perspective rather than the architect's and still less the inhabitant's.[10]

The cottage itself encourages Ruskin's ambivalent approach: both a type of essentially peasant housing, it is also a significant adjunct of picturesque parkscapes – even introduced simply as a visual ploy, which Humphry Repton did at Blaise Castle, near Bristol. Ruskin even makes the same point as Repton did in his Red Book for Blaise, when he insists upon the importance of smoke from a cottage chimney as giving an agreeable motion to a peaceful scene.[11] In their decorative function as scenic supplements, the cottage and its associated sub-types (rustic huts, summerhouses, etc) were the stock in trade of pattern books through Europe by the 1830s, at which genre of publication Ruskin glances snidely on several occasions. In almost all the major publications of that ilk – a line of English publications from P. Decker's *Chinese Architecture* and *Gothic Architecture* (both 1759) to James Malton's *Essay on British Cottage Architecture* (1798), and continental examples like Johann G. Grohmann's *Ideenmagazin für Liebhaber von Gärten* (1796 ff.), or Gijsbert van Laar's *Magazijn van Tuin-Sieraaden* ... (1802) – fabriques are represented with some scenic additions of a rather perfunctory, theatrical sort; but they confirm the assumption that what Ruskin calls «effect in scenery» is the desired aim of such structures. And Ruskin's own strategy is to expand such scenic hints into fullscale analyses of the topographical context, as he does with the Swiss mountain cottage.

The cottage, by the very nature of its humble origins and usage, is easily read as an outgrowth of the land into which it has been fitted. In a long paragraph on the Westmoreland cottage he notes how «Its colour is that of the ground» and that «the mass» of its individual stones «at a distance tells only as a large stone would»; placed in a valley, «the colour of these cottages agrees with everything ...».[12] The very inconspicuousness of the English Lakeland cottage, its design debt (as Ruskin claims) to nature herself, authorizes his slide from building into the surrounding landscape, which he treats in more detail and with more «poetry» than the building itself (I.46–8).

With the villa, inevitably, Ruskin has more difficulty pursuing its affinities with surrounding topographical materials. But the «whole glory of the design (of the Italian Lakeland villa) consists in its unison with the dignity of the landscape, and with the classical tone of the country», opportunities that the English imitation of such structures cannot share.[13] However, he again pays no attention to a villa's ground plan, concentrating instead upon its visual effect in the landscape, and he is concerned above all with its place in a series of graduated interventions in the landscape: «generally an apex of a series of artificial terraces, which conduct through its gardens to the water»,[14] but these terraces should not «extend to any distance from

7 These are I.79–80 and 81, of which the first – by a publishing accident, admittedly – got published separately. Some years ago, in an essay entitled «Œuvre and footnote», in: Hunt/Holland 1982, pp. 1–20, I tried to take Ruskin at his word and read his huge output as a fluid set of intertextual utterances, the status of any single one being liable to frequent repositioning and reformulating as it came to serve a new role in Ruskin's series of attempts to construct an œuvre, the shape and completeness of which would satisfy his current mindset. In these seemingly endless re-visions of his corpus, a large text could be pillaged for fragments that would then be allowed to stand alone or re-read as a simple gloss upon another: in 1875, for instance, he issued selections from *Modern Painters* as *Frondes Agrestes*, to which he added 34 new notes, and in 1884–1885 further «scientific portions» of *Modern Painters* on «the origin of form in clouds [and] mountains» were extracted for *In Montibus Sanctis* and *Coeli Enarrant*, which were in turn buttressed by cross-references to recent works like *Deucalion* and *Proserpina*. One published text could thus become a pretext, a gloss, an appendix, a note for another.

8 True, Ruskin largely mocks the fad for «ornamental summer-houses, or mimicries of wigwams ... erected as ornamental adjuncts to a prospect» (I.66).

9 Beeching terms this a «spectator's view of architecture». Cf. Helsinger's 1982, p. 80, phrase: «excursive viewing». Ruskin is, in fact, also following the line of reasoning about such structures propounded in Whately 1770; this seminal text on the new landscape style makes the point that buildings in landscapes have generally ceased to be considered for their function or usefulness and have become simply «objects» (Whately 1770, p. 117).

10 Understandably, as he has never – on his own admission (I.73 and 87) – had much experience of these buildings on the inside.

11 I.55 for Ruskin; for Repton's *Blaise*, see Hunt/Willis 1988, p. 362. Both Ruskin and Repton emphasise the need for movement in landscape.

12 Here he looks at the variety of colours of stones and lichens.

13 His very first examples in *The Poetry of Architecture* come from Regent's Park and the promontories of Derwent Water in the English Lake District, both recent examples of colonization by new villa sites.

14 I.83. This is a clear example of what elsewhere I have called the «three natures», and it suggests both the longstanding need for such a declension of artifice as one moves away from the house and Ruskin's own (maybe unconscious) reliance upon such design theory; see Hunt 2000. On an analogous, though very differently argued, discussion of siting see Leatherbarrow 2000.

the house».[15] In this insistence upon a «link between nature and art, a step of transition» Ruskin touches upon an essential and long-standing topic in landscape architectural design;[16] he does so, too, with an emphasis reminiscent of Humphry Repton, who came by the end of his career to allow, even insist upon, regular forms, mainly terracing, near a house.

Ruskin's discussions of siting imply some rivalry between 'architecture' and 'landscape architecture'. This is another topical theme: probably Ruskin knew Francis Bacon's claim that gardening was a «greater perfection» than architecture because humans turned to it later in their cultural development. In his overall focus upon sites rather than buildings, Ruskin seems to bend towards that view as well; he also denies the claim of architecture to the «mere preparation of convenience», acknowledging architecture only when it addresses itself to «the mind» or to «the play of the imagination» (I.105). Yet it is largely the landscape context of this architecture that (as we shall see) exercises the mind and brings the imagination into play.

III.

Much of Ruskin's discussion of siting involves a reciprocity or dialogue between the building and what is called the 'character' of the site. This is another well-established term and topos in landscape design literature. Repton had began his first treatise, *Sketches and Hints on Landscape Gardening* (1795), with the assertion that «All rational improvement of grounds is, necessarily, founded on a due attention to the CHARACTER and SITUATION of the place to be improved».[17] When Ruskin makes fun of «peacable old gentlemen, who never smelt (gun)powder in their lives, (eating) their morning muffin in a savage-looking tower, and (admitting) quiet old ladies to a tea-party under the range of twenty-six cannon ... pointed at the drawing-room windows» (I.153), he is not only probably echoing a similar satiric attack on inappropriate garden design by Repton and joining him in urging a return from «heroics to common sense»,[18] but he is also arguing for attention to the overall idea or character of the site to be designed and inhabited. The «only means of obtaining character», Ruskin proposes, is via «decorations» (I.136), a position which both lures him to concentrate on architectural details where decoration is readily introduced (windows, chimneys) and draws him to consider landscape architecture where interventions enhance or «animate» the given features or character of a site in a manner analogous to architectural decoration.[19]

Like Repton, Ruskin knew that landscape architecture was still in dire need of some «fixed and undoubted criterion»,[20] and it is on the issue of 'character' that he can draw upon a certain body of already available theory. Here we can identify several strands in largely eighteenth century and turn of the century discourse. The theme of propriety, of matching the manner or mode of some landscape design with its subject, owner or function, derives from a whole matrix of enquiry into generic form and vocabulary in the established arts – music, painting, literature, architecture – which landscape theorists borrowed to enhance the dignity of their discipline. Then there is the tendency – also followed in the interest of letting landscape gardening lay claim to beaux-arts status – to categorize, to invent a structure of abstract principles: Thomas Whately exemplifies this tactic in *Observations of Modern Gardening* (1770) when he discusses three types of character in design, establishes categories of site (farm, park, garden, riding) or reviews the constituent elements of landscape work (woods, water, rocks, buildings). We see a reflection of this schematic enquiry and some borrowing of its vocabulary when Ruskin divides topography into four categories (woody, green country; cultivated, blue; wild, grey; hilly, brown). A third cluster of established ideas Ruskin could have drawn upon comprises both an emphasis upon genius loci,[21] following Alexander Pope's famous injunction to «consult the genius of the place in all», and an element of later associationism that singles out leading elements of a scene the better to capture a strong idea of it.

It will help elucidate Ruskin's place in the literature of architectural and landscape architectural 'character' to look at the work of the architectural writer, Robert Morris, beginning in the late 1720's.[22] Himself not an original thinker, Morris

15 I.156 – in other words, some sense of balance or proportion between the effects of art and the pull of the natural scene must be maintained.

16 I use the term 'topic' in the sense set out by Leatherbarrow 1993, chapter one. See also Hunt 2000, p. 6.

17 Loudon 1840, p. 39. For Repton see Daniels 1999.

18 I.161. On this aspect of Repton's work see Hunt 1992, pp. 139–169.

19 This is the thrust of his opening paragraph, too long to quote here, in Chapter II., where «giving animation» to a scene results from embellishing the natural features of a landscape and thus drawing out or giving to it 'character'.

20 The phrase comes from his essay on the design of memorials (I.247), also contributed to Loudon's *Architectural Review*, and usually printed with *The Poetry of Architecture*. Cf. Repton's lament that landscape gardening was «the only Art which every one professes to understand, and even to practise, without having studied its Rudiments» (Loudon 1840, p. 409).

21 Cf. Ruskin's remarks on Lake Como that its «elevation of character ... brings it into harmony of its locus ...» (I. 101).

22 Once again, I am not concerned with the sources of Ruskin's pronouncements, for which perhaps Shaftesbury's ideas of 'character' might have been an alternative source with which to connect Ruskin. Equally, the essay by Home 1785, might be a place in which to track the sources of some of Ruskin's ideas, since the two writers tackle several topics in common. Kames would perhaps be more usefully invoked as a demonstration of some basic eighteenth-century ideas on landscape architecture, with which Ruskin clearly had both knowledge and affinity.

«acted as a barometer whose writings reflected contemporary changes ...».[23] He can interest us for his sustained examination of siting or situation as it contributes to and modifies 'character' in architecture. In his *Lectures on Architecture* (1734 and 1736) he insisted that «the first care in respect to (architectural) decoration is justly appropriating the design to the situation ... So blending art and nature together». 'Situation' became the principal subject of his later *Essay Upon Harmony, as it relates chiefly to Situation and Building* (1739), a title that would also have served Ruskin's purposes in *The Poetry of Architecture*. Further, as David Leatherbarrow has proposed, Morris's concept of situation was close to that of painters and their theorists. The influential Roger de Piles,[24] for instance, had defined situation as «the view, prospect or opening of a country», an aesthetic response to place that painters should consider when composing a scene which should be both coherent and (because of various types) «represented according to the country the painter is thinking of».[25] De Piles then notes that country can be «either open or closed, mountainous or watery», a categorizing that Morris maintains when he writes that: «Every Country, has its peculiar Enchantment of Situation; either in Extent of Prospect, its Woods, Rivers, Vales, Pastures, or something to attract, some Beauty, some Image, to allure our Eyes or Attention and fill us with agreeable Ideas».

Just as Ruskin would typify different kinds of country, Morris isolates grave, jovial and charming situations and requires the architect to make his work appropriate to «the several Scenes which Art or Nature have produced, in different Situations». And in his pattern books, *Rural Architecture* (1750, reissued as *Select Architecture*, 1755 and 1757) and *The Architectural Remembrancer* (1751, reissued in 1755 and 1757 as *Architecture Improved*), Morris not only represented designs for garden pavilions in rudimentary landscapes (a format we have already noticed in the pattern books generally) but commented upon their appropriateness, via siting and use, and upon their contribution to 'character'.

Robert Morris's treatment of architecture via its setting, his rehearsal of received ideas generally in the air, and the elaboration of the same topics in subsequent landscape literature allow *The Poetry of Architecture* to be read as a work emanating from eighteenth century traditions of landscape architectural commentary. One instance of Ruskin's obvious debts to this body of work is an, again unsurprising, vacillation between two points of view about 'character'. The first of these insists upon a single, unitary character – a «truth of the scene» (I.26) or «unity of feeling» (I.8), both of which tend to be premised upon a unique, perspectival viewing of the scene – thus Morris had insisted that objects be «strictly circumscribed by the Eye at one View» or otherwise they «cannot be comprehended in the [one] idea». The other approach, upon which later associationists preferred to concentrate, is contrariwise based upon a desire to move through landscape: it allows for a multiplicity of ideas and so privileges the train of reflection rather than its objective stimulus.[26]

IV.

'Character' and its other analogues ('truth of scene' or 'unity of feeling') are givens in landscape as well as ideas brought to the landscape by its visitors: Ruskin investigates both the inherent qualities of a topography, and the imaginative skills needed in a visitor to adduce sufficient meaning or poetry, without bothering to distinguish between them. We have already seen how the Italian villa responds to the «dignity of the landscape» and «the classical tone» of the country: these are at least as much attributed to Italy by the visitor (like Ruskin, coached by his readings in the poetry of Samuel Rogers and Byron) as assumed to be inherent in its scenery. In the activity of cultivating a sympathetic understanding of a site in which meaning may already be supposed to adhere, Ruskin is able to draw instinctively upon two fundamental aspects of his early education: the evangelical faith in the readability and meaning of God's other book of nature, and the repertoire of picturesque theory and practice that directed how to behave within different sceneries. The first was his mother's legacy, the second, a passion of his father's.[27]

The actual invocation of pictures as a means of structuring the experience of, especially unfamiliar, landscape is not something that Ruskin bothers much to discuss. It is, I take it, something he simply assumed: he would write about the «proper shape of pictures and engravings» for Loudon's edition of Repton's *Landscape Architecture*. In *The Poetry of Architecture* he connects the idea of a scenery with its being viewed as a picture (p.31) or best seen through a window: «the breaking out of the distant features in little well-composed morceaux» (I.170); he writes of how a garden or wicket fence will «complete a picture» of an English cottage (I.12); he invokes – as Repton, Price and Knight all did, with varying degrees of seriousness – different schools of paintings: «Claude, Salvator, and Poussin» (I.112) – as models for scenery and scenic experience. And if he did understand the term 'land-

23 See Leatherbarrow 1985, pp.48–59 (here p.50). I am indebted to this article in what follows.
24 His *Cours de peinture* was published in Paris in 1708 and in an English translation in London in 1743.
25 Quoted Leatherbarrow 1985, p.50. Cf. Ruskin, who also links the dominant idea of a scenery to its being pictured to the eye (I.28).
26 This interest in a variety of elements within a given scene, which Ruskin identifies particularly in his descriptions of the «cultivated, or blue, country (Chapter XIII), seems close to the kind of picturesque that Everett 1994 has termed 'Tory', an apt linkage for Ruskin.
27 I have treated Ruskin's picturesque in an essay of that title, collected in Hunt 1992, pp.193–212, and have endeavoured to repeat myself here as little as possible.

scape architecture' as applied to the depiction of buildings in landscape paintings, it would have given him added justification for applying pictorial structures to what his mentor, Loudon, may have told him about the 'new' meaning of that term and its debts to picturesque theorists. He was also firmly committed to the fundamental picturesque deployment of word and image in his essays, which display, as *The Times* praised: «the mind of a poet as well as the eye and hand of an artist» (I.xliii, note). Thus Ruskin not only is able to have his original essays illustrated with woodcuts after his own drawings, but contrives topographical descriptions or ekphraseis in terms which suggest painterly models;[28] he also silently appropriates a passage of Roger's poem, «Italy», with its vignettes by Turner, to conclude his essay on Italian villas, thus drawing upon the visual and verbal resources of a prime specimen of picturesque travel publication.

Yet it is also important to note Ruskin's mockery of the excesses of the picturesque – his swipe at the obelisk on the top of Whitlaw near Carlisle an «an insane lamp post in search of the picturesque» (I.249, note), or his scorn for designs that awaken «every possible conception which would be picturesque, and every imagination which would never be rapturous, to the mind of chimney-sweeps» (I.65). And above all, he follows a traditional satiric line on any picturesque «wild struggle for novelty» (I.8) that derives from the lack of taste displayed by «ruralizing cheesemongers» (I.102). Ruskin's distaste for «edificatorial fancies», pilloried especially in Chapter XII on «The Principles of Composition», recalls eighteenth century mockery of inept application of picturesque design among those who aspire to mimic patrician taste in landscape.[29]

The picturesque movement was omnivorous and inclusive; it addressed the issues already discussed – the relation of buildings to landscape, and the different 'characters' to be discovered in the latter – as well as other topics which seem central to Ruskin's approach in *The Poetry of Architecture* – the relation of meaning to form, of the whole to its parts, of emotions to the intellect, of the eye to the mind, of 'poetry' to science in picturesque experience. Most of those, sometimes distinct themes were gathered together, as they are in Ruskin's essays, in the picturesque concern with association, which, in its turn, was dedicated to understanding the relationship of scenery to its visitors.

Ruskin may deride the excess of the picturesque, but his essays nonetheless draw considerable nourishment from its substantial and serious concerns with the creation or discovery of meaning in landscape, thus with the larger theme of the encounter between visitor (subject) and scenery (object). This is a fundamental concern for all landscapists – whether painters, poets, gardeners or psychologists –

during the eighteenth century; it was a theme Ruskin would certainly have traced in his readings of Shaftesbury, Addison and Pope, and it continued to absorb and to be enhanced by later Romantic poets, especially Wordsworth, whom Ruskin also read and admired.

While Ruskin proves a slippery exponent of these issues, partly because he seems somewhat cavalier with his terminology, it is also clear that he is concerned throughout to address the issue of how a visitor respective viewer responds or relates to scenery, which at its most vital or satisfying must appeal to the eye, to the feelings and to the mind. At opposite extremes, a landscape response involves what Ruskin calls 'science' as well as 'poetry' – the former being the very first word of his first essay, the latter providing his title. The required, scientific attention to topography and terrain that Ruskin expects is clearest in separate essays he wrote for Loudon's *Magazine of Natural History* on the cause of colour in the River Rhine or on the strata of Mont Blanc,[30] however it surfaces in the essays for *The Architectural Review* when he considers (in a footnote) different kinds of avalanche (I.81, note) or analyses watery reflections (I.90–1). But this discussion of reflections also invokes other responses, where the language is that of «beguile», «fairy land» and «dreams unattainable and illimitable», which are stimulated by the watery depths of a lake.

The scientific element is Ruskin's own version of the picturesque attention to the form and texture of details in the landscape; these anchor the attentive eye and provide both its pleasures and one kind of meaning. He displays a typical picturesque interest in both detail and overall effect, in «long oblique shadows on the white surface» (I.22): in «the form of every stone in its walls (which) is a study» and which also in combination produce a design which no architect on earth could ever equal, sculptured by a chisel of unimaginable delicacy, and finished to a degree of perfection, which is unnoticed because it is everywhere» (I.48). As there, the feelings and the mind make their own demands of landscape experience, and these receive a greater amount of Ruskin's attention in, what is after all called, *The Poetry of Archi-*

28 The «perfect» view of «a populous and highly cultivated plain» taken through «rugged ravines» or past «some tall, vast and voiceless mountain» (I.43) and distant views of flat country «lost in richness of vegetation, ... or broken with masses of forest, or with distant hills» (I.176) of both conjure up a variety of Dutch and Flemish landscape paintings.

29 One wonders if the Ruskin family, known to have enjoyed eighteenth-century essayists, had read the famous piece on «Squire Mushroom», published in *The World*, no. 15 (12 April 1753); it was collected by A. Chalmers, the prolific Edinburgh publisher, in his multi-volumed *The British Essayists* (1823), XII, pp. 75–81.

30 These are reprinted in I.189–196.

tecture.[31] Yet they are instigated or triggered, in consonance with eighteenth-century psychological theories, by details in the physical world – the stones of a ruin, the leaf and bough of woodland chiaroscuro.[32]

Generally, Ruskin gives primacy to what he calls quite conventionally the trains of meditation in the mind» (I.5). Thus «the cottage should ... tell as a building on the mind as well as the eye» (I.185); though at times Ruskin seems willing to contrast or oppose these responses instead of seeing them in alliance (I.43), the more frequent assumption is that they function in some form of complicity or union. The mind's responses are themselves influenced by the feelings (I.47), where a distinction is also sometimes drawn, along the lines of Coleridge's separation of fancy and imagination in *Biographia Literaria*, between the liberties taken by the «light fancy» and «the deep feeling, of the mind».[33] None of the «trains of meditation» that Ruskin explores are anything but conventional, nor is his analysis of how the various responses – formal/visual, emotional, mental – mesh and reinforce each other, indeed: it recalls Repton's insistence, again in *Sketches and Hints*, that it must be «the understanding, which is able to compare, to separate, and to combine, the various sources of pleasure derived from external objects, and to trace them to some pre-existing causes in the structure of the human mind».[34]

However, where we may see some distinctive, because somewhat old-fashioned, emphasis in Ruskin's exploration of picturesque associationism is in its refusal to respond solely to formal effects and values. In eighteenth century landscape architecture, formal moves had seemed to dominate the work of «Capability» Brown and his imitators, and much of Repton's early designs make their appeal quite openly to merely formal effects. Ruskin is not immune to similar appeals; the relation of architectural shape and angle to those of surrounding trees is a theme treated explicitly by Repton and on several occasions by Ruskin, though with some characteristically 'scientific' precision: «with pines or larches», he writes, «the angle [of roofs] should not be regulated by the form of the tree, but by the shape of the branches» (I.70). But it is perhaps due to his evangelical instincts that Ruskin is led more usually to insist upon the 'meaning' of scenery, upon «sensation ... made almost equal with thought» (I.150). Here his characteristic formula is to invoke the figure of speech called 'prosopopeia', whereby something in the landscape speaks to its visitors, «tells» them something of its history, is «voiceful» (I.31), «speaks» to their feelings (see, for instance, I.17 or 68), or recalls experiences previously articulated in other literature, as when Ruskin recalls Isaac Walton and Armstrong's *The Art of Preserving Health* (I.38) in the same breath as the Swiss mountain cottage. But the most insistent 'message' that Ruskin hears and transcribes from these speaking topographies is that different sceneries declare ideas of national culture. And here he is again tapping into long-established themes in the profession of landscape architecture.

V.

At the height of enthusiasm for 'natural' landscape architecture in the writings of Horace Walpole, Whately, Gilpin, Uvedale Price, Richard Payne Knight and Repton among others, it was an essential aspect of this 'modern' style that it was indisputably and ineluctably English. It had been invented by the English (according to Walpole, as long ago as mediaeval deer parks), it had been brought to a «perfect perfection» by the English (Walpole singles out William Kent as the prime mover here), and its imagery spoke wholly and fully of Englishness, especially English laws and liberties; it had even been purveyed abroad by the English in a form of aesthetic empire building. By the time Ruskin comes to focus upon the national qualities of landscape architecture, very different attitudes were in the air, of which John Claudius Loudon was certainly aware.

To start with, landscapists in different European nations had – shortly after Ruskin, would A.J. Downing in the United States – deliberately adapted English landscaping theory and practice to their own social, political, geographical and climatic needs.[35] Whether Ruskin knew – through Loudon – of works by such French theorists as Jean-Marie Morel or Joseph de Laborbe, by the German C.C.L. Hirschfeld or Ercole Silva in Italy, he could scarcely by the late 1830s have been ignorant of fundamental changes in the demands made upon landscape architects, for these are exactly the social and national issues he attempts to address in *The Poetry of Architecture*. He had, after all, traveled on the continent, where the designed landscapes could not have appeared the same as back home – indeed, in his essays he is alert to the effect of different European political systems upon the prevalence and design of villas (I.102–103); he also registers distinctions within similar categories: «Italy, for example, is blue country; yet it has not the least resemblance to English blue country» (I.72–73), and early in the series of essays he announces with all the

31 Beeching draws attention to John Summerson's discussion of Sir John Soane's use of the phrase «poetry of architecture» to signal the way in which the eye could bypass rather than be halted by walls or ceilings.

32 I.69. See also Ruskin's claim that «The most minute objects (leaf, flower, stone), while they add to the beauty, seem to share in the sadness, of the whole» (I.20). Beeching argues in his thesis that Ruskin's debts are to associationists before Archibald Alison, who tended to play down the importance of the object as stimulus in favour of the train of stimulations itself; Ruskin, it is true, is firmly committed to the provocation of the object, whether building or landscape.

33 I.128; yet the term 'fancy' is also used by Ruskin in the more conventional eighteenth-century sense of Imagination (I.16), where it works to recover a sense of the past.

34 Loudon 1840, pp. 37–38.

35 I have taken this up more fully in Hunt 2001.

assurance of a twenty-year old that «The mind of the inhabitant of the continent, in general, is capable of deeper and finer sensations than that of the islander» (I.50).

But even in England, the hegenomy of 'pure' English landscape taste, as championed by Walpole and codified by Whately among others, no longer held sway, if only because the practice and theory of English landscape architecture were themselves having to adapt to different social needs as well as to respond to the realization that there were different topographical Englands as well as social ones in which to design. Repton had certainly become uncomfortably aware of these new professional constraints by the end of his career, while Loudon had responded positively to them, his garden writings specifically addressing a new social, mainly suburban class of property owner. Indeed, the Ruskin family may have been over-sensitive on this issue; the son's unease about social mobility and change is surely what lies behind his lament (in a footnote) that «the most perfect schools of architecture have arisen in districts whose character is unchanging» (I.118, note).

The huge literature of picturesque travel also promoted an awareness of different sceneries, at home and abroad, that the connoisseur would need to appreciate. Gilpin's tours had alerted travelers to the varied characters of different parts of the England, Wales and Scotland. Ruskin's separation of geologies that are responsible for what he categorizes as «simple blue ... picturesque blue ... natural green» countries in England (I.139 ff.) owes much to the discriminations which picturesque travel literature had established.[36] Yet this conventional identification of categories of terrain, distinctions to which he contributes his youthful geological interests, lands Ruskin in some trouble. On the one hand, the cottage is a building type that accommodates itself readily to different types of scenery: «we shall find a difference existing between every range of hills, which will demand a corresponding difference in the style of their cottages» (I.72). But the English country seat or villa is another matter. Since it cannot be seen to accommodate itself to the diversities of scenery, it tends towards a generic blandness – here Ruskin repeats what had been a frequent criticism of Lancelot Brown's designs: «our English park scenery, though exquisitely beautiful, is sometimes, we think, a little monotonous» (I.73). The discriminations of different topographies and in particular his passionate celebration of «picturesque blue country» for its grace, mystery and sensuality cannot now serve his turn where the villa is concerned;[37] frustrated by the very diversity of landscape characters that his own interests and those of picturesque connoisseurs had promoted, he cannot formulate enough guidelines for the more elite architectural insertions: «There never was, and never can be, a universal beau ideal in architecture, and the arrival at all local models of beauty would be the task of ages» (I.116); it is all «very discouraging» (I.117).

Yet the pull of traditional assumptions in landscape architecture is strong. Ruskin is clearly indebted to two basic notions of the English landscape movement: first, that, as Joseph Addison put it in an early formulation, a landowner may «make a pretty landskip of his own possessions», namely – given the painterly denotation of landskip – present a portrait of himself through his landscape; second, that, as Walpole and others announced it, an English landscape design should portray or represent England and Englishness. Ruskin's whole sequence of essays is premised upon similar assumptions: that a nation's «prevailing turn of mind» as well as that of individual inhabitant's is mirrored and therefore readable in the artistic productions of a particular country. To this tradition, he grafted parallel eighteenth-century discussions of the contribution of climate and topography to the development and form of the arts.[38]

But Ruskin draws more upon Walpole's contention than upon Addison's; for one thing, the latter's perspective would require detailed and particular examples that Ruskin's ambitious attempts at general principles cannot tolerate. Ruskin will, of necessity, make local topographical 'character' subservient to larger 'national' characteristics when it comes to considering the character of country estates or villa design. Happily the peasant, according to Ruskin «a being of more marked national character than man, the educated and refined» (I.74), will find that his dwelling, the cottage, comfortably expresses locality and nationality. With the villa and its owner, however, concessions have to be made to conditions and associations of nationality: hence, Ruskin's allowance, even promotion, of brick as a building material – «brick is peculiarly English in its effect» (I.142–143); hence his somewhat reluctant admission of Elizabethan forms of both architecture and garden layout as the «only style of villa architecture which can be called English» (I.121). Questions of scale are also vital in England and to interventions into English landscape: «England is a country whose every scene is in miniature» (I.14).

But perhaps the most important debt of Ruskin's analysis to established thinking on English landscape architecture is his occasionally awkward acknowledgement of both nature and art in forming landscapes. Their joint contribution to Walpole's vision of the perfect 'natural' landscape was a contradiction that Walpole chose to ignore, as Ruskin would later. Both writers drew upon the visual structuring of

36 See, for example, Dalrymple 1823, pp. 6–7, where four kinds of terrain are identified.

37 I.148–9; later in this section he laments, in a footnote, that «there must always be a difficulty in building in picturesque blue country in England; for the English character is opposed to that of the country: it is neither graceful, nor mysterious, nor voluptuous», with the result that either national characteristics or 'character' of scenery is sacrified to the benefit of the other (p. 153, note).

38 Again, I am not in search of Ruskin's sources: Du Bos's *Critical Reflections*, published in an English translation in 1748, would have been one instance of this idea being advanced.

landscape experience in which paintings and engravings had played a substantial role; yet both equally needed to celebrate the «natural» attributes of such landscapes, whether designed (largely Walpole's topic) or discovered (to which Ruskin devotes more attention). «Kata Phusin» was a pseudonym that announced Ruskin's faith in nature. As a guiding principle of design, this 'nature' is rarely expounded, but it is ubiquitous in the essays as the guiding light of design: «For architect and for employer, there can be but one rule: to be natural in all that they do ...» (I.168, note). Ruskin seems to rely upon two key notions of the natural: one is derived from the forms of natural materials, which are never out of proportion, strive for perfect forms (especially the curve) and should be copied assiduously from the material world; this announced what will become a familiar Ruskin obsession, and need not be pursued here. The other coincides with the idea of 'natural' as being in consonance with one's true nature or character: «The mistake of our architects in general is that they fancy they are speaking good English by speaking bad Greek» (I.168 note).

Here, we have come full circle in this analysis to Ruskin's concern with 'character', its connections with both local and national identity and its debts to painterly types of landscape representation. Yet it is worth noting here that the formulation of Ruskin's remark on «good English» echoes, doubtless coincidentally, an early eighteenth-century claim by the landscape gardener, Stephen Switzer, that in matters of landscape design, foreign borrowings must be taught to speak good English.[39] But Ruskin's concern to chide and chivy his compatriots into thinking fully about an apt and proper national style, in contradistinction to the Italian, French or Swiss, rests upon a long eighteenth-century concern to argue that the «landscape garden» was a truly English invention in whose attention to natural effects and freedom from constraints and artifice the whole political and social structure of that country was magnificently represented. So when Ruskin insists that in brown, cultivated country «All should be pure, but all should be English» design (I.181), he places himself squarely in the nationalistic rhetoric of landscape architectural writing. Like Walpole, Ruskin laments the sad state of England's (landscape) architecture in comparison with its painting; both writers, of course, bring painterly ideas to bear upon improving that theoretical and practical vacuum. For notwithstanding his youthful fascination with Italy and alpine Switzerland that leads him into enthusiastic and rhetorical claims for their scenery and buildings,[40] it is ultimately his own country that concerns him. He will castigate bad effects in England, especially the blandness of neo-Palladian design; he will denigrate English villa life as «preposterous» in contrast to the Italian, which is «full of imagination and emotion» and, above all, evinces «great nationality and great beauty» (I.95). His highly wrought, Byronic view of Italy: «the ancient system of Italian life, where every man's home had its dark, secret places, the abodes of his worst passions» (I.114) cannot be matched with any comparable fiction of Englishness. To redress that imbalance, he draws upon his detailed and truly informed understanding of English scenery in all its different varieties to sketch out the options for a genuine and indigenous design style.

VI.

The abrupt termination of the series in Loudon's *Architectural Review* may have contributed to Ruskin's inabilities to produce an adequate guide for contemporary English design. But the later history of nineteenth-century English architectural design would prove his frustrations only too legitimate. Which leaves us with the final question as to why Ruskin never really pursued the study of landscape architecture, which (as I hope to have proved) became in fact a substantial element of *The Poetry of Architecture*.

Two, speculative answers are possible. First, that Ruskin would have found Loudon's landscape architectural writings too uncongenial, whatever his indebtedness in other regards to that «literary patron», to have tempted him into more work in landscape architecture. In this connection we might recall his father's worried query in 1846 as to what forms 'real knowledge' would take for his son; what John James did not seem to realize perhaps is that his son was still engaged in a search less for the forms than for the very nature and substance of 'real knowledge' itself. On the basis of his assessment of Loudon's contributions to his chosen profession, perhaps Ruskin at least intuited that 'real knowledge' did not lie there.

Secondly, Ruskin's so evident enthusiasm for foreign places distracted him from pursuing an adequate and (as he realized) lengthy determination of the role played by local factors in national schemes of landscape architectural design. His one characteristic contribution to the literature of English landscape architecture – in this, for instance, quite unlike Walpole's xenophobic taunts – had been to engage in comparative analysis of English design with French, Italian and Swiss; these European examples would, through both his personal excursions and the example of

39 See Hunt 2000, pp. 201–206.
40 See, for instance, the peroration of Chapter VIII, which anticipates in its sense of the poetry of Italian gardens the much later essay by Sitwell 1909.

Turner's foreign travels, be sufficient to lead him into the alpine researches and Venetian analyses that constitute the next phases of his career.

In the spirit of true Ruskinian paradox, though, it may be worth arguing that in two respects he did continue to be absorbed with landscape architecture. The whole of his Venetian work is the examination of a large, urban landscape, in whose structures may be discerned both individual and cultural histories and through whose scenery, on two famous occasions in *The Stones of Venice*, he leads his reader as if through some elaborate and complex picturesque design.[41] And, on a much smaller scale, once he had purchased Brantwood, sight unseen, his future home overlooking Coniston Water in the English Lakes, he was simply fulfilling his own prophecy enunciated forty years before in *The Poetry of Architecture*: «all that we ought to do in the hill villa is, to adapt it for the habitation of a man of the highest faculties of perception and feeling» (I.182).

41 I have analysed the picturesque component of Ruskin's Venetian work in another paper, delivered at the Fondazione Giorgio Cini, Venice, in December 2000.

«St. Gothard», by J.M.W. Turner, in: John Ruskin, *Lectures on Landscape*, London 1897

John Gage

Ruskin and Turner: The formal vision

Ruskin has been abundantly interesting to biographers, but this paper is not about Ruskin the man. What interests me is the way in which a belief in the ultimate authority of nature (and, of course, behind nature, of God) could lead Ruskin to a notion of art which denied the possibility of absolute truth to nature, which proposed an extreme version of aesthetic subjectivism; and how radical view was rooted in a study of the works of Turner.

'Nature' had of course been a touchstone of aesthetic virtue since the Renaissance, and especially in the Neo-Classical climate in which Turner had been brought up, as a student at the Royal Academy.[1] But 'Nature' was – and is – a slippery concept, and Turner gave it a very particular inflection in a well-known note to the published lectures of his academic colleague, John Opie, about 1810 (at a time, be it said, when, according to Ruskin, Turner was still in thrall to the Old Masters):

«Every look at nature is a refinement upon art; each tree, and blade of grass or flower is not to (the artist) the individual tree grass or flower, but what it is in relation to the whole, its tone, its contrast and its use ...».[2]

Turner's important reference to the 'whole' in this note might well seem to be at odds with Ruskin's manifest interest in the fragments, the piecemeal elements of nature, which is so often exemplified in his drawings, and particularly in his approach to colour. Yet in *The Elements of Drawing*, his practical handbook of 1857 which, I shall argue, was his most important publication for the history of art, Ruskin similarly maintained that:

«... in a great picture every line and colour is so arranged as to advantage the rest. None are inessential, however slight; and none are independent, however forcible. It is not enough that they truly represent natural objects; but they must fit into certain places, and gather into certain harmonious groups ...». (III. 190)

Note that here Ruskin is talking of pictures, where Turner was talking of nature (although he also remarked in his note to Opie that the study of nature and art were entirely reciprocal), and it is clear that even in the first of his published manifestos on Turner, *Modern Painters*, Volume I (1843), he had begun with chapters on

1 For a still useful listing of texts, Lovejoy 1927, pp. 69–77.
2 Finberg 1961, p. 230.

tone, colour and chiaroscuro: all elements of picture-making rather than of 'nature'.

In the *Elements* Ruskin also spoke of the unifying effect of colour:
«... many noble pictures are painted almost exclusively in various tones of red, or grey, or gold, so as to be instantly striking by their breadth of flush, or glow, or tender coldness, these qualities being exhibited only by slight and subtle use of contrast ...».

Some of his own most complete and unified compositions were in monochrome, often the sepia which he had learned to love from his study of Turner's *Liber Studiorum*, and articulating his belief in the supreme value of tone.[3]

Turner himself, and notably in the period of his work which Ruskin admired most, had developed the unifying device of the «colour-beginning», first in watercolour and then in exhibited oils which, from the early 1830s, were often sent for display barely roughed-in and then finished in the presence of the other, delighted, exhibitors.[4] It is these «colour-beginnings», many hundreds of which survive in Turner's 'Nachlass', now at the Tate Gallery in London (Tate Britain) which have fuelled a notion of the painter as a proto-abstract painter, although he never seems to have considered them to be independent works. For Ruskin, who sifted through them in the late 1850s, at the time he was teaching the course on drawing at the Working Mens' College which became the basis of *Elements of Drawing*, they brought home the nature of art as process.[5]

Process was something which linked Ruskin's dynamic view of nature to his understanding of the functioning of the human mind. When, at the time of Turner's death in 1851, the new school of the Pre-Raphaelite Brotherhood came to be supported by Ruskin, also under aegis of «Truth to Nature», he was bound to examine the two very different routes to this «truth» followed by his old and his new heroes. He wrote in his 1851 pamphlet, *Pre-Raphaelitism* that:
«... it is always to be remembered that no one mind is like another, either in its powers or perceptions; and while the main principles of training must be the same for all, the result in each will be as various as the kinds of truth which each will apprehend; therefore, also, the modes of effort, even in men whose inner principles and final aims are exactly the same. Suppose, for instance, two men, equally honest, equally industrious, equally impressed with a humble desire to render some part of what they saw in nature faithfully ... But one of them is quiet in temperament, has a feeble memory, no invention, and excessively keen sight. The other is impatient in temperament, has a memory which nothing escapes, an invention which never rests, and is comparatively near-sighted.

Set them both free in the same field in a mountain valley. One sees everything, small and large, with almost the same clearness; mountains and grasshoppers alike; the leaves on the branches, the veins in the pebbles, the bubbles in the stream; but he can remember nothing and invent nothing. Patiently he sets himself to his mighty task; abandoning at once all thoughts of seizing transient effects, or giving general impressions of that which his eyes present to him in microscopical dissection, he chooses some small portion out of the infinite scene, and calculates with courage the number of weeks which must elapse before he can do justice to the intensity of his perceptions, or the fulness of matter in his subject.

Meantime the other has been watching the change of clouds, and the march of the light long the mountain sides; he beholds the entire scene in broad, soft masses of true gradation, and the very feebleness of his sight is in some sort an advantage to him, in making him more sensible of the aerial mystery of distance, and hiding from him the mutitudes of circumstances which it would have been impossible for him to represent ... as for his sitting down to 'draw from Nature', there was not one of the things which he wished to represent, that stayed for so much as five seconds together: but none of them escaped, for all that: they are sealed up in that strange storehouse of his; he may take one of them out perhaps, this day twenty years, and paint it in his dark room, far away... the first is John Everett Millais, and the second Joseph Mallard William Turner».[6]

I need hardly stress how remarkable it was that Ruskin, never one to withhold devastating and comprehensive criticism when he felt it was required, allowed equal value in this, on of his greatest set-pieces, to two widely divergent styles of landscape, and explained their differences on the basis of the artist's respective temperaments. We seem to be approaching the close of that long tradition of art-criticism which emphasized binary difference and its eclectic synthesis: Michelangelo versus Titian, Poussin versus Rubens, Delacroix versus Ingres, or their union in the Carracci or Chasseriau. Ruskin heralds that easy-going 'Stilpluralismus' so characteristic of our own times, not that he was ever easy-going himself.

As it happens, the criticism of Turner which dominated London during the late 1830s, when Ruskin was refining the critical armoury which was to explode in *Modern Painters*, related specifically to colour, and was articulated along the polar opposites of the «Neri» and the «Bianchi». Early in the century, Turner had been associated with a group of London-based artists described disparagingly by the amateur painter and collector of Old Masters as «the white painters». Now, in a book by a pupil of Sir Thomas Lawrence, Frank Howard, illustrated precociously in chromolithography, *Colour as a Means of Art* (1838), Turner was characterised as

3 Gage 1994.
4 Gage 1987, pp. 84–94.
5 Warrell 1995.
6 Ruskin 1906a, pp. 21–22.

the leader of the modern «Bianchi», raising the key and colouring of painting to an unprecedented degree and also radically simplifying the pictorial structure of landscape. Turner was only too happy to assume the role of «Admiral of the Whites» and celebrated it in a re-working of his very early academic success, *Dutch Boats in a Gale* (Private Collection), which had been praised for its Rembrandtesque chiaroscuro when it was exhibited in 1801, as *Dutch Fishing Boats: Hucksters bargaining for Fish* (1837; Chicago Art Institute), where the high overall key, if not brillance of colour, is particularly striking. Turner seems to have hoped that the two paintings would hang side-by-side in the collection of the Duke of Bridgewater, as evidence of how far his art had come, but it was not to be.[7]

Howard also placed particular emphasis on Turner's late flouting of the traditional academic view – especially promoted by Sir Joshua Reynolds – that paintings should be predominantly warm in tone. During the 1830s, in compositions such as the two *Burning of the House of Parliament* of 1834 and 1835, Turner had certainly underlined the capacity of preceived «colour-temperatures» to create a strong pictorial structure, although, at least in exhibited works, he was usually concerned to identify specific phenomena or objects with these classes of colour. Ruskin, in *Elements of Drawing* had an especially interesting take on «warm» and «cold» colours. He was anxious to show that traditional interpretation of blue as receding and red as advancing was mistaken:

«Neither blue, nor yellow, nor red, can have, as such, the smallest power of expressing either nearness or distance: they express them only under the peculiar circumstances which render them at the moment, or in that place, 'signs' of nearness or distance». (III. 184)

Here he is arguing – as modern colourists such as Josef Albers have argued – that colours have no direct physiological capacity to articulate the perception of space; they do so by association only, and this was something which was also felt by Turner, who was probably the source of Ruskin's observation. Time and again Turner reverses the expected warm-cold sequence by bringing cool blues into his foregrounds and painting his distances warm.

Ruskin's remarks on warm and cool colours were part of his argument, first articulated in *The Seven Lamps of Architecture* (1849, IV, xxxvi), that colour did not support form, but acted as a counterpoint to it. Colour and form were independent. 'Colore' had of course long been set against 'disegno', but one of the most important discoveries of nineteenth-century aesthetics was that there was no sense of hierarchy here, and this discovery was based largely on the investigation of subjective colour-effects such as after-images and contrast, which were brought into the arena of art particularly by the French chemist M.E. Chevreul. Chevreul's work was certainly known in England by the late 1840s although it was not translated until the following decade; but for Ruskin, who never, it seems, mentions the French scientist, a prime authority on these phenomena must have been his old teacher James Duffield Harding, whose *Principles and Practice of Art* (1855) included a quiet remarkable chapter on colour-effects.[8]

Of «complementary» constrasts of blue and orange, for example, Harding wrote:

«Great attention must be paid to the results of this opposition, as all the beauty of colouring depends upon it. It must be remarked that there is no actual change either in the blue or orange, the change is in their effect on us; they are not actually brighter by this opposition, but they appear so. We are made sensible, by reason of this opposition, of an increased brillancy of hue, or, in other words, of a colour which has no existence except in our sensations, and is to be ascribed to the effect which the opposition has on the optic nerve. ... It is quite clear that each of these colours must affect the other when in opposition, and produce hues of every variety of delicacy and intensity; whether we see and feel them or not depends on our vision being sensitive by nature, and being made more so by education ...». (p. 120)

Parallel to these effects of contrast was the psychological attempt at colour-assimilation which has come to be known as optical mixture, where small patches of more or less pure colour appear to blend at a certain distance from eye. Ruskin was by no means the first to identify this method of mixing, but in *Elements* he made it the keystone of his method, corresponding to the «gradation» which he felt was the universal principle of natural colour. «Breaking one colour in small points through or over another», he said, «is the most important of all processes in good modern oil and water-colour painting», and he likened the effect to mosaic or chopped straw (III. 172). This is what commended *Elements* to the French pointillists at the close of the century; and the Impressionists, notably Monet, were also impressed by Ruskin's idea that

«We see nothing but flat colours ... The whole technical power of painting depends on our recovery of what may be called the innocence of the eye; that is to say, a sort of childish perception of these flat stains of colour, merely as such, without consciousness of what they signify – as a blind man would see them if suddenly gifted with sight». (I. 5, note)

Elements was translated into French in the 1890s in the circle of the Neo-Impressionists, and I have elsewhere traced the impact of these ideas on the aesthetics of

7 Gage 1987, p. 132, Gage 1993a, pp. 7–8.
8 For Chevreul in England, Roque 1997, pp. 193–194. Ruskin recommended Harding's books several times in *Elements*.

Monet and Matisse.[9] But it now seems to me that there are even more striking parallels with the ideas and practice of Cézanne, parallels that are probably fortuitous, but which nevertheless link him, by way of the interpretation of Ruskin, with the radically perceptualist approaches of Turner.

Cézanne was perhaps the last painter of the European mainstream to insist that the realisation of his sensations should be tied to his experience of nature; and in this he was in the direkt line of Turner and Ruskin. But Ruskin in *Elements*, laid out in some detail the material obstacles to representing nature directly, because of the limitations of the artist's media:

«Good drawing», said Ruskin, «is ... an abstract of natural facts, you cannot represent all that you would, but must continually be falling short, whether you will or no, of the force, or quantitiy of Nature ...». (III. 234)

We are reminded vividly of Cézanne's despairing letter to his son on September 8 1906, in which he said that he was becoming more clear-sighted before nature, but

«I cannot attain the intensity that is unfolded before my senses, I have not the magnificent richness of colouring that animates nature ...».

Ruskin continued:

«You remember, in your first studies of colour from Nature, you were to leave the passages of light which were too bright to be imitated, as white paper. But, in completing the picture, it becomes necessary to put colour into them; and then the other colours must be made darker, in some fixed relation to them. If you deepen all proportionately, though the whole scene is darker than reality, it is only as if you were looking at the reality in a lower light: but if, while you darken some of the tints, you leave others undarkened, the picture is out of harmony, and will not give the impression of truth ...». (III. 235)

Cézanne was not prepared to lower his tonal scale and so, in so many of his late works, he never filled in the lights; and in the well-known case of his portrait of Vollard, after 115 sittings he left two blank points in the hands because he could not find the colour to fill them and, had he chosen the wrong tone, he felt he would certainly have had to repaint the whole.[10]

What Ruskin was arguing – and again he was not alone in this in the 1850s – was that the very attempt to translate the visual perception of nature into painting necessarily implied a departure from «truth». The artist must paint his impressions, and in the matter of colour, these impressions were hard to pin down because of colour's essential relativity.

«Every hue throughout your work is altered by every touch that you add in other places ... so that every touch must be laid , not with a view to its effect at the time, but done being previously considered». (III. 152)

«You may easily understand», added Ruskin, «that, this being so, nothing but the devotion of life, and great genius besides, can make a colourist».

So it was colour, with a life of its one, which undermined the whole notion of a viable representational art, and this in the heyday of Pre-Raphaelitism! Ruskin's formal vision, aided and stimulated by his intimate knowledge of Turner's working procedures, made him in this, as in so much else, into an aesthetic prophet.

9 Gage 1994.
10 I have discussed Cézanne's method more fully in Gage 1993b, pp. 209–211.

«Venga Medusa», Taf. 71 in: John Ruskin, *Modern Painters*, vol. V, London 1860

Werner Oechslin

Ruskins «Science of feeling»: die Herausbildung einer ganzheitlichen Kunstauffassung aus Natur und Kunst, Kunstgeschichte und Religion

> «... The first of these, or the theoretic faculty, is concerned with the moral perception and appreciation of ideas of beauty. ... The second great faculty is the imaginative, which the mind exercises in a certain mode of regarding or combining the ideas it has received from external nature, and the operations of which become in their turn objects of the theoretic faculty to other minds».
>
> John Ruskin, *Modern Painters* II, «Of the Imaginative and Theoretic Faculties», London 1846, S. 9.

Leben und Werk John Ruskins lassen sich nicht trennen oder in irgendeiner Weise auseinanderdividieren: das ist einer der geläufigsten Topoi der Ruskin-Literatur. Und vielleicht ist es auch der Grund dafür, dass ein Grossteil dieses Schrifttums so deutlich biographisch – und oft ausschliesslich biographisch – ausgerichtet erscheint, dass gleichsam alles aus seinem Leben erklärt und herausgelöst und wiederum dorthin zurückgeführt wird. Es gibt jedoch noch andere Möglichkeiten, diesen Zusammenhang von Leben und Werk sinnvoll zu deuten. Ruskin ist ein unentwegter Schreiber, der im Schreiben alles zusammenführt, was er beobachtet und aufnimmt und verarbeitet, womit er auch absichtlich die verschiedenen Formen von Erfahrung und Einsicht, von Praxis und Theorie ständig mischt und so den Schreibfluss umsomehr aufrechterhält.[1] Schreibend schafft er auf diese Weise eine 'zweite Welt', die sich für den Lesenden – trotz des gleichsam in jeder Zeile akribisch bewiesenen Bezuges zur Wirklichkeit – letztlich doch als eine andere, davon und vom Leben Ruskins abgelöste, neue Welt darstellt, so wie eben gemäss Ruskin selbst der «imaginative Akt» – eines Künstlers oder eines Schriftstellers – zu Resultaten führt, die so oder anders wiederum zum Objekt der Erkenntnis anderer Menschen werden («which become in their turn objects of the theoretic faculty to other minds»).[2] Unser 'Erkenntnis-Objekt' ist demzufolge Ruskins Sichtweise, wie sie

1 Vgl. Ruskins einleitende Erörterungen zu den theoretischen Möglichkeiten in: Ruskin 1843–1860, II, 1846, (Part III. Of Ideas of Beauty. Section I. Of the theoretic faculty), S. 8: «Science and art are either subservient to life or the objects of it. As subservient of life, or practical, their results are, in the common sense of the world, useful. As the object of life or theoretic, they are, in the common sense, useless; and yet the step between practical and theoretic science is the step between the miner and the geologist, the apothecary and the chemist; and the step between practical and theoretic art is that between the builder and the architect, between the plumber and the artist, and this is a step allowed on all hands to be from less to greater ...».

2 Vgl. oben das einleitende Zitat; Ruskin 1843–1860, II, 1846, S. 9.

sich eben in Ruskins Schrifttum umfassend darstellt. Es käme letztlich einer unverzeihlichen Herabminderung von dessen hoher Bedeutung gleich, wollte man darin nur nach biographischen Hintergründen oder nach episodenhaft vereinzelten Einsichten oder Ansichten zur Kunst suchen. Obwohl den Schriften Ruskins das 'Prozesshafte' Seite für Seite anzumerken ist, und obwohl das Projekt der *Modern Painters* durch andere Buchprojekte unterbrochen und verzögert wird, ist das Ganze, an dem Ruskin arbeitet, erkennbar und von ihm selbst auch immer wieder durch die kontinuierlich angewandten und wiederholten Argumente, durch wiederholt versuchte Neuansätze eines systematischen Zugriffs und übrigens auch durch häufige Verweise in Erinnerung gerufen.

Dass ein solches Ganzes komplex und dessen Bewältigung sehr anspruchsvoll ist, und dass die Schreibweise Ruskins das Ihre zur erhöhten Schwierigkeit eines einigermassen adäquaten Verstehens beigetragen hat, steht ausser Zweifel. Jenen Topos vom untrennbaren Zusammenhang von Leben und Werk hat John Dixon Hunt denn auch überzeugend mit Ruskins eigener, selbstkritischer Bemerkung zu seiner Schreib- und Komponierweise aus *The Crown of Wild Olives* von 1873 illustriert: es gehöre nämlich zu einer seiner schlechten Gewohnheiten, die Hälfte der Bücher in Vorworte zu packen.[3] Und er ergänzte diese Feststellung mit der Bemerkung des Herausgebers der Briefe Ruskins zu dessen Unfähigkeit, sich in irgendeiner Art (des Schreibens) zu beschränken. Dieses Uferlose und Überbordende und die Tatsache, dass Kürzungen oder Einschränkungen ohne wesentliche Verluste gar nicht erst denkbar sind, zeichnen Ruskins Schrifttum aus, in dem er sich und seine Erfahrungen in innigster Verbindung mit Kunst und Kunstauffassung darstellt und – bis ans Ende – auch auslebt.[4] Inmitten der nicht abgeschlossenen *Praeterita*, des literarischen Rückbezugs auf sein schriftstellerisches Leben, scheint auch sein tatsächliches Leben stillzustehen. Für einen solchen radikalen Zugang sind Bezeichnungen oder Kategorien, so vermutet man vorerst, wenig brauchbar oder schlicht zu eng. Kein 'Diskurs', schon gar keine 'Theorie' ('theoretic faculty' ist ja 'nur' eines unter andern Vermögen!); und auch «poetry» erscheint trotz des frühen, absichtlichen Gebrauchs dieses Begriffs durch Ruskin selbst – ausgerechnet in der Paarung mit Architektur – als zu einseitig, weil bei ihm Theorie und Diskurs in jedem Fall in ein solches 'Poetisches' hineinverwoben sind. Das wenige, was sich andererseits wie ein 'Traktat' gibt, kommt nur in zweiter Linie zustande, wie das 'Pamphlet' *On the Nature of Gothic Architecture*, das – dem vielzitierten allumfassenden Titel zum Trotz – nur einen Auszug aus dem zweiten Band der *Stones of Venice* darstellt.[5] Und was soll man in Anbetracht der ersten Zeilen der *Seven Lamps*, dieses Meilensteins der Architekturliteratur des 19. Jahrhunderts sagen, wenn man gleich zu Beginn des Buches liest: «The memoranda which form the basis of the following Essay have been thrown together during the preparation of one of the sections of the third volume of 'Modern Painters'».[6] 'Thrown together'! Ein Abfallprodukt seines grösseren Projektes der *Modern Painters*! Nicht genug, Ruskin ergänzt diesen ersten Satz – entsprechend obiger Bemerkung – gleich mit einer Fussnote, in der er ausführlichst die Umstände und Verzögerungen im Fortgang seiner schriftstellerischen Tätigkeit ausbreitet. Dort hat er natürlich für «the inordinate delay», zu denen sich prompt das Versprechen gesellt, es dabei zu keinem weiteren Schaden kommen zu lassen, einen sehr viel schwerwiegenderen Grund anzugeben: «His (= Ruskins) whole time has been lately occupied in taking drawings from one side of buildings, of which masons were knocking down the other ...».[7] Es kommt also – in Entsprechung des zitierten Topos – auch noch die 'Praxis', das tatsächliche Leben, die 'vita activa', hinzu, die Schrifttum und Leben in ein unauflösliches, stets dramatisch bewegtes Ganzes hineinstellt. Was für Ruskin selbst gilt, fordert er für die Sache und den Rest der Welt. Kein Zweifel, er tut dies im Sinne von 'Ganzheitsvorstellungen', des alles mit allem Zusammensehens und Verknüpfens. Und dieses Ganze ist dementsprechend keineswegs ein reines Produkt des Geistes, sondern aus tausenden von Einzelbeobachtungen und -urteilen, die sich in täglicher und stündlicher Modifikation einstellen, zusammengefügt. Kein Begriff der konventionellen Ästhetik oder Kunstgeschichte – schon gar nicht der der 'Romantik' – würde dies adäquat abbilden. Ganzheitsvorstellungen erfordern viel. Das «art has to be taken seriously or not at all» stellt eine ultimative Forderung dar.[8] Und dass sich Kunstvorstellung und Religiosität hier – wie bei anderen Künstlern (selbst bei Gottfried Semper) – berühren, ist mehr als nur einleuchtend, aber natürlich noch lange kein Grund, die Wirklichkeit zu vernachlässigen.

Kurzum, man muss sich auf Ruskin selbst (und auf seine Texte) einlassen, auf das Risiko hin, doch immer nur – trotz eines noch so ausgeweiteten Blickes – der einen oder anderen Sichtweise auf zufällige oder verkürzte Weise wenigstens ein bisschen auf die Schliche zu kommen. Um Ruskins Sichtweisen – und insofern eben doch um 'mehr' als die häufige (blosse) An- und Zurückbindung künstlerischer und kunsttheoretischer Vorstellungen an seine Biographie und andere 'Wirklichkeiten' – geht es allemal. Dabei sind Einschränkungen und Risiken in Kauf zu nehmen, zu denen die Konstruktion jenes (geläufigen) – und damit bereits voreilig unterstellten – 'idealen' Zusammenhangs gehört, gemäss dem beispielsweise ein

3 Vgl. Hunt 1982, S. ix.

4 John Dixon Hunt schloss daraus völlig zurecht auf den Vorrang eines «fresh model of that complex personality» gegenüber einer Forschung gemäss dem Prinzip des «hitherto unpublished» (ebd., S. ix)!

5 Der (zweiten) Version, einem fünfzigseitigen, kleingedruckten Heftchen in Klein 8.0 von 1854 (London, published by Smith, Elder, & Co., 65, Cornhill), entnehmen wir einige bezeichende, besondere Umstände: dem Untertitel («and herein of the True Function of the Workman in Art») 'entspricht' der Vermerk: «The profits arising from the sale of this pamphlet will be offered to the WORKING MEN'S COLLEGE, 31, Red Lion Square, London».

6 Vgl. Ruskin 1849, S. (v). Natürlich erscheint hier Ruskin bereits auf der Titelseite als «Author of 'Modern Painters'».

7 Ebd., Fussnote (*).

8 Vgl. dazu: Paul 1971, S. 286ff.; insbes. S. 314.

24. The Towers of Fribourg

25. Things in general.

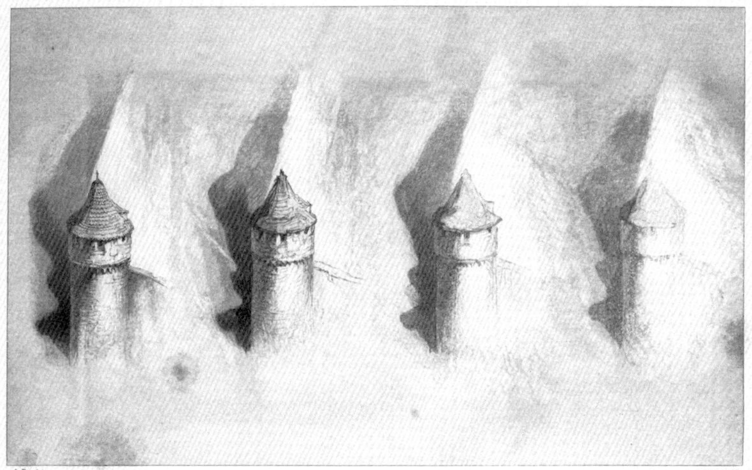

26. The Law of Evanescence

Atmosphärisch/gegenständlich: «The Towers of Fribourg», Taf. 24 in: John Ruskin, *Modern Painters*, vol. IV, London 1856

«Things in general», Taf. 25 in: John Ruskin, *Modern Painters*, vol. IV, London 1856

«The Law of Evanescence», Taf. 26 in: John Ruskin, *Modern Painters*, vol. IV, London 1856 stets vorausgesetzter Universalismus in Ruskins Vorstellung von Natur und Kunst gegeben sei. Gerade dieser wird jedoch oft und immer wieder abrupt und unvermittelt in die Formen unendlich verästelter Naturbeobachtung, kunstgeschichtlicher Analyse und freiem künstlerischem Empfinden überführt, sodass am Ende folgerichtig nur die kunstvolle Sprache allein – und keine irgendwie geartete, systematische Einfassung – als passendes Gefäss übrigzubleiben scheint. Doch darin darf man nicht das Ziel, sondern muss man die notwendige Bedingung der so fein verästelten Vorgehensweise Ruskins erkennen, der im übrigen keine noch so aufwendige, in die kleinste Einzelheit eindringende Analyse scheut. Begriffsscheu oder ahistorisch ist diese Ruskinsche Betrachtungsweise gerade deshalb keineswegs; noch steht sie überhaupt Wissenschaft und Intellekt 'trotz' hoher künstlerischer Sensibilität in irgendeiner Weise feindlich gegenüber.[9] Ruskins 'Ganzes' ist umfassend und schliesst alle nur erdenklichen Zugänge und Methoden und Formen des Grübelns und Nachdenkens mit ein, so sie denn ihm dem vertiefenden Erkennen dienen.

Gerade darin lässt sich allenfalls das 'Zeittypische' Ruskins erkennen, wenn denn danach gefragt sein sollte. Es sei dies mit einem – aus einem völlig anderweitigen Kontext zitierten – Urteil von Rudolf Virchow illustriert, das dieser aus Anlass der Totenfeier von Johannes Müller 1858 in Berlin formulierte. Rückblickend und natürlich in erster Linie auf deutsche Verhältnisse bezogen, schreibt dort Virchow: «Durch Schelling's Naturphilosophie hatte man gelernt, alle Erscheinungen aus der Idee des Absoluten abzuleiten».[10] Aus dieser «Verirrung» heraus, so Virchow weiter, hätte man es sich gestattet, «ohne Forschung das System zurecht zu legen». Die Gegenbewegung sei nun durch die «sorgfältigste Beobachtung» oder eben – Goethe darauf behaftend – das «Princip der Beobachtung» im Sinne der zu ihrem Siegeszug ansetzenden Naturwissenschaften – und richtig aufgefasster Forschung – ausgelöst worden.

Das beschreibt die Zeit, in der Ruskin seine reiche schriftstellerische, kritische Tätigkeit entfaltete. Und man darf dies – das «Princip der Beobachtung» – durchaus als gegebenen Ausgangspunkt nehmen, zumal dies ja keine deutsche Exklusivität darstellt. Immerhin zitiert Ruskin unter der äusserst knapp geführten Rubrik «Books which have influenced me» (1887) Alexander von Humboldt, was doch mehr als ein zufälliger Fingerzeig ist.[11] Humboldt steht für Ruskin als «central model» der Reiseliteratur und die lässt sich sowieso nicht dem einen oder an-

9 Ich sehe also keinen Grund, Ruskin als einen «der wirksamsten Wortführer des Irrationalismus» (vgl. Paul 1971, S. 315) zu bezeichnen; noch ist es überhaupt opportun, die Welt nach solchen Kriterien zu unterteilen.
10 Vgl. Virchow 1858, S. 16.
11 Vgl. Ruskin, Brief vom 14. Mai 1887, in Cook/Wedderburn 1903–1912, XXXIV, 1908, S. 605/606. Dort findet sich auch die Bemerkung, er würde systematisch keine englische, dafür (ausschliesslich) französische wissenschaftliche Literatur lesen: «All fine French divinity and science. I never read English sermons or scientific books, and only Humboldt (translated) of German».

deren Wissenszweig zuordnen.[12] Der Hinweis – notabene auf die beschreibende Reiseliteratur – ist also in mancher Hinsicht, eben auch bezüglich der Darstellungsform wie des disziplinären Zuschnitts der Schriften Ruskins aufschlussreich. Denn selbstverständlich hat Ruskin sein Gedankengebäude aus Natur und Kunst unabhängig von Schellings Naturphilosophie entwickelt. Es ist all dem lediglich noch hinzuzufügen, dass genaueste Beobachtung natürlich keine ausschliessliche Domäne der Naturwissenschaften darstellt, auch wenn diese Form von radikaler Kuriosität und ausgeprägtem Wissensdurst häufig genug in erster Linie unter diesem Paradigma geführt wird; und dass umgekehrt das 'Absolute' oder auch das 'Ideale' keineswegs bloss der Philosophie vorbehalten ist. Ruskins Persönlichkeit unterläuft auch eine solche, allzu eng gefasste, im späteren Vorurteil des Gegensatzes von Natur- und Geisteswissenschaft kodifizierte Unterscheidung. Kunst und Kunstbetrachtung bilden gemäss seiner Auffassung ein Gefäss, in dem dies alles undiskriminiert Platz findet.

Der folgende Beitrag will also insbesondere – verengt aber modellhaft – von einem (vermeintlichen) pantheistisch gefärbten ruskinschen Natur-Universalismus in der Tradition des alten, in der Imitationslehre verhafteten Natur-Kunst-Gegensatzes wegführen, um den Akzent umsomehr auf Ruskins ständig sich verändernde und bereichernde, auf unermüdliche Beobachtung gestützte, kulturgeschichtlich komplexe Sichtweise zu legen, die die Einzelbeobachtung dem Ganzen zuführt und dabei – im Einzelnen wie im Ganzen – auch noch das Religiöse mit in Betracht zu ziehen vermag.

I. Zugänge zu einer umfassenden Materie und zu einem grenzenlosen Projekt.

«... it is, or ought to be, a science of feeling more than of rule ...».

Kata Phusin (John Ruskin), *The Poetry of Architecture*, 1837.

«Whatever I have asserted throughout the work, I have endeavoured to ground altogether on demonstrations which must stand or fall by their own strength, and which ought to involve no more reference to authority or character than a demonstration in Euclid».

John Ruskin, *Modern Painters* I, 1843, Preface.

«[I] found that *demonstration* in matters of art was no such easy matter, and the pamphlet turned into a volume».

John Ruskin, «Brief an Rev. Osborne Gordon, 10. März 1844», in: E.T. Cook/A. Wedderburn (Hg.), *Complete Works* III, 1903, S. 665/666.

Trotz der erwähnten, notwendigen Einschränkungen darf man also voraussetzen, dass Ruskin in keiner Weise 'naiv' an den Gegenstand herangeht. Ganz im Gegenteil: er führt sein ganzes, sich ständig erweiterndes Wissen in seine Begegnung mit Natur und Kunst ein. Und so ist ihm auch stets klar, um welche möglichen rationalen Zugänge oder vielmehr um welche Gefühle es dabei geht. «The Idea had come into my head in the summer of '37, and, I imagine, rose immediately out of my sense of the contrast between the cottages of Westmoreland and those of Italy».[13] Nachdem er sich der Beschreibung, dessen was er unmittelbar am Wegrand wahrnahm, gerade hingegeben hatte, kam ihm eine 'Idee' – unmittelbar seiner Sinneswahrnehmung entspriessend – und mischte sich auch schon mit der Erinnerung an unterschiedliche Häuser, als Ausdrucksformen unterschiedlicher Kultur in England wie in Italien. In einem Satz beschreibt und fasst Ruskin rückblickend in den *Praeterita* zusammen, wie in ihm im spontanen Einfall und in ebenso unmittelbarer Assoziation eine – auf diese Weise auch historisch fundierte – 'Idee', also eine (theoretische) Vorstellung entstand. Was ihm damals eingefallen sei und was später sein halbes Leben ausgefüllt und bestimmt hätte, liesse sich nicht in kürzere Worte fassen: «I could not have put in fewer, or more inclusive words ...».[14] Es geht um den Titel des unter dem Pseudonym Kata Phusin 1837 in Loudons *Architectural Magazine* publizierten Erstlingswerks «The Poetry of Architecture; or, The Archi-

12 Ebd., Brief vom 13. Januar 1886, S. 583. (Diese Äusserung bezieht sich auf die Frage der *Pall Mall Gazette* nach den «Best hundred Books» von 1886.)

13 Vgl. Ruskin 1886/1887, S. 413.

14 Ebd.: «... the definition of what half my future life was to be spent in discoursing of ...».

tecture of the Nations of Europe considered in its Association with Natural Scenery and National Character».[15] Zugegebenermassen kein kurzer Titel! Aber, wie sagte es Ruskin zurecht: kürzer wäre es wohl kaum gegangen, wenn – und das gehörte ganz offensichtlich zur programmatischen Absicht (schon) dieser Schrift – Poesie, Landschaft und kulturelle Vielfalt gemäss Nationalcharakter und geographischer Gegebenheit unter einen Begriff gebracht werden sollten. Ruskin hatte in *Praeterita* zusätzlich auf das «According to Nature» als einem «nom-de-plume» verwiesen. Er bezog dies, damit man auch dies richtig verstehe, auf die Kraft des eigenen Urteils: «The adoption of a nom-de-plume at all, implied ... a sense of a power of judgement in myself ...».[16] Bei aller späteren Kritik an den früheren beschränkten Möglichkeiten und am jugendlichen Eifer, hält er auch noch spät an diesen Urteilen und Entscheidungen fest. Und er weiss sich auch zu erinnern, dass er diese Möglichkeiten eben aus der Sprache – der Bibel und Johnson – geschöpft hätte.[17] Nein, naiv-romantisch ist Ruskin auch als Jüngling keineswegs, und dies nicht nur wegen der verklärten späteren Sicht der *Praeterita*!

Jener Aufsatz von 1837 begann, wie es dem jugendlichen Eifer Ruskins entsprach und jedwelchem jugendlichen Eifer zu entsprechen scheint, mit dem Lob der 'Wissenschaft Architektur' als einer der nobelsten Errungenschaften des menschlichen Geistes, was dann im zweiten Satz – gegen alle Konvention und gegen alle möglichen Vorurteile – in einer These zurechtgestutzt und gleich wieder erweitert wird: «It is not merely a science of the rule and compass, it does not consist only in the observation of just rule, or of fair proportion: it is, or ought to be, a science of feeling more than of rule, a ministry to the mind, more than to the eye».[18] Auf diese Weise des Widerspruchs zur konventionellen Vorstellung einer regelschaffenden, in der Geometrie gegründeten Theorie der Architektur haben natürlich schon vor Ruskin beispielsweise Etienne-Louis Boullée und Nicolas Le Camus de Mézieres die Öffnung gesucht. Boullée forderte die Umkehrung der Argumentationsweise Vitruvs («Vitruve prend l'effet pour la cause»); und Le Camus de Mézieres empfahl gleichzeitig die Ergänzung der Lehre der fünf Ordnungen um die Berücksichtigung der «affections de l'âme».[19] Längst also war vieles in Bewegung geraten. Dementsprechend ist dies, die Erweiterung des Blickwinkels in Sachen architektonisches Regelwerk, für Ruskin alias Kata Phusin der Weg, um jener Diskussion etwas entgegenzusetzen, die kurz zuvor in Loudons Zeitschrift zu 'Stil', zu «copied architecture» oder «imitative architecture», geführt wurde.[20] Ruskin bricht früh mit dieser üblichen Diskussion, die er als «at a miserably low ebb in England» brandmarkt. «Gothic in form and Grecian in detail»: nichts davon, von solchen «monstrosified pepper-boxes», gehört für ihn zum Thema einer Architektur-Wissenschaft.[21] Dieser Blick auf die «so miserably debased» Architektur-Schule ist aber nur gerade der Ausgangspunkt, von dem aus Ruskin auf den ersten wenigen Seiten

– und mit knappen Hinweisen auf «unity of feeling», auf «feelings and manners» entsprechend Nation und «scenery»[22] – seinen Aufbruch beschreibt: an den er sich spät in den *Praeterita* als der unmittelbar aus den Sinnen aufgegangenen «Idee» 'entsinnt'.

In der «Preface» zum ersten Band der *Modern Painters* wendet sich Ruskin 1843 gleich im ersten Satz – ähnlich dezidiert und polemisch – gegen «the shallow and false criticisms of the periodicals of the day on the works of the great living artists to whom it principally refers».[23] Auch hier ist also ein radikaler Schnitt mit der üblichen Kunstkritik der Ausgangspunkt. Und was vorerst als «a short pamphlet» gedacht war, und worin er sich schnell als «compelled to amplify» genötigt sah, wird bald einmal zu einem mehrbändigen Lebenswerk. Auch dieses Werk beginnt wie die als «science of feeling» apostrophierte *Poetry* von 1837 durchaus mit einem Theorie-Verdacht. «The True, the Beautiful, the Intellectual» – bezogen auf die Werke der Kunst der modernen Meister und insbesondere J.M.W. Turners – umschreibt dies Ruskin im Untertitel seines wohl berühmtesten Werkes. Da die «superiority» gegenüber den alten Meistern in Sachen Landschaftsmalerei schon zuvor benannt ist, denkt man an eine Neuauflage des klassischen 'paragone' oder eine neu-adaptierte 'querelle'.[24] Doch zeigen die drei fettgedruckten und in altertümelnden Lettern gesetzten Epitheta, dass es um mehr, mithin um eine Kennzeichnung der Reichweite von Kunst überhaupt – entsprechend den genannten, umfassenden philosophischen und ästhetischen Kategorien – geht. Wie 1837, als es – bezogen auf Architektur – um «science» ging, sind es hier also die grossen Begriffe und Gefässe wie das der 'Wahrheit', von denen Ruskin ausgeht, um sich dann wiederum sehr schnell in den kapillaren Strukturen und in der einzelnen Beobachtung (scheinbar) zu verlieren, oder eben zu vertiefen. «Whatever I have asserted throughout the work, I have endeavoured to ground altogether on demonstrations

15 In den *Praeterita* (Ruskin 1886/1887, I, S. 413) ist der Titel ungenau als «Introduction to the Poetry of Architecture ...» und das Pseudonym in einem Wort als «Kataphusin» gegeben. Der entsprechende Passus erscheint 1893 zu Beginn der «Prefatory Notes» in der von George Allen besorgten, aufwendigen, illustrierten Neuausgabe der *Poetry of Architecture*.

16 Ebd., S. 413/414.

17 Vgl. dazu unten.

18 Vgl. Loudon 1837 (Reprint London 1972), S. 505.

19 Vgl. Boullée 1953, S. 27; Le Camus de Mézieres 1780, S. 1/2: «Jusqu'ici on a travaillé d'après les proportions des cinq Ordres d'Architecture ... Mais, combien d'Artistes n'ont employé ces Ordres que machinalement ...».

20 Vgl. «Amicus», Notes on modern Architecture, n. 2, in: Loudon 1837, S. 474ff. – Dem Autor geht es um die Behauptung, dass sich die gotische Architektur analog zu den Säulenordnungen der Griechen in «character and form» auffassen und unterscheiden lasse.

21 Vgl. Ruskin 1837–1838, S. 505/506.

22 Ebd., S. 507.

23 Ruskin 1843–1860, I, S. (vii).

24 Zur Präzisierung sei hier der vollständige Titel des ersten Bandes der *Modern Painters* wiedergegeben: «MODERN PAINTERS:/ THEIR SUPERIORITY/ IN THE ART OF LANDSCAPE PAINTING/ TO ALL/ THE ANCIENT MASTERS/ PROVED BY EXAMPLES OF/ *The True, the Beautiful, and the Intellectual*,/ FROM THE/ WORKS OF MODERN ARTISTS,/ ESPECIALLY/ FROM THOSE OF J.M.W. TURNER, ESQ.R.A./ BY A GRADUATE OF OXFORD ...».

which must stand or fall by their own strength, and which ought to involve no more reference to authority or character than a demonstration in Euclid».[25] Auf höhere wissenschaftliche Ansprüche kann man sich kaum berufen. Aber natürlich ist dies zuvor und danach durch Einschränkungen («I have not entered into systematic criticism of all the painters of the present day ...») und Enschuldigungen («... I have to apologise for the imperfection of a work ...») in die Wirklichkeit zurückgeholt. Würde man bloss der Auflistung der Kapitelüberschriften in der «Synopsis of Contents» folgen, so könnte man in der Tat ein hochphilosophisches Werk, und in Anbetracht des ab Seite 52 durchgehend applizierten Prinzips der Wahrheit ein solches von geradezu metaphysischem Tiefgang vermuten. Doch wird man andererseits sehr schnell bemerken, dass es am Ende um so 'konkrete' Fragen wie «Truth of Chiaroscuro» oder «Truth of Clouds» geht. Eine 'Metaphysik', wenn schon, der künstlerischen Interpretationen der Natur!

Der Bezug auf Euklidische Axiomatik – oder gar Normativität – steht nur stellvertretend für den Anspruch einer letztlich völlig andersgearteten wissenschaftlichen Radikalität, die in jener präzisen Beobachtung der Wirklichkeit ihren Grund findet. Als ob man dies durch jenes erklären müsste, um in Sachen 'Theorie' – oder eben was man darunter konventionellerweise verstand – ernstgenommen zu werden. Eine 'Theorie' in statu nascendi sollte es allemal sein. Man muss sich des jugendlichen Alters Ruskins erinnern, der damals in rascher Abfolge die italienische Bildungsreise und das Naturerlebnis von Chamonix hinter sich bringt und beides, Kunst und Natur, in ihren jeweils herausragendsten Erscheinungsformen nebeneinander zu verarbeiten sucht. Anekdotenhaft und verklärt erscheint dabei in seiner Biographie der doppelte Entschluss von Mitte Juli 1842 in Genf, ein Pamphlet und daraus resultierend ein Traktat über die Landschaftsmalerei zu schreiben, und andererseits in Mannheim am 31. Juli 1842 die Architektur an den Nagel zu hängen.[26] Dazwischen, so Ruskin selbst im Rückblick von 1844, meditiert er rheinabwärts, um festzustellen: «[I] found that demonstration in matters of art was no such easy matter ...».[27] Spielt hier auch noch die klassische Differenz von Architektur und bildender Kunst eine gewisse Rolle? Ruskin ist sich der unterschiedlichen Eignung architektonischer respektive künstlerischer Gegenstände für einen systematisierenden Zugriff bewusst; entsprechende Ansätze finden sich in

25 Vgl. Ruskin 1843–1860, I, Preface, S. x.

26 Die Genfer Episode rekonstruiert Ruskin in einem Brief an seinen damaligen Begleiter Rev. Osborne Gordon vom 10. März 1844 (vgl. Cook/Wedderburn 1903–1912, III, S. 665f.; vgl. u.a.: Hunt 1982, S. 129ff.; Sawyer 1985, S. 34ff.). Der entscheidende Passus lautet dort: «... and that forenoon in church (it's an odd thing, but all my resolutions of which anything is to come are invariably formed, whether I will or not, in church – I scheme all thro' the litany) – that forenoon, I say, I determined to write a pamphlet and blow the critics out of the water».
Nichts davon findet sich in Ruskins Tagebuch, das dieser 1875 verschenkt hatte und das ihm bei Abfassung der *Praeterita* nicht zur Verfügung stand. Dort steht hingegen der Eintrag vom 31. Juli in Mannheim mit dem – scheinbaren – Verzicht auf Architektur. (Vgl. Evans/Whitehouse 1953–1956, III, 1956, S. 231).

27 Vgl. Cook/Wedderburn 1903–1912, III, S. 666.

Grade des Naturalismus
in der Kunstgeschichte:
«Early Naturalism»,
Taf. 16 in: John Ruskin,
Modern Painters, vol. III,
London 1856

«Advanced Naturalism»,
Taf. 17 in: John Ruskin,
Modern Painters,
vol. III, London 1856

seinen Schriften bunt gemischt. Doch jetzt scheint er die Architektur aufgeben zu wollen. «A great deal of interest in the Architecture ..., but I fear I shall have to give up Arch: too many irons in fire», schreibt er am 31. Juli 1842 ins Tagebuch. Aber Zeilen später notiert er wiederum seine architektonisierenden Beobachtungen («Note the conglomerate rocks ...»; «Note the calcareous formation ...»), die erahnen lassen, dass er Architektur natürlich nie aus seinem Blickfeld verlieren wird. Er will sie bloss – wie schon 1837 behauptet – ausserhalb der engeren vitruvianischen Wissenschaft und der Reduktivität eines Regelwerkes – natur- und geistesgeschichtlich umfassend angehen dürfen. So ist er natürlich immer mal wieder versucht, der Natur eine architektonisch-systematisierende Sichtweise aufzuzwingen. Andererseits lässt sich der Eindruck des Strassburger Münsters eben kurz – und prägnant – mit «a brilliant barbarism» fassen.[28] Es soll hier – und dafür ist die Sprache das adäquate Mittel – auch nicht die feinste Beobachtung unterschlagen werden. Denn gerade in solchen unscheinbaren Beobachtungen liegt der Schlüssel der Erkenntnis und der alleinige Zugang zur Wahrheit.

Natürlich ist bei Ruskin schon damals der genaue Blick auf die unendliche Vielfalt der Natur religiös überhöht – und wird es auch stets bleiben. In den *Praeterita*, in denen ansonsten wenig Präzises zu den zuletzt genannten Ereignissen steht, ist zumindest im Rückblick dieser Grundzug deutlich gemacht: «The first sight of the Alps had been to me as a direct revelation of the benevolent will in creation».[29] Diese Erinnerung steht in einem präzisen Kontext. Dem Satz zur göttlichen Schöpfung ging die Erörterung des Vesuvs voraus. Und danach folgte der Verweis auf Homer und Dante, sodass sich am Schluss dem «visible Paradise» von Lauterbrunnen im Berner Oberland auf überzeugende Weise die «visible Hell» des Vulkans kontrastreich gegenübergestellt findet. Beides bezieht sich auf obligatorische Stationen der italienischen sowie der neueren, 'alpinen' Bildungsreise, deren unterschiedliche Beobachtungen nun auf diese Weise zusammengeführt werden. Nichts kommt ohne solche Verknüpfung, ohne solche Bilder aus. Und diese Hermeneutik wird schon innerhalb der Sprache selbst, so spontan und zufällig sie geformt sein mag, kenntnisreich entwickelt. Wenn es etwa um jenes sublime Erschrecken im Anblick der alpinen Naturgewalt geht, so wird eben vorerst die Verwendung des Wortes «horrid» bei John Evelyn, der diese Bezeichnung auch schon benützte,[30] untersucht: ganz im Sinne jener allgemeinen Feststellung, wonach früher geäusserte Ideen nun eben selbst zum Objekt «of the theoretic faculty to other minds» würden.[31] Das Universale bricht sich im Konreten, hier wie beinahe überall.

II. Natur und Kunst: das alte Begriffspaar auf universalem Hintergrund, neuaufgelegt und präzisiert.

«By truth of earth, we mean the faithful representation of the facts and forms of the bare ground, considered as entirely divested of vegetation, through whatever disguise, or under whatever modification may be occasioned by the clothing of the landscape».

John Ruskin, *Modern Painters* I, 1843, S. 259.

«Mountains are, to the rest of the body of the earth, what violent, muscular action is to the body of man».

John Ruskin, *Modern Painters* I, 1843, S. 261.

«Forms of earth ... why I do not say rocks or mountains ...?»

John Ruskin, *Stones of Venice* I, 1851, S. 218.

«It may be noted in passing, that this wall which with its regular fosse defends the Riffelhorn on its western side ... are curious intances of trenchant precipice ...; hard, green as a sea wave, and polished like the inside of a shell ...».

John Ruskin, *Modern Painters* IV, 1856, S. 239.

Auf diesen Prämissen, dem selbstverfassten 'Reisebericht' in den Alpen, der auf die klassische kunsthistorische Bildungsreise gestülpt wird, soll letztlich die Landschaftsmalerei als die neue, allumfassende Kunstgattung, die den Primat der Historienmalerei ablösen soll, aufgebaut und herausgestellt werden. Sie war in der Kunst J.M.W. Turners längst in unübertrefflicher Weise vorgegeben. Natur- und Kunststudium in konsequentester Anwendung finden hier ideal zusammen. Man könnte also durchaus verführt sein, seinerseits alles mit allem zu vergleichen und zu verbinden. Natürlich hat schon Scheuchzer in dieser Frühphase stratigraphischer Studien an den steilaufsteigenden Felswänden am Urnersee die naturgeschichtlichen Einsichten dem biblischen Schöpfungsakt zugeordnet und auf diese Weise sein Werk als *Physica Sacra, oder geheiligte Wissenschaft* respektive, leicht gewandelt, als *Physique sacrée ou histoire-naturelle de la Bible* ausgegeben und – aktuell und 'wissenschaftlich korrekt' – illustriert. Natürlich stellen sich in einem Blick die Bilder der Basaltformationen und die entsprechenden architektonischen Phantasien bis hin zu Bruno Tauts geometrisch-architektonischer Verformung der Alpen in seiner *Alpinen Architektur* (1919) ein. Fingals Höhle, Jakow Tschernichows Variationen geometrisch-architektonischer, stalaktitähnlich aufgereihter Körper und selbst das (gesetzeskonforme) 'set-back' der New Yorker Wolkenkratzer in der modell- und

28 Vgl. Evans/Whitehouse 1953–1956, S. 232.
29 Vgl. Ruskin 1886/1887, II, S. 87f.
30 Ebd., S. 3.
31 Vgl. oben.

schemenhaften Darstellung des ‘renderers’ Hugh Ferriss in «Metropolis of tomorrow» (1929) ähneln sich und scheinen derselben universalen – besser: verallgemeinernden – Sichtweise einer ‘architektonischen’ Natur nachgeformt zu sein. Aber diese formalen Analogien erweisen sich in Anbetracht des detaillierten Interesses Ruskins als zu formalistisch und oberflächlich.[32]

Bei Ruskin sind solche älteren oder eben auch jüngeren universalistischen und naturreligiösen Betrachtungsweisen jedoch längst in die konkrete Bedingung naturgeschichtlicher und kultureller Konkretheit hineingesetzt. Zwar bemüht auch er vorerst die – abstrahierende – Zurückführung der Natur auf ihre ‘nackte Wahrheit’. «Truth of Earth» wird im ersten Band von *Modern Painters* bezogen auf das, was er «general structures» nennt, mit einer entsprechenden Definition eingeleitet: «By truth of earth, we mean the faithful representation of the facts and forms of the bare ground, considered as entirely divested of vegetation, through whatever disguise, or under whatever modificiation may be occasioned by the clothing of the landscape».[33] Auffällig ist dabei aber, dass diese nackte, entkleidete – scheinbar abstrakte – Landschaft, genauer deren ‘Wahrheit’, mit «faithful representation» verknüpft wird, was – mit diesem Beiwort einer ‘getreuen’ Abbildung ausgestattet! – unmöglich auf jener abstrakten Ebene einer idealisiserten Urlandschaft aufgefasst werden kann. Anders gesagt: auch dies, diese nackte Wahrheit, obwohl sie erst durch das Wegnehmen von Vegetation und Kleidung überhaupt erkennbar wird, ist konkrete Natur und insofern ein Objekt der unmittelbaren (künstlerischen) Natur-Darstellung. (*Modern Painters* ist reich an Reproduktionen von Bildern, die in diesem Sinne ‘abstrahierend’ sind, jedoch stets erkennbar Landschaftsmalerei verkörpern.)

Umso besser begreift man nun den nächsten Satz, der die gesamte Kunsttheorie gemäss der alten Imitationslehre gleichwohl zu subsumieren scheint: «Ground is to the landscape painter what the naked body is to the historical».[34] Man ist dank der Einsicht in eine solche Analogie schnell bereit, eine entsprechende Theorie zur Landschaft und zur Landschaftsmalerei entgegenzunehmen. Vergleichbarkeit und Vergleichung sind die Voraussetzung jeder Methode. Mit einer Mischung von Vorkenntnis und Ahnung begegnet man den weiteren Argumenten: «laws of the organization of the earth». Sie kann man «without knowledge of the interior mechanism» erkennen. Sie liegen den Sinnen offen, sichtbar in der Landschaft ausgebreitet. Mit dieser Einschränkung führt Ruskin – notgedrungen – von der Erdwissenschaft weg und in die Kunstgeschichte hinein; er führt ein in die Art und Weise, wie Künstler mit solchen ‘Gesetzen’ umgehen und stets umgegangen sind. (Das ‘wie’ wird ja später – im «of realization» überschriebenen Kapitel im dritten Band von *Modern Painters* (1856) – gleichsam zum Paradigmawechsel in Ruskins Betrachtungsweise!)[35] Gleichwohl wird das Bild der einmal gewählten Analogie Landschaft/Körper weitergesponnen: «Mountains are, to the rest of the body of the earth, what violent, muscular action is to the body of man».[36] Ja gerade dies, dass der Natur wie dem menschlichen Körper «convulsive energy»,[37] «expression», «passion» und «strength» eingegeben sei, macht Ruskin zum «first grand principle of the truth of the earth».

Ruskin führt also mittelbar dank solcher Analogie von der Konkretheit zurück zum Prinzip. Umgekehrt ist er andernorts auf geradezu ängstliche Weise darum bemüht, keine unzulässige Verallgemeinerung und Schlussfolgerung aufkommen zu lassen. Eine solche klärende, methodische Anmerkung – mit Bezug auf 'Wahrheit' – findet sich in der Preface des vierten Bandes (1856) der *Modern Painters*. «General truth», so liest man dort, beziehe sich nicht auf das Seite 185 gezeigte Diagramm, sondern lediglich auf die zugehörigen ausgemessenen Winkel.[38] Diagramme, auch wenn sie auf präzis gemessenen, 'objektiven', Daten basieren, bleiben Hypothesen, sind mathematische Hilfskonstruktionen. Die Wahrheit sucht Ruskin in der Natur selbst, aber eben auch nicht in einer oder ausgerechnet in der 'typischsten' Erscheinungsform, deren unbestrittene Eindrücklichkeit beispielsweise Bruno Taut dazu bringt, den «Fels Matterhorn» (aus der berühmten Zermatter Sicht!) tale quale zur Architektur zu erklären.[39] Ruskin verweigert sich der künstlerischen Sehweise keineswegs. Gerade er geht ja von solchen eindrücklichen Bildern («strong impressions») aus. Er spricht von «peakedness» und «spiry separatness», bildet gleichsam eine begrifflich gefasste Phänomenologie der Berggipfel, um dann gleichwohl dies als nur «partially true» zu relativieren.[40] Es geht Ruskin eben gleichermassen auch um die wissenschaftlich korrekte Beschreibung des Matterhorns, die er – deshalb nicht beschränkt auf die übliche, 'typische' Erscheinungsform – im Umschreiten und somit aus verschiedenstem Blickwinkel erfasst und 'wahrheitsgetreu', teilweise unter Zuhilfenahme von Diagrammen, darstellt. Wahrheit im Zusammenhang von Natur und Kunst ist ein heikles Ding, und Ruskin, der ja selbst seine Einbildungskraft nicht zügeln mag und die Kontur eines Berggipfels mit derjenigen des Daches eines alten französischen Hauses vergleicht,

32 Der Schreibende ist dieser verführerischen Analogie (vgl. Oechslin 1984, S. 44ff.) selbst erlegen, was hier kritisch vermerkt sei.
33 Ruskin 1886/1887, I, S. 259.
34 Ebd.
35 Vgl. Ruskin 1843–1860, III, 1856, S. 17: «In the outset of this inquiry, the reader must thoroughly understand that we are not now considering what is to be painted, but how far it is to be painted ...».
36 Ebd., S. 261.
37 Solcherlei Beschreibungen dienen später der Kunstgeschichte als Erklärungsmodell der – ansonsten 'nicht beschreibbaren' – barocken Kunst. (Vgl. Riegl 1908, S. 3: «Das Ausserordentliche packt uns in der Antike und Renaissance, im Barockstil stösst es uns ab, wir empfinden es störend, wie eine lästige Unklarheit; z.B. eine Figur, die betet und sich dabei in konvulsivischen Bewegungen krümmt».)
38 Ruskin 1843–1860, IV, 1856, S. vii.
39 Vgl. Taut 1919, 3. Teil: Der Alpenbau, Blatt 20. Der Fels Matterhorn.
40 Ruskin 1843–1860, IV, 1856, S. 182.

breaking wave is indicated; and note farther, how different a thing good drawing may be from delicate *drawing* on the one hand, and how different it must be from ignorant drawing on the other. Woodcutting, in Durer's days, had reached no delicacy capable of expressing subtle detail or aërial perspective. But all the subtlety and aërial perspective of modern days are useless, and even barbarous, if they fail in the expression of the essential mountain facts.

§ 26. It will be noticed, however, that in this example of Durer's, the recognition of straightness of line does not exist, and that for this reason the hills look soft and earthy, not rocky.

So, also, in the next example, Fig. 64., the crest in the middle

Fig. 64.

X.

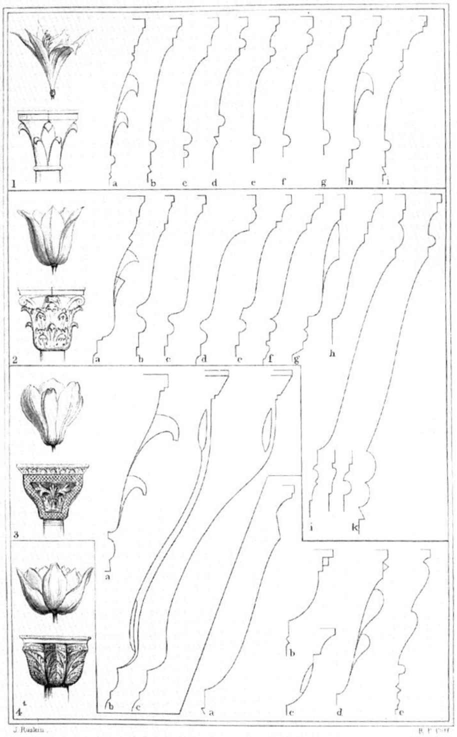

The Four Venetian Flower Orders.

VII.

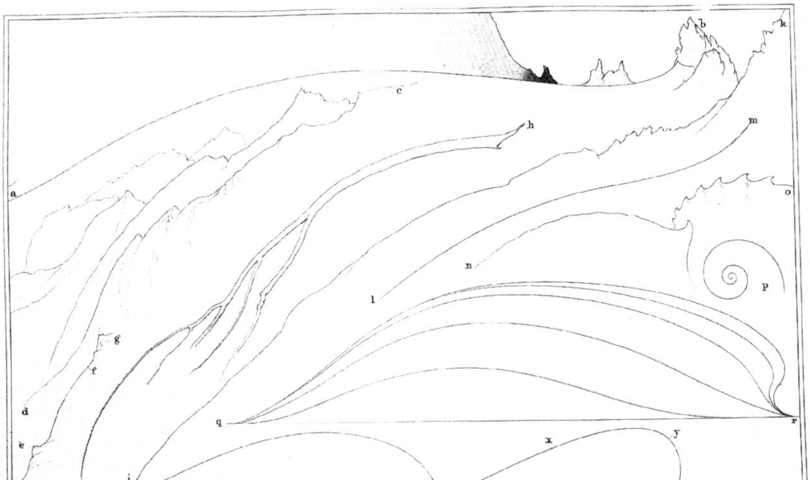

Abstract Lines.

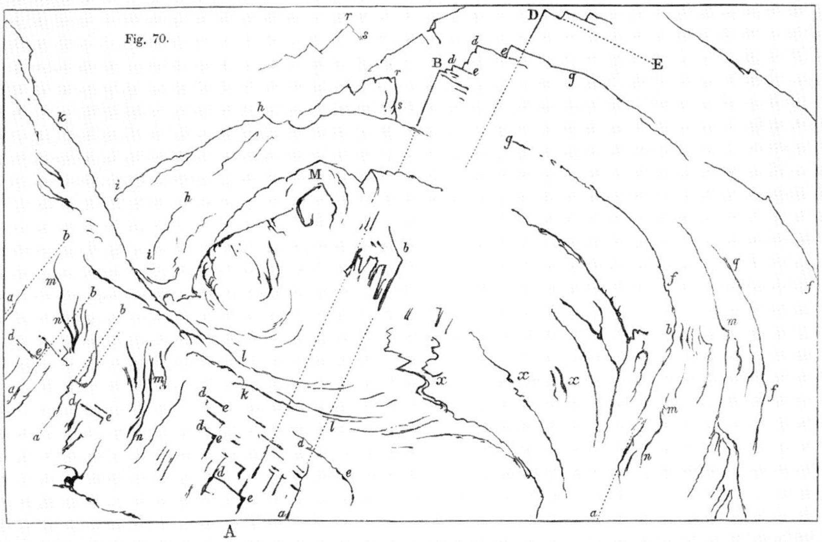

Linie/Malerei-Naturerfassung:

«Crests», Fig. 64 in: John Ruskin, *Modern Painters*, vol. IV, London 1956, S. 222

«The Four Venetian Flower-Orders», Taf. X^1 in: John Ruskin, *The Stones of Venice*, vol. II, London 1853

«Abstract Lines», Taf. VII in: John Ruskin, *The Stones of Venice*, vol. I, London 1851

«Crests», Fig. 70 in: John Ruskin, *Modern Painters*, vol. IV, London 1856, S. 228

«Rocks in Unrest», Taf. 81 in: John Ruskin, *Modern Painters*, vol. V, London 1860

81 Rocks in Unrest

weiss sehr wohl zwischen Naturgegebenheit und Bild zu unterscheiden.[41] Wenn schon liegt hier die Wahrheit in der Konkretheit einer Felsformation, gleichsam im Detail und eben nicht in der eindrücklichen Silhouette aufgereihter Berggipfel versteckt. Dieser wird eine Teilwahrheit zuerkannt und die gilt es genauer zu beschreiben. Denn Begriffe wie «obelisk», Felsobelisk für das Matterhorn, wie ihn der von Ruskin ansonsten hochgeschätzte Forbes verwendet, sind ihm dann doch zu symbolhaft abstrakt.[42] Ruskin ist zweifelsohne auf der Suche nach der Wahrheit; er forscht deshalb nach 'Tatsachen', sucht sie aus den idealen Vorstellungen – ohne diese zu zerstören – herauszulösen, um so der Sache auf den Grund zu kommen. Das lässt ihm die Möglichkeit, den Winkel eines Felsabhangs mit der gleichen Aufmerksamkeit festzustellen, wie er andererseits eben Bergformationen mit den Wellen des Meeres oder einer Muschel vergleicht: das Universale im Konkreten!

So oder anders weist die Argumentation Ruskins seine physikalisch korrekte Ordnung auf. Er geht von der Schöpfung aus, kommt zu den «Materials of Mountains», deren Kompaktheit und Körperhaftigkeit wiederum zur Betrachtung «of the Sculpture of Mountain» führen, was dann Stratifizierungen und die Gestalt von Bergspitzen ins Zentrum der Aufmerksamkeit rücken lässt. Nach einer derartigen Ausbreitung des «broad aspect of things» beginnt erst die eigentliche Untersuchung. Sie gilt den «resulting forms». Ruskin wählt die «Aiguilles» als Demonstrationsobjekt. Die Seriosität seiner Absicht unterstreicht Ruskin mit der Aussage: «We must now consent to take more pains, and observe more closely».[43]

Was folgt, kann man sowohl als geologische Untersuchung als auch als peinlich genaue kunstgeschichtliche (Bild-)Analyse verstehen. Formgebung von Natur und Kunst, das war ja vorgegeben, sind in irgendeiner Weise analog und vergleichbar. Also lassen sich die entsprechenden 'Methoden' oder Sichtweisen vergleichen und gelegentlich auch vermengen. Dass hier irgendeinmal ein Dürerscher Holzschnitt – genauer ein Landschaftsausschnitt mit fernen Gebirgszügen – in der Diskussion auftauchen würde, überrascht niemanden. Und auch die – spektakuläre – 'Rückführung' der Aiguilles auf eine Befestigungsmauer, von der aus in einem Prozess der «dilapidation» der ruinöse Zustand hergeleitet wird, den die Natur in der Tat in jahrtausendlanger Erosion geschaffen hat, überrascht nach den Erläuterungen zur Ruskinschen Vorgehensweise niemanden mehr.[44] Alles, was hier detailliert analysiert, auf «resulting form» hin geprüft und wörtlich von allen Seiten her beleuchtet wird, ergibt sich aus dieser grundsätzlichen Absicht des Erkennens und Analysierens von Formschaffungs-Prozessen.

Darin also finden Natur und Kunst zusammen. Und Ruskins Schriften illustrieren tausend Facetten dieser ewigen Begegnung in ihren tatsächlichen Ausprägungen und Erscheinungsformen. Wenn er anderswo – im ersten Band der *Stones of Venice* (1851), die ja zwischen den zweiten und dritten Band der *Modern Painters* 'geschoben' wurden – auf die «Forms of Earth» zu sprechen kommt, ist es gerade diese Dynamik, die im Vordergrund steht. «We are to follow the labour of Nature», empfiehlt er hier, nachdem er zuvor gefragt hat, weshalb er von «Form of Earth» und nicht beispielsweise von «rocks or mountains» gesprochen hätte.[45] Letzteres würde doch wiederum ein blosses Festhalten eines zufälligen Naturausschnittes begünstigen. Ruskin verlangt – in guter Tradition – mehr von der Kunst. Noch wäre eine künstlerische Darstellung mit dieser Vorgabe einer perfekten Reproduktion überhaupt möglich, noch wäre sie erwünscht. «Their scale cannot be represented, not their accident systematised».[46] Der 'Grösse' der Natur wird auf der kleinen Leinwand keine massgetreue Abbildung entsprechen können; und aus Zufälligem kann man kein System bilden. Auch vor dem Mikrokosmos der Natur, den Spuren eines Felsabbruches beispielsweise, steht der Künstler mit einer bloss reproduzierenden Zielsetzung hilflos gegenüber: «No sculptor can in the least imitate the peculiar character of accidental fracture: he can obey or exhibit the laws of nature, but he cannot copy the felicity or her fancies, nor follow the steps of her fury».[47]

Keine exakte Kopie von Natur und deren Zufälligkeiten und Launen – aber auch keine blosse idealisierende 'Darstellung' von Naturgesetzen. «The very glory of a mountain is in the revolutions which raised it into power, and the forces which are striking it into ruin».[48] Aus der Dynamik der Natur ist zu lernen. Und das präzisiert Ruskin im Nebensatz des zitierten Postulats «We are to follow the labour of Nature», was nun fortgeführt wird: «but not her disturbance; to imitate what she has deliberately ordained*, not what she has violently suffered, or strangely permitted».[49] Man darf das durchaus so lesen, dass Ruskin in seinem Parallelismus von Natur und Kunst auch der Natur gleichsam künstlerische Kriterien unterstellt: der reinen Zufälligkeit etwa im Erosionsprozess der Berge stellt er einen Prozess entgegen, dem eine gewisse Ordnung, ein 'Sinn' unterstellt wird. Für diese 'Mittelstellung' bezüglich der Analogie von Natur und Kunst verweist er an diesem Ort (*) auf das Beispiel des Matterhorns. Und damit auch wirklich keinerlei deterministische Vorstellungen dieses ausgewogene Verhältnis von Natur und Kunst stören und in Kausalitäten verkehren können, gibt er noch einmal die Extrempunkte des

41 Ebd., S. 183 und fig. 130.

42 Ebd., S. 184. – Forbes Alpenbeschreibung setzt Ruskin in seiner Wertschätzung an die Seite Humboldts in seiner Liste der Bücher, die ihn beeinflussten. Vgl. Cook/Wedderburn 1903–1912, XXXIV, 1908, S. 583: «Forbes (James Forbes in Alps) is essential to the modern Swiss tourist–of sensse».

43 Ruskin 1843–1860, IV, 1856, S. 177.

44 Ebd., S. 187.

45 Vgl. Ruskin 1851–1853, I, The Foundations, S. 218.

46 Ebd.

47 An dieser Stelle ist ein Vergleich mit Semper aufschlussreich, der in den Prolegomena zum *Stil* (1860) das Künstlertum ebenfalls – mit abweichender Beurteilung – an dieser Nahtstelle beschreibt. (Vgl. Oechslin 2002).

48 Ruskin 1851 1853, I, S. 218.

49 Ebd., S. 218/219.

möglichen Naturbezuges der Kunst zu bedenken. Kristallines («the completely systematised natural structure») findet sich überall in der Kunst; dessen Anwendung ist unbegrenzt und stets schön, so Ruskin. Doch, das entsprechende künstlerische Verursacherprinzip steht im Zeichen des «not knowingly»![50] Der Künstler kommt aus eigenem Antrieb zu analogen, regelmässigen Formen: «I do not suppose a single hint was ever actually taken from mineral form».[51] Selbst die Stalaktit-Gewölbe der Araber wären nicht durch solche direkte Übernahme von Naturformen entstanden. Auf der anderen Seite steht jener schon im zweiten Kapitel «The Virtues of Architecture» geäusserte Satz: «And all noble ornamentation is the expression of man's delight in God's work.» Aber auch dies ist 'bloss' eine Asymptote der künstlerischen Formfindung, die «of our own invention» bleibt.

III. Turner: der 'Grund' der Konkretheit der Theorie und der Kunst in Ruskins Betrachtung.

«... it was in September, I believe, of 1832 ... 'There', said my father, 'is Mr. Turner, the great sea* painter'».

John Ruskin, *Dilecta* I, 1886, S. 1.

«I shall be content with directing the reader's attention to the facts in nature, and in Turner ...».

John Ruskin, *Modern Painters* IV, 1856, Preface, S. vi.

«Of no man but Turner, whom I have ever known, could I say this».

John Ruskin, *Modern Painters* V, 1860, «Peace», S. 345.

«Of Mountain Beauty» ist vol. IV «containing Part V» von *Modern Painters* betitelt. Als Frontispiz dient ihm eine berggesäumte, aufgewühlte Seelandschaft, die Ruskin mit «The Gates of the Hills» überschreibt. Und auf dem Titel figuriert ein Gedicht von Wordsworth, das mit «Accuse me not / Of arrogance, ... / If, having walked with Nature» ansetzt und in wenigen Zeilen neben der Natur auch «Truth», «Divinity» und die «Philosophers» anspricht, die Seele und «transcendent universe» zusammenführen. Er möchte eigentlich keine Einleitung schreiben, überlegt Ruskin. Doch, jetzt, nach zehnjährigem Arbeitsunterbruch, gedenke er doch einiges vorauszuschicken. Landschaften, genauer «mountain-drawings», von Poussin und Salvator Rosa hätte er zusammentragen und an die Seite Turners stellen wollen. Daraus entsteht nun letztlich das umfassende, Natur und Kunst vereinigende, auf (beidseits) präzis erforschter Grundlage stehende Gedankengebäude: «facts in nature, and in Turner».[52]

Für 'Vegetatives' vertröstet er hier auf den nächsten Band. Im Vordergrund stehen die beigefügten – und lediglich als «guides», Andeutungen zu lesenden – Reproduktionen von Bildkompositionen Turners. Sie fassen jene «facts» – abstrahierend und gleichwohl expressiv, summarisch und präzis – knapp im Bild zusammen. So ist es im Frontispiz modellgebend vorgezeichnet: «sketch from nature, taken at sunset from the hills near Como».[53] Der bewegte Himmel, eigentlich «a little too heavy», um zur Landschaft zu passen. Aber eben: «facts»! Ruskin insi-

50 Ruskin 1851–1853, I, S. 219.
51 Ebd.
52 Ruskin 1843–1860, IV, 1856, Preface, S. vi.
53 Ruskin 1843–1860, IV, 1856, S. vii.

stiert: «It was there».[54] Und daran und an seiner verlässlichen Feststellung ist nicht zu rütteln. Dafür steht als Garant Turner und dessen Kunst.

So eingeleitet wird man mit dem Glauben an die Lektüre herangehen, dass Ruskin unbestechlich und 'wahr' seine Naturstudien betreibt, Tatsachen registriert und zudem seine künstlerischen Einsichten zu eben diesem Zweck einsetzt. Man wird also zurecht vermuten, dass er die Natur nicht nur sehr hoch einschätzt, sondern in ihr alles zu erkennen glaubt, was denn überhaupt vorstellbar und andererseits für die Kunst von Bedeutung ist. Allein, zu kurz gegriffen wäre die Meinung, er komme deshalb ganz ohne Modell oder Metapher aus. Bei genauerem Hinsehen wird eben von Anfang an klar, dass er diese Vorstellungen nur korrigieren und präzisieren und in diesem Sinne um die gesamten, vielfältigsten Einsichten in die Natur bereichern will. So wie das – in der Kunst selbst – Turner geleistet hat. Auf diese Weise kommt die Synthese aus Natur- und Kunstgeschichte zustande und wird ihr die Apotheose William Turners folgerichtig einbeschrieben. Turners Kunst kommt dabei – dank der überragenden künstlerischen Sensibilität des Malers – die Aufgabe zu, die Möglichkeit solcher feinster Beobachtungen und Erkenntnisse überhaupt erst unter Beweis zu stellen, sie als künstlerische Optionen einsehbar zu machen.

Die Tragweite und die Radikalität dieses Vorgehens lässt sich nur am Einzelfall genauer ablesen. Das Oszillieren von universaler und mikroskopischer Betrachtungsweise findet bei Ruskin innerhalb einzelner Analysen im stetigen Wechsel statt. «Mountain Beauty» wird – in *Modern Painters* IV – mit Beobachtungen zum «Turnerian Picturesque» eingeleitet. Wie sollten diese Bemerkungen denn ohne die Kunst auskommen, da der Künstler – alter Ciceronianischer Weisheit zur Folge – erwiesenermassen am meisten von der Kunst versteht. Also ist auch von einer «Turnerian Topography» die Rede.[55] Und «things in general» werden – am Beispiel der Stadtbefestigung von Fribourg erläutert – mit künstlerischen Augen gesehen, was erst recht dann vonnöten ist, wenn die Wirklichkeit 'atmosphärisch' gefiltert zur Darstellung gelangen soll: «the Law of Evanescence». Was mal als Gesetzmässigkeit ausgegeben wird, wird andernorts als unenträtselbare «mental chemistry» beschrieben.[56] Und für all dies liefert Ruskin das gemeinsame Dach

54 Das erinnert an die berühmten Postkarteneffekte (und deren angezweifelte 'Wahrhaftigkeit') und die entsprechenden modernen 'psychologischen' Überlegungen zum Zusammenhang von Bilderwissen und Realität.

55 Ruskin 1843–1860, IV, 1856, S. 16ff.

56 Ruskin 1843–1860, IV, 1856, S. 28: «The kind of mental chemistry by which the dream summons and associates ist materials, I have already endeavoured, not to explain, for it is utterly inexplicable, but to illustrate, by a well ascertained though equally inexplicable fact in common chemistry». Wohlgemerkt, diese Anmerkung zu den Grenzen der Erkenntnis in künstlerischen Belangen, bezieht sich auf Komposition und Imagination in Turners Kunst. – «Chemistry» ist andererseits auch in Ruskin 1843–1860, III, 1856, S. vii, ein Bezugspunkt, um Methode und Dogmatik in die richtige Relation zu setzen.

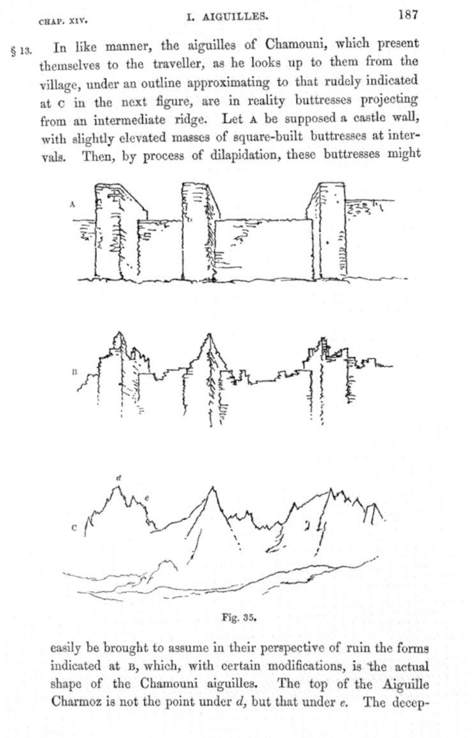

CHAP. XIV. I. AIGUILLES. 187

§ 13. In like manner, the aiguilles of Chamouni, which present themselves to the traveller, as he looks up to them from the village, under an outline approximating to that rudely indicated at C in the next figure, are in reality buttresses projecting from an intermediate ridge. Let A be supposed a castle wall, with slightly elevated masses of square-built buttresses at intervals. Then, by process of dilapidation, these buttresses might

Fig. 35.

easily be brought to assume in their perspective of ruin the forms indicated at B, which, with certain modifications, is the actual shape of the Chamouni aiguilles. The top of the Aiguille Charmoz is not the point under *d*, but that under *e*. The decep-

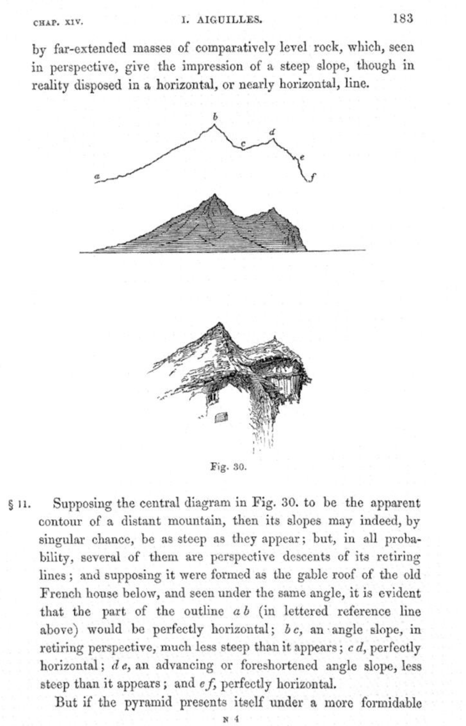

CHAP. XIV. I. AIGUILLES. 183

by far-extended masses of comparatively level rock, which, seen in perspective, give the impression of a steep slope, though in reality disposed in a horizontal, or nearly horizontal, line.

Fig. 30.

§ 11. Supposing the central diagram in Fig. 30. to be the apparent contour of a distant mountain, then its slopes may indeed, by singular chance, be as steep as they appear; but, in all probability, several of them are perspective descents of its retiring lines; and supposing it were formed as the gable roof of the old French house below, and seen under the same angle, it is evident that the part of the outline *a b* (in lettered reference line above) would be perfectly horizontal; *b c*, an angle slope, in retiring perspective, much less steep than it appears; *c d*, perfectly horizontal; *d e*, an advancing or foreshortened angle slope, less steep than it appears; and *e f*, perfectly horizontal.

But if the pyramid presents itself under a more formidable

N 4

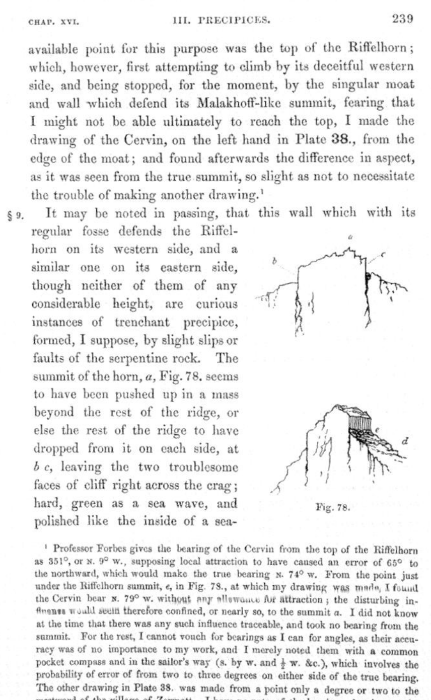

CHAP. XVI. III. PRECIPICES. 239

available point for this purpose was the top of the Riffelhorn; which, however, first attempting to climb by its deceitful western side, and being stopped, for the moment, by the singular moat and wall which defend its Malakhoff-like summit, fearing that I might not be able ultimately to reach the top, I made the drawing of the Cervin, on the left hand in Plate 38., from the edge of the moat; and found afterwards the difference in aspect, as it was seen from the true summit, so slight as not to necessitate the trouble of making another drawing.[1]

§ 9. It may be noted in passing, that this wall which with its regular fosse defends the Riffelhorn on its western side, and a similar one on its eastern side, though neither of them of any considerable height, are curious instances of trenchant precipice, formed, I suppose, by slight slips or faults of the serpentine rock. The summit of the horn, *a*, Fig. 78. seems to have been pushed up in a mass beyond the rest of the ridge, or else the rest of the ridge to have dropped from it on each side, at *b c*, leaving the two troublesome faces of cliff right across the crag; hard, green as a sea wave, and polished like the inside of a sea-

Fig. 78.

[1] Professor Forbes gives the bearing of the Cervin from the top of the Riffelhorn as 351°, or N. 9° W., supposing local attraction to have caused an error of 65° to the northward, which would make the true bearing N. 74° W. From the point just under the Riffelhorn summit, *e*, in Fig. 78., at which my drawing was made, I found the Cervin bear N. 79° W. without any allowance for attraction; the disturbing influence would seem therefore confined, or nearly so, to the summit *a*. I did not know at the time that there was any such influence traceable, and took no bearing from the summit. For the rest, I cannot vouch for bearings as I can for angles, as their accuracy was of no importance to my work, and I merely noted them with a common pocket compass and in the sailor's way (S. by W. and ½ W. &c.), which involves the probability of error of from two to three degrees on either side of the true bearing. The other drawing in Plate 38. was made from a point only a degree or two to the westward of the village of Zermatt. I have no note of the bearing; but it must be about S. 60° or 65° W.

Das Architektonische in der Natur – symbolisch:

«Aiguilles», Fig. 35 in: John Ruskin, *Modern Painters*, vol. IV, London 1856, S. 187

«Aiguilles», Fig. 30 in: John Ruskin, *Modern Painters*, vol. IV, London 1856, S. 183

«Precipies», Fig. 78 in: John Ruskin, *Modern Painters*, vol. IV, London 1856, S. 239

eines «Turnerian Mystery», was dann gleich zu ernsten Bedenken und Fragen führen muss: «»But, is Turner right in doing this?»[57] Natürlich ist er. Jenes 'mystery' ist – künstlerisch begriffen – 'fact': «The truth is indeed so.»

Solcherlei Ausführungen werden hier nicht als Schlussfolgerungen allgemeiner Naturbeobachtungen zugunsten künstlerischer Praxis mit dem Ziel eines entsprechenden Regelwerkes aufgestellt. Es wird vielmehr umgekehrt von jenen 'künstlerischen Tatsachen' auf die Notwendigkeit und auf die Art und Weise des Naturstudiums geschlossen. Danach, nach diesen Turnerschen Einsichten, beginnt erst die 'eigentliche' Analyse der «Mountain Beauty». Die Aufgabe stünde nun an, so Ruskin zu Beginn des sechsten Kapitels, zu erfahren, was die angemessene Wirkung der Naturschönheit auf den Menschen – entsprechend den Erfahrungen Turners – sei, genauer: zu sein habe («ought to be on the human mind»).[58] Mit den Bergen würde er «for the sake of convenience in illustration» ansetzen.

So beginnt jetzt Ruskin radikal und grundsätzlich mit dem Firmament, dem Schöpfungsakt gemäss dem Genesis-Bericht, wobei er gleich hier, am zweiten Schöpfungstag – Scheuchzers Vorgehen in seiner «histoire naturelle de la Bible» insofern vergleichbar[59] – in die Bibelexegese direkt eingreift. Um aus der unklaren Terminologie von «heaven» oder «firmament» herauszuführen, bemüht er Miltons *Paradise Lost*. Und er dreht die Dinge so lange, bis seine eigene Deutung auch allen plausibel erscheinen muss, dass nämlich jener zweite Schöpfungstag ganz konkret unseren wolkenbesetzten Himmel zum Resultat hatte: «I understand the making of the firmament to signify that, so far as man is concerned, most magnificent ordinance of the clouds».[60] Das ist die Bestätigung für Ruskins Argumentations- und Vorgehensweise: von der Kunst ausgehend führt er über die Weltschöpfung zurück zur Kunst und landet so am Ende wieder auf Turners Staffelei.

IV. Die Aufgabe der Kunst: doch eine neue Kunsttheorie, oder eben eine auf der Dynamik und Wechselhaftigkeit des Lebens und der Natur gegründete Morallehre der Kunst.

«... that the minutest portion of a great composition is helpful to the whole ...»

John Ruskin, «The Task of the Least», in: *Modern Painters* V, 1860, S. 168.

«We have to inquire into the various Powers, Conditions, and Aims of mind involved in the conception or creation of pictures».

John Ruskin, *Modern Painters* V, 1860, S. 157.

Eine enggefasste, Natur und Kunst in ein klares Verhältnis zwingende Imitationslehre und Kunsttheorie kann daraus nicht werden. Allein schon der ständige Rückgriff auf Turner lässt dies kaum zu. Zu komplex sind die Vorgänge der Natur und enstprechend anspruchsvoll die Antwort der Kunst. Eines ist dabei ohnehin gewiss: die Naivität spontaner Kunst ist längst verloren. Ruskin entnimmt der *Encyclopedia Britannica* (1797) die übliche Beschreibung der von einem festen Standort aus gefertigten Landschaftsdarstellung: «at the time when Claude, Poussin, and Salvator were in the zenith of their reputation».[61] Das entlockt ihm ein müdes Lächeln und die Fussnote: «What a comfortable, as well as intelligent, operation, sketching from nature must have been in those days!»[62] Es reicht jetzt nicht mehr aus, die Natur einfach abzubilden, wie sie – entsprechend der verbreiteten ästhetischen Maxime – 'ins Auge fällt'. Am Beispiel der Turnerschen Darstellung des Pilatus bei Luzern wird demonstriert, wie aus einem vertieften Verständnis eines solchen Gebirges überhaupt erst der richtige Bildausschnitt bestimmt und das richtige Bildthema gewählt werden kann. Der Maler weiss mehr! Das ist in erster Linie eine Herausforderung.

Bei aller Wertschätzung Dürers stellt Ruskin die Grenzen seiner Landschaftsdarstellung fest. Der Holzschnitt lässt die Linien viel zu gleichförmig erscheinen, sodass felsige Hügel eben lediglich «soft and earthy» erscheinen. «Woodcutting in Durer's day, had reached no delicacy capable of expressing subtle detail or aerial perspective».[63] Kunst ist stets ein 'mehr'. Jener – in einem Holzschnitt eben unmöglich darzustellende – Dunst, der über einer Landschaft liegt

57 Ruskin 1843–1860, IV, 1856, S. 72.
58 Ruskin 1843–1860, IV, 1856, S. 83. – Diese 'Umkehrung' entspricht wiederum der von Boullée verfolgten Strategie des: «Non il faut concevoir pour effectuer ...». Vgl. oben.
59 Vgl. oben. Scheuchzer war ja in seiner Zeit bemüht, die neuesten naturwissenschaftlichen Ergebnisse just in die Bibelexegese zu integrieren. Vgl. dazu neuerdings: Müsch 2000.
60 Ruskin 1843–1860, IV, 1856, S. 88.
61 Ruskin 1843–1860, IV, 1856, S. 303.
62 Ebd.
63 Ruskin 1843–1860, IV, 1856, S. 222.

und den optischen Eindruck des Betrachters bestimmt, ist ein solches 'mehr' gegenüber dem (objektiven) Naturzustand. Und diesbezüglich fordert jetzt Ruskin: «If we see something different from what is there, then we are to paint that – nay, we must paint that, whether we will or not; it being for us, the only reality we can get at».[64]

Darin liegt das Geheimnis der Kunst überhaupt – und aus Ruskins Sicht auch eine Verpflichtung. Mit Bezug auf Turners Lichtmalerei beschreibt er die extremen Bedingungen dieser Anforderungen an den Künstler im Detail. Ein Berg fünf oder sechs Meilen entfernt an einem sonnigen Sommermorgen in der Schweiz würde sich gegenüber dem Himmel dunkel abheben; allein, im Vergleich mit dem Weiss des Papiers wäre der dunkelste Flecken jenes Dunkels immer noch weisser als das Papier.[65] Man 'löst' dieses Problem mit dem Hinweis auf «the apparent colour». Aber dahinter verbirgt sich mehr. Es geht stets um künstlerische Erfindungsgabe und Imagination. Und die beginnt erst jenseits der Natur, wie sie ist, wirksam zu werden. Auch dies beurteilt Ruskin im Kapitel der «Turnerian Topography». Zwei sich ausschliessende Möglichkeiten bieten sich an. Bezieht sich der Künstler bloss auf «the commonly visible facts» und versucht er diese gemäss üblicher Regeln oder geläufiger Kunstpraxis darzustellen, so verfügt er eben nicht über genuine Erfindungsgabe. Umgekehrt, wenn der Künstler Unberechenbares und 'Unreales' vorfindet und sich ihm dieser Zustand – vorerst eben völlig unkontrollierbar – gleichsam aufdrängt, dann ist er mit seiner Erfindungskunst in der Tat gefordert: «If visions of unreal things present themselves to him with or without his own will, praying to be painted, quite ungovernable in their coming or going, – neither to be summoned if they do not choose to come, nor banished if they do, – he has invention».[66] Wenn sich der Künstler also diesen Aufgaben stellt und diese – wie im Falle Turners vielfach erwiesen – auch noch bewältigt, dann wird man die «superiority», die im Titel von *Modern Painters* beansprucht wird, auch tatsächlich erreichen und beanspruchen können. Was man seit jenem naiven Zustand der Landschaftsmalerei, als der Holzschnitt noch seinen Dienst erfüllte, an methodischer Feinheit und Raffinesse der künstlerisch umgesetzten Naturerkenntnis hinzugewonnen hat, kann man der Zusammenstellung Ruskins entnehmen, in der er die unterschiedlichen Stimmungen und Lichtverhältnisse von frühmorgens bis spätabends und in die Nacht hinein und andererseits eine entsprechend 'vollständige' Serie von Bildern Turners auf die Reihe bringt.[67]

Das reicht nun in der Tat weit über die traditionelle Kunsttheorie mitsamt ihrer Natur und Kunst einbindenden 'idealen' und 'idealistischen' Imitationslehre hinaus. Längst hat Ruskin dieses bei Turner immer wieder herausgefilterte 'mehr' den 'facts' zugeordnet. Allein, wie soll man, was künstlerisch längst Wirklichkeit geworden ist, auch richtig einordnen? Zwischen Prinzipien, Gesetzmässigkeiten und «mental chemistry» scheint das Pendel frei hin- und herzuschwingen. Es geht mitunter – und insbesondere beim Betrachter – um Stimmungen. Darauf weist Ruskin seine Zuhörer in Edinburgh auf provokative Weise hin. Die George Street für sich allein wäre wohl kaum attraktiv, würde man nicht weiterblicken hin zum Firth of Forth und zum Castle Rock: «Take away the sea-waves, and the dark basalt, and I fear you would find little to interest you in George Street by itself».[68]

Als ob es der Kunst vorbehalten wäre, dies durch ihre Darstellungskunst aufzuzeigen und zu lösen. Natur und Kunst begegnen sich, so besehen, in der ständigen Überblendung der Naturvorstellung durch eine vertiefte oder gar verbesserte künstlerische Sichtweise. Wahrheit und Moral bilden Sammelbecken eines solchen synkretistischen Vorgehens.[69] «Virtues of Architecture», architektonische Tugenden, stellen das entsprechende Gefäss für die Architektur dar, in dem Platz findet, was mit den Forderungen nach «act well», «speak well» und «look well» umfassend beschrieben wird.[70] «Safeguard of highest beauty» entspreche genau dem, was mit «safeguard of conduct in soul» gemeint sei, führt Ruskin weiter aus, und was in der Kardinalstugend der 'temperantia' grundgelegt sei.[71] Bei der grundsätzlichen Erörterung der «Moral of Landscape» geht Ruskin ebenfalls von den «elements of pleasure» der Landschaftsdarstellung aus und fragt nach den «effects of this pleasure».[72] Als ob sich auch hier ein Grund fände, die Landschaftsmalerei in der Hierarchie der Gattungen der Historienmalerei anzunähern, suggeriert Ruskin, dass weniger «joy» als «duties of life» zur Debatte stünden. Moral der Landschaftsmalerei ist ein Thema! Auch dieses Argument wird sorgfältig aufgebaut, etwa davon ausgehend, dass «landscape-instinct» und niedere Gefühle und Leidenschaften sich anerkanntermassen ausschlössen.[73] Und natürlich sind gerade hier moralisierende und religiöse Überlegungen zur Hand. Ruskin bekennt sich zu utopischen Ansichten und Hoffnungen.[74] Zurück bei der Malerei angelangt wandelt er seine eigene Bezeichnung Turners vom «master of this science of Aspects» nunmehr zum «master of the science of Essence».

Die moralische Frage dient also der Verwesentlichung der Landschaftsmalerei. Unter der Rubrik der «Teachers of Turner» wird vorerst die Geschichte nachgeführt. Verkürzt in den Bildtafeln stellt sich das als «Botany of the Fourteenth Century», als «Geology of the Middle Ages» (Leonardo) und als «Latest Purism»

64 Ruskin 1843–1860, IV, 1856, S. 17.
65 Ruskin 1843–1860, IV, 1856, S. 39f.
66 Ruskin 1843–1860, IV, 1856, S. 17.
67 Ruskin 1843–1860, I, 1843, S. 256ff.
68 Vgl. Ruskin 1854, S. 3.
69 Das hat seine Wirkungen bis auf Le Corbusier, der ja in *Vers une Architecture* (1923) in ähnlicher Weise die moralischen Qualitäten mit den 'emotionalen' verknüpft, der von «moralité dorique» spricht und dies wiederum ganz konkret auf die Profilierungen der Triglyphenschlitze der dorischen Ordnung zurückbezieht.
70 Ruskin 1851–1853, I, S. 35f.
71 Ruskin 1851–1853, II, S. 4.
72 Ruskin 1843–1860, III, 1856, S. 286.
73 Ruskin 1843–1860, III, 1856, S. 301 («inconsistency with all evil passion»).
74 Ruskin 1843–1860, III, 1856, S. 310: «And I am Utopian and enthousiastic enough to believe, that the time will come when the world will discover this».

10. Geology of the Middle Ages.

29. Aiguille Structure.

GENESIS Cap.VII.v.21.22.23. Cataclysmi Reliquiæ.

I. Buch Mosis Cap.VII.v.21.22.23. Überbleibselen der Sündflüth.

Das Architektonische in der Natur-Struktur:

«Geology in the Middle Ages», Taf. X in: John Ruskin, *Modern Painters*, vol. III, London 1856

«Aiguille Structure», Taf. 29 in: John Ruskin, *Modern Painters*, vol. IV, London 1856

«Restes du Déluge», Taf. XLVI in: Johann Jakob Scheuchzer, *Physique Sacrée*, Amsterdam 1732

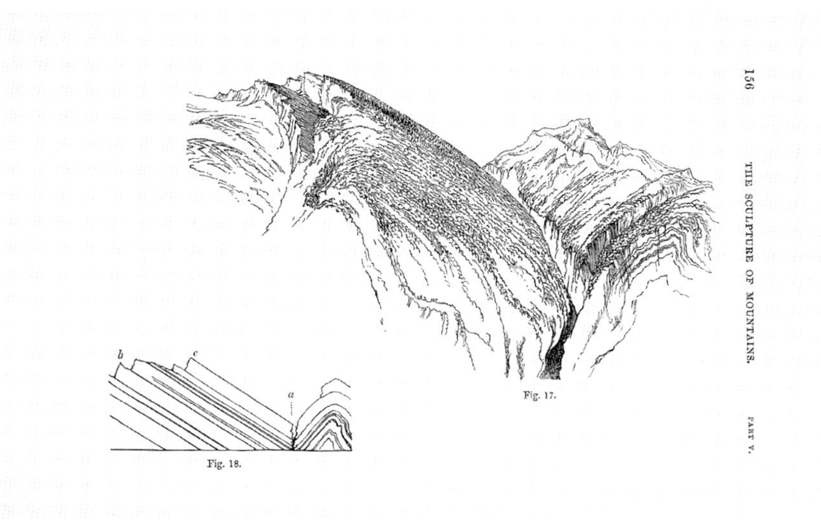

«The Sculpture of Mountains», Fig. 17–18 in: John Ruskin, *Modern Painters*, vol. IV, London 1856, S. 156

«Aiguilles and their Friends», Taf. 69 in: John Ruskin, *Modern Painters*, vol. V, London 1860

«Aiguille Drawing», Taf. 32 in: John Ruskin, *Modern Painters*, vol. IV, London 1856

(Raphael) dar, entwickelt sich vom «first Mountain-Naturalism» (Masaccio) zum «early Naturalism» (Tizian) und «advanced Naturalism» (Tintoretto). Eine kleine Kunstgeschichte der Landschaftsmalerei fundiert auf moralischen Prämissen!

Der Wissenschaft der objektiven Naturbeobachtung ist diese Darstellung längst entwachsen. An die Stelle des Ausmessens tritt (wieder) die Sprache und die benutzten Gradmesser, die bevorzugten 'Gesetzmässigkeiten' sind die der Abweichung und Unbestimmtheit.

Sprache! Dazu hat sich Ruskin im Rückblick auf seinen Erstling, die *Poetry of Architecture*, der als Auftakt seiner «science of feeling» gedacht war, in den *Praeterita* präzis geäussert. «The skill of language» wäre bei ihm schon früh als angenehmes Talent aufgefallen.[75] Die Bibel und Johnson – genauer: «Johnsonian symmetry and balance» – wären seine Muster gewesen. Zur 'moralischen' Qualität der Bibel braucht kaum etwas gesagt zu werden. Doch auch Johnson wird nun durchaus in diesem Sinne gewertet: «entirely sincere, and infallibly wise in the view and estimate he gave of the common questions».[76] (Englischer) 'commonsense' und Moral bewahren ihn, Ruskin, von der Tücke eines theoretischen Überbaues: «from being caught in the cobwebs of German metaphysics, or sloughed in the English drainage of them».[77]

«Commonsense» als Massgabe, um gleichwohl der komplexesten Wirklichkeit und einer adäquaten Kunst klare Kriterien zur Verfügung zu stellen! Sprache zur Einbindung der künstlerischen in die moralischen Vorstellungen! Jenen formalistischen, stilorientierten Umgang mit dem klassischen Gegensatz von 'Dorisch' und 'Gotisch' wollte Ruskin schon 1837 überwunden haben. 'Poetisch' – und moralisch verarbeitet – kommt das Argument in den *Seven Lamps* von 1849 zurück. Das venezianische Ornament stehe in seiner umfassenden Integration vegetaler und animalischer Formen für «the temperance of a man, the command of Adam over creation», sei insgesamt ein Zeichen «of human authority».[78]

Auch das Gesetz der Kurvatur («the Law of Curvature») ist dementsprechend nicht eine Grösse, die gleichsam aus Euklid hergeleitet wird und auf diese Weise einen höheren Grad der geometrischen Form erklimmt. Die Kurve wird vielmehr in der menschlichen Empfindung des Angenehmen geortet. Sie ist «the cause of loveliness in all form». Und das ist einmal mehr eine 'moralische' Feststellung: «But the great and temperate designer does not allow himself any violent curves; he works much with lines in which the curvature, though always existing, is long before it is perceived».[79] Natürlich wirkt sich 'temperance' als Garant gegen «over-refinement», der jede Malschule zum Opfer fallen würde, künstlerisch aus. Und gemäss diesem Prinzip der kaum bemerkbaren Kurvierungen wird die Kompositionslehre in *The Elements of Drawing* (1857) aufgebaut. «You may ascertain, by experiment, that all beautiful objects whatsoever are thus terminated by delicately curved lines, except where the straight line is indispensable to their use or stability ...».[80]

Ruskin 'gewinnt' seine sanften Kurven aus den venezianischen Blumen-Kapitellen. (Er nennt sie auch «the four Venetian Flower-Orders»![81]) Hier, in den *Stones of Venice*, bezieht er sich auf die vorausgegangene Erörterung der Schönheit der Linien in *Modern Painters* und fügt dem lediglich ergänzend hinzu, dass Linien stets «expressive of action or force of some kind» wären. Unter diesem gemeinsamen Dach – und dem (irritierenden weil exklusiven) Titel «Abstract Lines» vereinigt Ruskin «mountain-line» und «leaf-line», Linien, die er beim Matterhorn beobachtet hat, und solche die er von einer Nautilus-Muschel hernimmt. Und niemand wird sich nun wundern, dass Ruskin bei der Beschreibung vom Riffelhorn von einer Welle und einer Muschel spricht.[82] In der Tat, diese Linien-Diskussion ist der grösseren über das «Material of Ornament» einbeschrieben, in der gleich die Diskussion der «Forms of Earth»,[83] der «Forms of Water», der «Forms of Fire» und der «Forms of Air» folgt. Diese Auflistung wird mit der Feststellung eingeleitet: «The proper material of ornament will be whatever God has created».[84] Die einzelnen Beobachtungen finden also wieder im Zeichen der Schöpfung zusammen. Dieser universale Rahmen bietet sich hilfreich an, wo immer die 'facts' von Kunst und Natur für sich alleine genommen doch zu unbestimmt bleiben. Darauf kommt Ruskin immer wieder zurück.

«Zoologists often disagree in their descriptions of the curve of a shell, or the plumage of a bird, though they may lay their specimen on the table and examine it at their leisure.»[85] So liest man es gleich zu Beginn in den *Stones of Venice*, obwohl – genauer: gerade weil – Ruskin zuvor ein Bekenntnis zu seiner Methode abgelegt hat: «... I may be permitted to give this single and sufficient reason, that my account of every building is based on personal examination and measurement of it ...».[86] Das lässt nur einen Schluss zu: sosehr Ruskin sich um Genauigkeit und Zuverlässigkeit seines Beobachtens bemüht, sosehr weiss er, dass es keinerlei Objektivität bei der Beurteilung der so gewonnenen Resultate gibt. Er nimmt jetzt vorweg – ja, er schäme sich –, dass er wohl immer wieder sagen werde: «I am not sure». Im Kapitel «The Nature of Gothic» gerät dies zur doppelt formulierten Einsicht: «the demand for perfection is always a sign of a misunderstanding of the ends of art»;

75 Ruskin 1886/1887, I, S. 414.
76 Ebd., S. 416.
77 Ebd., S. 417.
78 Ruskin 1849, S. 88.
79 Ruskin 1851–1853, III, S. 5.
80 Ruskin 1857, S. 269.
81 Ruskin 1851–1853, II, pl. x.
82 Ruskin 1843–1860, 1856, IV, S. 239.
83 Vgl. dazu oben.
84 Ruskin 1851–1853, I, S. 214.
85 Ruskin 1851–1853, I, Preface, S. vi.
86 Ebd.

und: «... imperfection is in some sort essential to all what we know of life. It is the sign of life in a mortal body, that is to say, of a state of progress and change».[87]

Die übergeordnete Frage der Zielsetzung der Kunst verlangt nach einer adäquaten Antwort. Ruskin findet sie im Prinzip vom ewigen Wechsel und Fortgang der Dinge, «the infinite and unapproachable variety of nature». Im ersten Band von *Modern Painters*, gleichsam in die Darlegung des «Truth of Colour» versteckt, findet sich dieses Bekenntnis, in die Einzelheiten zerlegt, wieder: «And I wish to insist on this the more particularly, because it is one of the eternal principes of nature, that she will not have one line nor colour, nor one portion nor atom of space, without change in it. There is not one of her shadows, tints, or lines that is not in a state of perpetual variation: I do not mean in time, but in space».[88] Und weil sich Ruskin hier einmal mehr auf seine genaue Kenntnis der Natur beruft, ist das auch mit einer seiner konkreten Beobachtungen, einer «beautiful instance of an exception to general rules», zu illustrieren. Ruskin bezieht sich auf eine Zeichnung Turners, «Llanthony».[89] Fallendes Wasser würde – «universally» – eine konvexe Form beschreiben. Doch die «rocks in situ» würden das Wasser – im Kontrast zur Form der Felsen – in konkaver Weise niederstürzen lassen, was Turner eben genau beobachtet hätte. «The depth of that knowledge» des Künstlers ist 'regelhaft' und lässt immer wieder – gegen Konvention – «new evidence of knowledge, and fresh manifestation of thought» erkennen.[90] Das ist letztlich die Einlösung jener moralischen Forderung nach Wahrheit in Kunst und Natur.

V. Von der Moral zur Theologie.

> «The first sight of the Alps had been to me as a direct revelation of the benevolent will in creation».
>
> John Ruskin, *Praeterita* II, 1887, S. 87 f.

> «... (its an odd thing, but all my resolutions of which anything is to come are invariably formed, whether I will or no, in church – I scheme all thro'the litany) ...».
>
> John Ruskin, «Brief an Rev. Osborne Gordon, 10. März 1844», in: E.T. Cook/A. Wedderburn (Hg.), *Complete Works* III, 1903, S. 665/666.

> «Man being thus the crowning and ruling work of God, it will follow that all his best art must have something to tell about himself, as the soul of things, and ruler of creatures».
>
> John Ruskin, *Modern Painters* V, 1860, S. 201.

> «In this last division we have to consider its relations of art to God and man. Its work in the help of human beings, and services of their Creator».
>
> John Ruskin, *Modern Painters* V, 1860, S. 157.

Auf andere 'Regeln' als die der ständigen Veränderung kann und will sich Ruskin, der wie kein anderer Kunsttheoretiker vor ihm die Natur und die Kunst genau durchleuchtet und auf ihre 'Gesetzmässigkeiten' durchsucht hat, letztlich nicht einlassen. Dieser Weg führt zur Anerkennung der Schöpfung in ihrer ganzen umfassenden Komplexität. Und dass dies alles immer wieder in Religiosität mündet, ergibt sich zwangsläufig. Sosehr sich Ruskin der endlos verästelten Naturbeobachtung und Kunstanalyse mitsamt deren Ungewissheiten verschreibt, sosehr findet er jederzeit zu grundsätzlichen Fragen und Einsichten zurück. Das äussert sich zwar nicht in 'deutscher Metaphysik', wogegen sich Ruskin verwahrt, lässt sich aber gleichwohl in entsprechenden Formulierungen passend widerspiegeln. In der Reinholdschen Beurteilung des Fortgangs der deutschen Philosophie – um 1800 – gehört die Einsicht des notwendigen Zusammenhangs von Sein und Wissen zu den unumstösslichen Errungenschaften menschlicher Entwicklung überhaupt: «Mit dieser nothwendigen Verknüpfung des Seyns und des Wissens beginnt die Wissenschaftslehre».[91] Und selbst wenn Reinhold diesbezüglich einräumt, es würde dies und jenes unterschiedlich beurteilt, so hält er daran fest, dass «diese absolute Vereinigung des Seyns und des Wissens immer eine grosse Idee» sei. Daraus ent-

87 Ruskin 1851–1853, II, S. 170/171.
88 Ruskin 1843–1860, I, S. 165.
89 Ruskin 1843–1860, I, S. 322.
90 Ebd.
91 Vgl. Reinhold 1801, S. 147ff.; insbes. S. 167.

steht ein Satz, der den «denkenden Menschen» im Visier hat und dessen Prämisse so lautet: «Ein denkender Geist, der über sein eignes Wesen reflektiert, kann nicht anders für wahr und existierend halten, als was er eben durch diese Reflexion findet, er kann die Welt nicht anders ansehen, als er sie eben ansieht, für ihn giebt es kein andres Daseyn, als das, welches er als existirend annimmt».[92]

Ein «denkender Geist» in diesem Sinne ist Ruskin zweifelsohne, auch wenn die 'deutschen' Begriffe – in Anbetracht der spezifisch religiösen Brechungen in Ruskins Argumentationen – nicht unbedingt passen sollten. Zu Ruskin passt immerhin, dass in jener Formulierung die Reflexion – durchaus im Sinne der «Subjektivität seiner Vorstellungen» – und die Welterfahrung so nahe aneinandergerückt sind. Darin liegt ja wohl auch der Grund des so häufigen Oszillierens seiner Gedanken. Am Ende der *Modern Painters* kommt Ruskin einmal mehr zu den grossen Fragen von «perfectness» und «harmony» zurück. Wie stets zuvor relativiert er dies umgehend dahingehend, es sei alles, «all great work», bestimmten Bedingungen unterworfen: «reduced under certain conditions». Und auch dieser 'Satz' erfährt wiederum die übliche Brechung 'in eigener (künstlerischer) Sache' mitsamt dem persönlichen Bekentnnis, man würde sich voreilig mit den Skizzen zufriedenstellen: «we have put ourselves to produce sketches as an end instead of a means», was zu einer «scornful rejection of the things beyond ours» führe. Mit der Diskussion von 'Perfektion' wird also doch die Frage der Sinngebung von Kunst mit ins Spiel gebracht. Aber vorerst lässt sich Ruskin an dieser Stelle – bezeichnenderweise – auf die verschiedenen Formen der Skizzen («experimental», «determinant», «commemorative») ein und folgt dabei natürlich stets dem 'exemplum' Turners. Erst dann kommt notgedrungen wieder der Zweifel am Sinn und an der Bedeutung des Ganzen, dort, wo er nicht umhin kommt, bei Turner selbst das unzertrennliche Einhergehen künstlerisch-beobachtender und intellektuell-erkennender Befähigungen zu beschreiben und dies in die unbeantwortbare Frage eines künstlerischen Mysteriums einfliessen zu lassen: «I repeat – the power of mind which accomplishes this, is yet wholly inexplicable to me, as it was when first I defined it in the chapter of imagination associative, in the second volume».[93]

Jener scheinbar so losgelöste zweite Band der *Modern Painters* von 1846, der sich vergleichsweise wie ein theoretisch ästhetisches Traktat gibt, bleibt präsent.[94] Und gerade jetzt wird dies offenkundig, da Ruskin in der ersten Hälfte des fünften Bandes der *Modern Painters* einmal mehr der Schönheit in der Natur – von den Pflanzen zu den Wolkenformationen – systematisch nachgeht und formuliert: «We have to inquire into the various Powers, Conditions, and Aims of mind involved in the conception or creation of pictures ...».[95] Das impliziert eine Kunsttheorie im umfassendsten Sinne. Im einleitenden Abschnitt zuvor hat Ruskin das entsprechende Vorgehen zusammengefasst. Der Darlegung von Kunst als «consistent with physical or material facts» sei jene des Zusammenhangs mit den Gesetzmässigkeiten der Naturschönheit gefolgt. Und jetzt müsse dies in den grossen Rahmen von Gott und Mensch gestellt werden. «In this last division we have to consider its relations of art to God and man. Its work in the help of human beings, and service of their Creator».[96]

Natürlich würde man sich einmal mehr täuschen, würde man nun ein – endgültiges – Abheben in mystisch-religiöse Sphären erwarten. Ruskin bleibt sich treu: es gibt nichts, was sich nicht – und dort allen Unbestimmtheiten und 'mysteries' zum Trotz meist viel präziser – im Künstlerischen selbst feststellen und beschreiben liesse. Diese eben zitierten Gedanken zu Gott und Mensch und zu den Grundbedingungen künstlerischer Kreativität stehen unter der Überschrift von «Ideas of Relation» und von «Invention». Und von hier führen die Gedanken einmal mehr schnurstracks zu Kunst und Künstler zurück. «The task of the least», fügt sich hier als weiteres Kapitel konsequent an. Und das Credo, das Ruskin nun gleichsam als längst vermittelten roten Faden seiner Analysen erinnert, lautet schlicht: «The reader has probably been surprised at my assertions made often before now, and reiterated here, that the minutest portion of a great composition is helpful to the whole».[97] Auch das sei nicht einfach einsehbar: «But it is the fact».

Aber es geht um weit mehr: um «invention spiritual». Ruskin führt dies mit einem Blick auf die religiöse Erziehung des Kindes ein: «A child would, I suppose receive a religious lesson from a flower more willingly than from a print of one and might be taught to understand the nineteenth Psalm, on a starry night, better than by diagrams of the constellations».[98] Das ist natürlich nicht gegen (Darstellungs-)Kunst gerichtet, sondern zeigt nur den Anspruch Ruskins an, den er an die Kunst richtet. Und da er nun einmal an dieser zentralen Frage der Verbindung der Landschaftsmalerei «with humanity, or with spiritual powers» festhält, sieht auch er sich gezwungen grundsätzlich Kategorien festzulegen. «Picturesque» erscheint in einem solchen – 'theologischen' – Licht nicht mehr als «the degradation (or sometimes the undeveloped state) of the Contemplative».[99] Und vieles, was hier an Beispielen zusammengeführt wird, verdient kunstgeschichtlich besehen allenfalls die Bezeichnung «hybrid». Bei der Festlegung solcher «orders of art» hätte er sich einigen

92 Ebd.
93 Ruskin 1843–1860, V, S. 191.
94 Selbst Wolfgang Kemp kommt nicht umhin, hier Ruskin eines gewissen Dogmatismus zu bezichtigen (Kemp 1983, S. 137, zu *Modern Painters* vol. II: «... ein Werk der Unsicherheit, die durch dogmatischen Überschuss sowohl in ästhetischer als auch in religiöser Hinsicht kompensiert wird»). – John Dixon Hunt (Hunt 1982, S. 270) bemerkt umgekehrt zu Band fünf: «the tone is less dogmatic than in earlier volumes». – Ich kann beim besten Willen in *Modern Painters* insgesamt nichts Dogmatisches erkennen, ausser man wolle das ständige Bemühen um tiefere Erkenntnis – was bei Ruskin ja zudem bezogen auf seine Beobachtungen wie auf seine Folgerungen stets in Bewegung ist – mit diesem einseitigen Begriff charakterisieren (und damit letztlich auch tabuisieren oder gar verurteilen).
95 Ruskin 1843–1860, V, S. 157.
96 Ebd.
97 Ebd., S. 168.
98 Ebd., S. 197/198.
99 Ebd., S. 199.

38. The Cervin, from the East, and North-East.

view, taken from the Riffelhorn, is here the apparent summit. I was for some time in considerable doubt which of the appearances was most trustworthy; and believe now that they are *both* deceptive; for I found, on ascending the flank of the hills on the other

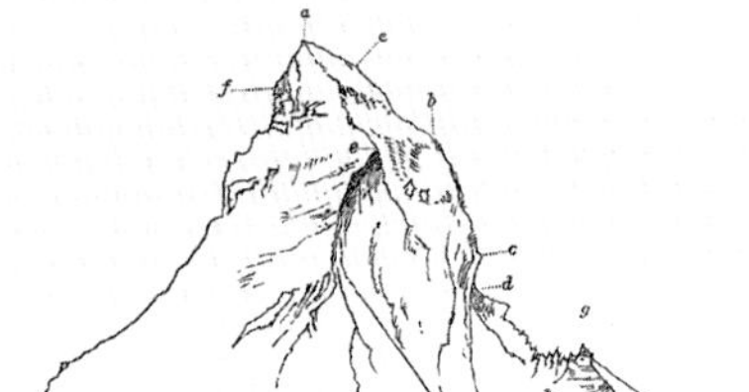

Fig. 33.

Angles with the horizon *x*, *y*.

a f - - -	56°	*c d* (overhanging) - -	79°
a e - - -	12¾	*a x* (irrespective of irregularities) -	56
e b (from point to point) -	44½	*a y* - - - -	38¾
b c (ditto, ditto) -	67¼		

side of the Valais, to a height of about five thousand feet above Brieg, between the Aletsch glacier and Bietsch-horn; being thus high enough to get a view of the Matterhorn on something like distant terms of equality, up the St. Nicholas valley, it presented itself under the outline Fig. 34., which seems to be conclusive for the supremacy of the point *e*, between *a* and *b* in Fig. 33. But the impossibility of determining, at the foot of it, without a trigonometrical observation, *which is the top* of such an apparent peak as the Matterhorn, may serve to show the reader how little the eye is to be trusted for the verification of peaked outline.

Fig. 34.

Fig. 31.

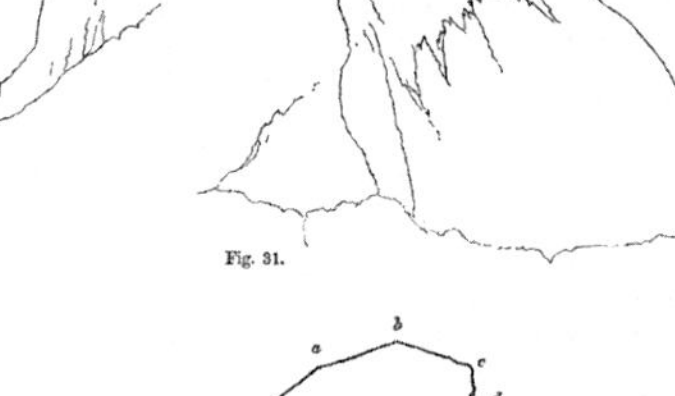

Fig. 32.

Angles with the horizon *x y*.

Of the line *a b* - - -	17°	Of the line *d y* (general slope, exclusive of inequalities)	35¾°
b c - -	20½	*a x* (ditto, ditto, to point of cliff above *x*) -	23½

39. The Cervin, from the North-West.

Idee Matterhorn:

«The Cervin, from the East, and the North-East», Taf. 38 in: John Ruskin, *Modern Painters*, vol. IV, London 1856

«Aiguilles», Fig. 33 in: John Ruskin, *Modern Painters*, vol. IV, London 1856

«Aiguilles», Fig. 31–32 in: John Ruskin, *Modern Painters*, vol. IV, London 1856

«The Cervin, from the North-West», Taf. 39 in: John Ruskin, *Modern Painters*, vol. IV, London 1856

«Der Fels Matterhorn», Taf. 20 in: Bruno Taut, *Alpine Architektur*, Hagen i.W. 1919

Schwierigkeiten ausgesetzt gefühlt, meint Ruskin in einer seiner vielen 'strategischen' Bemerkungen. Zuerst hätte er – in Übereinstimmung mit den in Band zwei dargelegten Grundsätzen – an «Romantic, Classic, Georgic, and Theoric» gedacht. Nun aber lautet die verbindliche Klassifizierung der künstlerischen Erfassung der Landschaft – mitsamt der Zuweisung ihres jeweils typischsten Vertreters – so: «HEROIC» (Tizian), «CLASSICAL» (Poussin), «PASTORAL» (Cuyp) und «CONTEMPLATIVE» (Turner).[100] Gerade der letzte Begriff, «contemplative», sei besonders schwierig, da er ebenso gut zur romantischen, pastoralen und modernen Auffassung der Landschaftsmalerei passen könnte.[101] Aber, so Ruskin, er töne besser und sei letztlich auch verständlicher.[102] Auch das fügt sich schliesslich nahtlos der 'religiösen' Erweiterung der Ruskinschen Argumentation an.

Also folgen nun erwartungsgemäss Analysen heroischer, klassischer, pastoraler und immer wieder moderner Turnerscher Landschaften: mit zunehmenden Einschüben religiöser Natur! «Man being thus the crowning and ruling work of God, it will follow that all his best art must have something to tell about himself, as the soul of things, and ruler of creatures».[103] Vorerst spricht Ruskin lediglich von den unterschiedlichen Kategorien der Landschaftsmalerei. Doch das scheint ihm in Anbetracht des merklich gehobenen Anspruchs nicht zu genügen. Er spricht nun viel dezidierter und allgemein von einer «contemplative reaction», die er generell in der modernen Kunst und im Zeichen des Begriffs «Christian» erkennt.[104] Und davon gilt: «it may be hoped a new spiritual art may be developed». Davon abgelöst zu betrachten sei die von «nobles naturalists» geprägte 'heroische Schule' und sowieso jene 'klassische' und 'pastorale' Landschaftsmalerei, die der Zeit des «sensual decline» angehöre.

Gemäss dieser Einschätzung, so kann man argumentieren, hat also die moderne Landschaftsmalerei – im Gegensatz zu ihren Vorgängerinnen – nicht nur die Gattungen der Porträt- oder der Historienmalerei ein- und überholt, da sie ja selbst den Menschen ganz in ihr Zentrum stellt. Sie ist, da jener Gottes krönendes Schöpfungswerk darstellt, mittelbar der (alten) religiösen Malerei gleichzustellen. Demgemäss stellt sich nun die Frage nach der religiösen Kunst schlechthin, die er, so Ruskin, eigentlich bis zu den Griechen und den Ägyptern – und deren Darstellung von Landschaften – zurück verfolgen müsste.[105] Stellvertretend sind es jetzt «the Lance of Pallas» und «the wings of the Lion», die solchen Erörterungen standzuhalten haben. Griechisches und Venezianisches im religionsgeschichtlichen Vergleich! «Therefore the Christian painters differed from the Greek in two main points. They had been taught a faith which put an end to restless questioning and discouragement».[106] «Deep horror which vexed the soul of Aeschylus and Homer» auf der einen Seite. Lazarus – statt Achill – auf der andern, was allerdings «a morbid influence» auf das Kunstschaffen nicht vermeiden liess.[107] Nun muss die Diskussion nicht nur auf «the last believing school of Italy», die venezianische, sondern auch auf das kommen, was mit «Roman Catholic» verbunden wird.[108] Auf die Unterschiede der modernen englischen Vorstellung von Religion und dem «temper of the Venetian Catholics» wolle er nicht eingehen und er beschränkt sich denn auch auf die Feststellung, dass diese sich stets im Akt des Betens, jene aber gerade nicht, darstellen liessen, was jedoch nichts mit Hypokrisie zu tun habe.[109] Nein, es geht – in Ruskins Sicht ohnehin – um echte religiöse Gefühle in der Kunst. Wen wundert es, dass er dabei auf die auch später (bis zu Hugo Ball) häufig vorgekehrte Frage kommt. Ruskin versteht es nicht, aber es sei «unquestionable»: «Up to the time of the Reformation it was possible for men even of the highest powers of intellect to obtain a tranquillity of faith, in the highest degree favourable to the pursuit of any particular art».[110] «But this possibility ceased at the Reformation».[111]

Ruskin beginnt nun der 'religiösen Malerei' in Turners Werk, angefangen bei dem «Nereid's Gard», «our English painter's first great religious picture» und ein «exponent of our English faith», nachzuspüren.[112] Also kommen wieder Licht und Farben, malerische – 'turnerische' Qualitäten! – in den Gesichtskreis des die Verbindung mit dem Religiösen aufsuchenden Ruskin. «Claude and Cuyp had painted the sunshine, Turner alone, the sun colour».[113] Und dann wird Farbe gleich wieder an alttestamentliche Symbolvorstellungen als «sanctifying element of visible beauty, inseparably connected with purity and life» herangerückt.[114] «Mystical connection between life and love» erkennt er im «Hebrew system of sacrificial religion». Und das macht allgemeine Feststellungen möglich: «Colour is therefore, in brief terms, the type of love».[115] Und in dem Mass, in dem gerade in diesen letzten Seiten von *Modern Painters* immer wieder Turner und noch einmal Turner ins Visier genommen wird («Of no man but Turner, whom I have ever known, could I say this»[116]), wächst sich Ruskins Kunstexegese und Kunsthermeneutik zu einer Kunstreligion oder sogar zu einer Kunsttheologie aus. So kommt also auch noch Gott selbst und «the communion of saints» in die Diskussion.[117] Und da «infedelity» und «ignorance» zusammengehen und nun andererseits Turner zum Inbegriff einer wirklich religiösen Kunst wird, muss er der grosse 'Unverstandene' sein, als der ihn seine Biographie ohnehin ausweist. Turners «condition of mind» fasst Rus-

100 Ebd., S. 198.
101 Ebd., Anm. 1, S. 199.
102 Ebd.: «... but would not have been pleasant in sound, not, to the genereal reader, very clear in sense».
103 Ebd., S. 207.
104 Ebd., hier bezieht sich Ruskin auf Rio und Lord Lindsay.
105 Ebd., S. 208.
106 Ebd., S. 221.
107 Ebd., S. 222.
108 Ebd., S. 223f.
109 Ebd., S. 223/224.
110 Ebd., S. 235.
111 Ebd.
112 Ebd., S. 317.
113 Ebd., S. 320.
114 Ebd., S. 324/325. – Das wird hier zusammen mit zusammenfassenden Formulierungen aus früheren Bemerkungen zur Farbe in ausführlichen Fussnoten ausgebreitet.
115 Ebd., S. 326.
116 Ebd., S. 345.
117 Ebd., S. 349.

kin so: «What I do must be done rightly; but I know also that no man now living in Europe cares to understand it; and the better I do it, the less he will see the meaning of it».[118] Kepler und Galilei konnten wenigstens ein Stück weit ihre Einsichten kundtun. Für Turner gilt: «Only another Turner could apprehend Turner».[119] Theologie. Ruskin erinnert Turners letzte Bemerkung zu einem Bild: «The priest held the poisoned cup».[120] Und aus solchen biblischen Bildern findet er, Ruskin, als er noch im Mai 1860 um den Abschluss seines opus magnum kämpfte, bis zum Schluss nicht mehr heraus. Einen grösseren 'Umfang' als den des Religiösen kann seine rastlose Suche nach dem Ganzen nicht finden. Nur knapp hat Ruskin zu diesem Zeitpunkt – 1860[121], einundvierzigjährig – die Mitte seines Lebens überschritten und ist noch weit von seiner späteren – 'prophetischen' – Zeit entfernt!

118 Ebd., S. 351.
119 Ebd., S. 352.
120 Ebd., S. 353.
121 Vgl. zu diesem zeitlichen Ablauf: Sawyer 1985, S. 227ff.

VI.

Types of Towers.

«Types of Towers», Taf. VI in: John Ruskin, *Stones of Venice* I, London 1851

Robin Middleton

Ruskin versus the rest

Ruskin upheld two buildings as supreme in *The seven lamps of architecture*, of 1849, the campanile of the cathedral at Florence, and the Doges Palace in Venice. The first was described as «the model and mirror of perfect architecture»,[1] the second as «the model of perfection» of the square form of building – «It would be impossible, I believe», he wrote, «to invent a more magnificent arrangement of all that is in building most dignified and most fair».[2] Again and again the Doges' Palace serves Ruskin as a point of reference, and is extolled as a natural emanation, almost, of all those principles that he has laid down as the proper beginning for the making and understanding of architecture – Sacrifice, Truth, Power, Beauty, Life, Memory and Obedience.

«Do not let it be supposed», Ruskin notes, «that I imagine the Byzantine workman to have had these various principles in their minds as they built. I believe they built altogether from feeling, and it was because they did so, that there is this marvellous life, changefulness, and subtlety running through their every arrangement; and that we reason upon the lovely building as we should upon some fair growth of the trees of the earth, that know not their own beauty».[3]

Ruskin touches here on so much that mattered to him in architecture, its closeness to nature, its age and the expression given to it by each individual workman. Two years later, when the first volume of *The stones of Venice* appeared, the Doges' Palace had become «the central building of the world»[4] and it was used to define the particular felicity of the Gothic of Italy, all that he had loved of the Gothic of the north – Chartres and Amiens – being cast rudely aside almost, in the torrent of praise: «The Gothic of the Ducal Palace of Venice is in harmony with all that is grand in the world: that of the north is in harmony with the grotesque northern spirit only».

Fittingly, a whole chapter of the second volume of the *Stones of Venice*, appearing in July 1853, is devoted to the Doges' Palace; it takes up one third of the book – more even than «The Nature of Gothic», also included, which was to be regarded by William Morris as «one of the very few necessary and inevitable utterances of the century». Even if the two be not compared, there is little denying that Ruskin's account of the Doges' Palace is disappointing, it comes as a rude anti-

1 Ruskin 1849, p. 135.
2 Ibid., p. 72.
3 Ibid., p. 152.
4 Ruskin 1851–1853, I, 1851, p. 17.

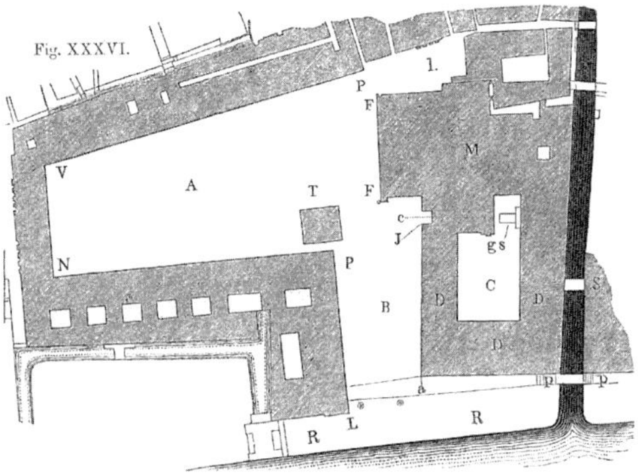

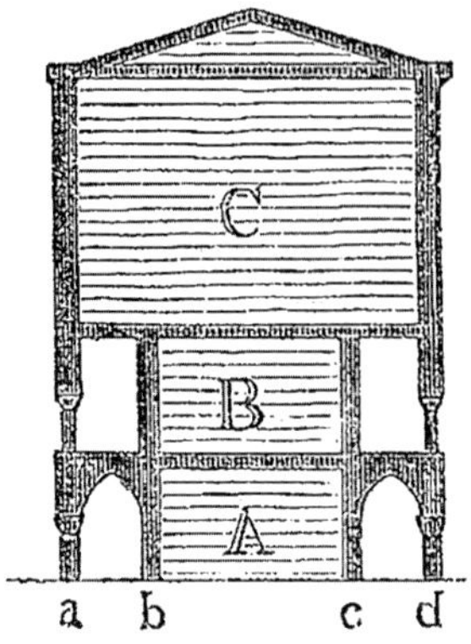

Fig. XXXVII.

Plan and aerial perspective of the Doge's Palace, Venice, in: John Ruskin, *The Stones of Venice* II, 1853, fig. XXXVII.

Diagrammatic section through the Doge's Palace, Venice, in: John Ruskin, *Stones of Venice* II, London 1853, p. 284.

Façade of the Doge's Palace as constructed in timber, in: Eugène Emmanuel Viollet-le-Duc, *Entretiens sur l'architecture* 2, Paris 1872, p. 206.

climax. There is, unusual for Ruskin, an undue emphasis on the history of the building, and this, even more unusual, is accompanied by a site plan and a bird's-eye view. These, it must be stressed, are not included to explain the organization of the building or to indicate anything of its architectural distinction, merely to make clear the historical evolution of the various parts. He liked best the earliest parts. And though he liked the incremental nature of the building and the way in which it had survived and been transformed after fires, attaining always to nobility and grandeur, he gave only the scantest attention to the subsequent work. The interiors, he dismissed, as having been replaced and refitted after fires – «the severe and religious work of Guariento and Bellini has been replaced by the wildness of Tintoret and the luxury of Veronese».[5] Though, of course, he had something to say about the restoration of their paintings.

Near the beginning of his historical account Ruskin slips in another unusual drawing – not only unusual but almost unprecedented in all his voluminous writings – an architectural section. This is no more than a diagram showing how the top-most floor of the building is supported by two lower floors, recessed, and

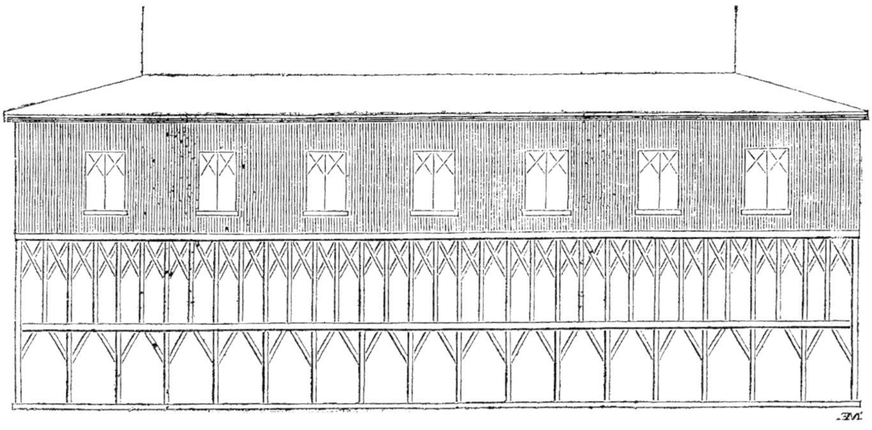

screened by sustaining columns. The subdivisions within, however, having been changed over the centuries, are not to be allowed to trouble his readers. That is all there is of the structure and internal workings of the architecture. Having dealt thus with the arrangement and the history of the building there is evident relief that the real analysis can be begun – «Now, therefore, we are at liberty to examine some of the details of the Ducal Palace, without any doubt about their dates».[6] This, about a quarter of the way throught the chapter. The remainder is devoted almost entirely to a description of the carving on the three exposed corners and the capitals of the columns of the lower order, facing onto the Piazzetta. The capitals on the lagoon front are not explained, having been carelessly restored. The great expanse of wall, he claimed, required that some prominence and importance be given to the corners, lest the whole should seem meagre. This is established, almost, as a principle of Gothic architecture. The Vine angle (the Drunkenness of Noah), the Fig-Tree angle (the Fall of Man) and the Judgement angle (the Judgement of Solomon) are described and analyzed as to their biblical meaning. Then follows an extraordinarily detailed description of the thirty-six ground floor capitals, one by one in succession, face by successive face on occasion, itemizing the steps to virtue represented there, with reference to St. Ambrose, St. Francis and others. It is a nice piece of scriptural exegesis. And undoubtedly illuminating, but it serves hardly at all, one might think, to illuminate the architecture. Only right at the very end does he turn to that, and then he extolls it as something of the order of nature, something, almost, of the hand of god. Though once again, it is an evasion of the architectural issues, as generally understood. His final paragraph requires to be quoted in full:
«... sometimes when walking at evening on the Lido, whence the great chain of the Alps, crested with silver clouds, might be seen rising above the front of the Ducal

5 Ibid., II, 1853, p. 370.
6 Ibid., II, 1853, p. 304.

Palace, I used to feel as much awe in gazing on the building as on the hills, and could believe that God had done a greater work in breathing into the narrowness of dust the mighty spirits by whom its haughty walls had been raised, and its burning legends written, than in lifting the rocks of granite highter than the clouds of heaven, and the veiling them with their various mantle of purple flower and shadowy pine».[7]

Ruskin is not at his best here, he was more magical by far in conjouring up the crestings of waves and the sea-foam on the façade of St. Mark's. Usually, of course, Ruskin could rise to the occasion. But even when he is at his best, there is always the sense that the architecture has eluded him. Even his memorable walk through Venice offers no more than glimpses of architectural details. The poetry is there, but it is a poetry applied, set off by some architectural feature, some notion of the world from which it has sprung, or the spirit of the craftsman who fashioned it. Ruskin's categories – and in «The Nature of Gothic» he added a new array, Savageness, Changefulness, Naturalism, Grotesqueness, Rigidity and Redundance – do not really serve to describe the qualities with which the designers of buildings – or indeed, the makers – are actively concerned.

Ruskin's arch rival, Viollet-le-Duc, almost contemporary, towering over all other expositors of architecture in France, as Ruskin did in England, sharing a great deal in common with him – a deep love of Gothic, an intense interest in geology and the Alps – never once made mention of him. Ruskin's name does not occur in his endless writings. Yet he must have known of him. Viollet-le-Duc's close friend, Prosper Mérimée, thought to write an article on Ruskin in 1850, soon after their return from England, but nothing came of it. But articles on Ruskin were published in France from 1856 onwards, though the real vogue for his writings dates from the closing years of the century.

Ruskin, on the other hand, was self-consciously concerned by Viollet-le-Duc. He had nightmares that Viollet-le-Duc refused to speak to him. He admitted to being jealous of the *Dictionnaire raisonné de l'architecture française*. But he felt bold to recommend it to his students in Oxford – «the best informed, most intelligent, and most thoughtful of guides», he pronounced, and he went on at some length as to Viollet-le-Duc's virtues, but ended by remarking on his vice – «his professional interest in the mere *science* of architecture, and comparative insensibility to the power of sculpture».[8] That was in 1873.

The only acknowledgement Viollet-le-Duc made of Ruskin – if indeed it was an acknowledgement – was made in the previous year, in his fifteenth *Entretien*. The reference was oblique, but pointed. It occurred in an analysis of surface revetment. Viollet-le-Duc had dealt with the Masjed-i-Shah in Isphahan. He had explained how the enclosure was essentially a precinct in which one could cleanse and purify oneself in order to communicate with god. No imagery was required. But some adornment was needed to provide distinction. A decorative revetment was devised that sprung from the forms and geometry of the plan – «elle tient à l'édifice, non comme le vêtement, mais comme les muscles et la peau tiennent à l'homme».[9] This of course, is no more than a rhetorical application of his critical vocabulary of approval. He turns then to something different, something producing a similarity of effect, but made of stone: the Doges' Palace.

«Laissons de côté», he writes, «si l'on veut, le détail décoratif qui n'est pas d'un goût irréprochable; voyons l'ensemble».[10] A thrust at Ruskin, one assumes. For he begins in the same way, describing the section of the building, the spacious halls on the uppermost floor, supported by two floors of service spaces, accessed by galleries, screened by an array of struts and columns. The expression of this is quite direct. And he illustrates how it might have looked if built in timber, with posts, cross-bracing and vertical planking above. But stone was the material to be employed. The programme was thus expressed, scrupulously, in stone.
«L'architecture vénitienne a scrupuleusement rempli ce programme, et son œuvre emprunte toute sa décoration à l'expression rigoureuse, absolue de la structure».[11]

Viollet-le-Duc leaves one in no doubt as to his criteria of excellence. The ornamental detail, he repeats, plays little part in the general effect, yet it is not insignificant.
«L'architecte, par l'arrangement excellent des angles (point délicat) a su donner un aspect robuste à ce quillage soutenant une boîte massive en apparence».[12] Perversely, he includes a large engraving of the corner detail. To lighten the effect of the mass red and white stone is used, as a great mosaic almost, in the eastern manner. And to set off this great surface, intricately modelled capitals and carvings are introduced, underlining by contrast the unity of the whole, but not destroying it. «A nos yeux, la meilleure architecture est celle dont la décoration ne peut être distraite de la structure».[13] As a final thrust, he warns, however good a piece of carving may be, if it can be removed without altering the essential form of the building, better that it did not exist.

Whether or not Viollet-le-Duc was responding to Ruskin scarce matters. Both men loved the Doges' Palace, and both failed in their attempt to grasp and convey the distinction of the architecture. Viollet-le-Duc's system could not encompass it – the form of the building did not express any organizational complexities, the structure was too straightforward. Ruskin liked breadth – «one needs

7 Ibid., II, 1853, p. 374.
8 Cook/Wedderburn 1903–1912, v. 33, p. 465.
9 Viollet-le-Duc 1863–1872, II, 1872, p. 205.
10 Ibid., II, 1872, p. 206.
11 Ibid., II, 1872, p. 207.
12 Ibid., II, 1872, p. 207.
13 Ibid., II, 1872, p. 208.

sheer vertical mass of walling»,[14] he wrote in reference to the great expanse of the wall, or «veil» as he preferred to call it – but the wall was too big for him, he turned to the minutest of details instead, and remained with them.

The Doges' Palace can be set aside now. I would like, briefly, to consider how Ruskin's contemporaries in England were trying to devise a critical approach to architecture and to suggest how it might be best applied in the making of architecture. Forget, for the moment, A.W.N. Pugin, who provided the springs of all Ruskin's criticism, and look at three highly popular books published at almost the same moment as the *Seven Lamps... – The orders and their aesthetic principles*, of 1848, by W.H. Leeds, *An historical enquiry into the true principles of beauty in art, more especially with reference to architecture*, of 1849, by James Fergusson, and a *Rudimentary treatise on the principles of design in architecture as deducible from nature and exemplified in the works of the Greek and Gothic architects*, of 1850, by Edward Lacy Garbett.

Leeds was an interesting critic, writing in the new architectural periodicals such as the *Civil Engineer and Architect's Journal* he could be sharp and perceptive. He was good on both Soane and Barry. His book on the Orders does not, inevitably, exhibit his range; but it does serve to demonstrate his cast of mind. He was very matter-of-fact in approach. He rejected all notion that Greek architecture was a transposition in stone of timber forms; the proportions of the Orders, he noted, had nothing to do with human proportions and the Vitruvian account of the origin of the Corinthian capital was sheer humbug. Concepts of beauty in architecture were essentially established prejudices, the fluting of the Doric column had first been done for effect, no more, and had fixed taste, just as the approved slope of the pediment was no more than a taste accepted. Taste, in fact, looms large in many of his judgements, in his definition of architecture even: «... architecture is building with something more than a view to mere utility and convenience, it is building in such a manner as to delight the eye by beauty of forms, to captivate the imagination, and to satisfy that faculty of the mind which we denominate taste».[15]

There is not much in this to inspire or even to guide one. The book emerges as nothing much more than a late, sensible account of the Orders and their application, freely interpreted if required. But he did address the propriety of simply applying a style in the fashioning of a contemporary architecture. Gothic should not be re-installed either as a national or as a catholic style because, as he said, «it would be eminently artificial in principle»,[16] altogether at variance with contemporary habits and tastes. Taste again. The result, he sneered (no doubt at Pugin) would be «Old-maidish Gothic». The only sensible style for the nineteenth century, he finally recommended, was that of the Renaissance or the Greco-Italian, as exemplified in the work of Charles Barry, as «it is by no means yet worked out»,[17] as he said. Once again not much to inspire one.

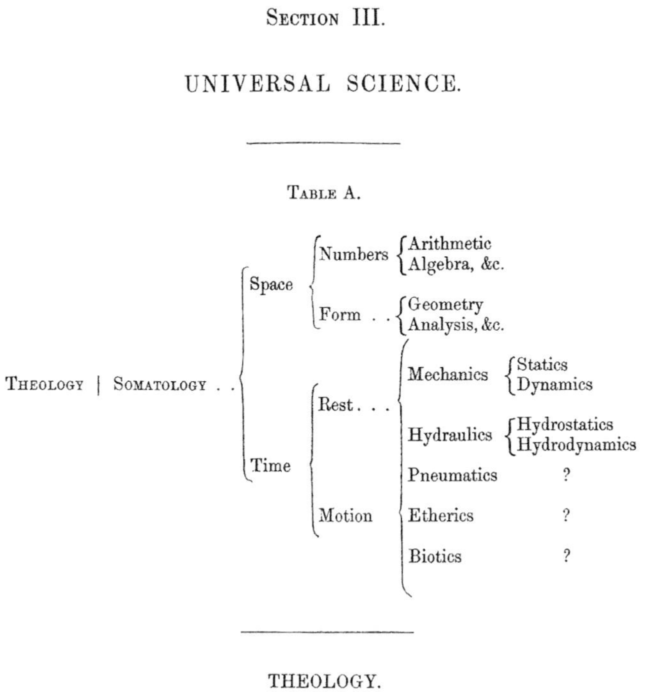

SECTION III.

UNIVERSAL SCIENCE.

TABLE A.

THEOLOGY | SOMATOLOGY . .
Space
Numbers: Arithmetic, Algebra, &c.
Form . . Geometry, Analysis, &c.
Time
Rest . . .
Mechanics: Statics, Dynamics
Hydraulics: Hydrostatics, Hydrodynamics
Motion
Pneumatics ?
Etherics ?
Biotics ?

THEOLOGY.

Table A. Universal science, in: J. Fergusson, *An historical enquiry* ..., London 1849, p. 27.

James Fergusson's book was altogether different. He is remembered for his suffocating histories of architecture, the prelude to Banister Fletcher's, and there is something of this in his *Historical enquiry...*, but it is the introduction, 170 odd close-packed pages, that I intend to focus on, as outlining his approach to architecture, indeed to all art and knowledge.

Fergusson aimed to encompass all forms of architecture – whether Buddhist, Hindoo or Mexican. He had been an indigo grower in India. The object of his despite was «the monkey styles of Europe». He presented himself as an honest, Protestant gentleman, immensely proud of the British system of government and the state of the manufacturing arts of that country. He did not think much though, of the state of the arts themselves. The governing classes had relinquished their responsibilities, they had provided no intellectual lead in the realm of the arts. Once, the architecture of England had indeed been superior, superior even to that of Greece itself «with all their disadvantages, our forefathers surpassed the Greeks, not only in the constructive skill and magnitude of their edifices, but in their knowledge of effect, and the general grandeur of conception and appropriateness of detail displayed in every part».[18] That however, was time past. The upper classes must be roused from their slumbers, a great and truthful architecture might yet arise. But

14 Ruskin 1849, p. 70.
15 Leeds 1848, 10th edition, 1874, p. 2.
16 Ibid., 10th edition, 1874, p. 121.
17 Ibid., 10th edition, 1874, p. 122.
18 Fergusson 1849, p. 13.

Section IV.

PHYSICAL SCIENCES.

Table B.

- Astronomy
  - Space . . Stellar / Planetic / Telluric
  - Time . . History
- Etherology
  - Space . . . Chemistry / Etherography / Geography
  - Time . . . ?
- Mineralogy
  - Space . . . Chemistry / Crystallography / Meteorology? / Morphology / Geography
  - Time . . . Geology / History
- Botany
  - Space . . . Chemistry / Anatomy / Physiology / Phytography / Geography
  - Time . . . Palæophytology / History
- Zoology
  - Space . . . Chemistry / Anatomy / Physiology / Ontology / Zoography / Geography
  - Time . . . Palæozoology / History

PHYSICS.

Table B. Physical sciences, in: J. Fergusson, *An historical enquiry* ..., p. 40.

Table C. Anthropics. Physical description of man, in: J. Fergusson, *An historical enquiry* ..., p. 58.

first, what was required, was a general classification of knowledge, marking the affinities and the distinctions between science and art, the better to isolate the generative principles of the latter – science being defined as a knowledge of nature's workings, art of man's. And so he begins, breaking science down into three categories – Universal Science, Physical Science and Anthropics (the physical description of man). Universal Science is based in Theology/Somatology, which divides into Space and Time; Space divides into Numbers and Form, Time into Rest and Motion, and these then divide further into Arithmetic, Algebra, Geometry, Analysis, Mechanics, Hydraulics, Pneumatics, Etherics, Biotics, with even more subdivisions indicated, Statics, Dynamics, Hydrostatics, Hydrodynamics, and some yet undefined (like the elements of the rare earth group on old school charts). There is a skirmish with the existence of God at the beginning of the explanation of this section, but Fergusson moves swiftly on to detailed discussion of each of the categories named. Physical Science is broken down in ever-dividing categories in much the same way, and explained to tedium, as is the Science of Anthropics, the physical description of man. This is the section in which architecture is to be embraced. But before he gets on to it there is a lot more of general definition and specific

Section V.

ANTHROPICS.

PHYSICAL DESCRIPTION OF MAN.

Table C.

Chemistry.		
	Simple Substances	Oxygen, Hydrogen, Carbon, &c.
	Compound „	Albumen, Fibrine, Gelatine, Urea, &c.
Anatomy.		
	Cellular and Vascular Tissues	Bones, Ligaments, Muscles, &c.
	Vessels	Absorbent, Circulative, Secretive, &c.
	Nerves	Sympathetic, Vertebral, Cerebral, Sensous, &c.
Physiology.		
	Mechanical Functions—	Organisation and Combination of Textures, Connexion of Parts, Muscular Action, Functions of Osseous Fibre, &c.
	Chemical „	Assimilation, Chylification, Sanguinification, Secretion and Excretion, Nutrition, &c.
	Sensorial „	Organisation of Nerves, Ganglia, External Senses, Touch, Taste, Smell, Hearing, Vision, &c.
	Mental „	Recurrence and Association of Impressions, Volition and Voluntary Motion; Automatic, Instinctive, and Involuntary Motions; Sleep; Voice.
	Generative „	Fecundation, Utero-Gestation, Parturition, Lactation, &c.
	Mutative „	Growth, Disease, Decay, Death.
Ontology.		
	Instincts	Nutrition, Amativeness, Love of Offspring, Gregariousness, Self-preservation, &c.
	Propensities	Acquisitiveness, Combativeness, Self-love.
	Emotions	Joy, Hope, Love, Benevolence, Pride.
	Sentiments	Friendship, Veneration, Justice.
	Intellect	Attention {Comparison, Analysis} {Combination, Synthesis} Induction.
	Memory	{Spontaneous Association, Habit} {Voluntary Recollection., Thought.}
	Nosology	Silliness, Idiotcy, Mania, Ramollissement, Paralysis.
Morals		
Religion.	(See Table G.)	

analysis of various art forms. Fine art in general, he makes clear, is in essence an intellectual pursuit.

«The highest aim of all», he writes, «is always an appeal to the intellect. Sense and sentient beauty may be, and in most art generally is, the vehicle through which the appeal is made; but in the highest arts it is neither the aim nor the end, and phonetic or euphonetic, would be a better term to apply: but some loftier expression than even this ought to be used to express those artistic utterances which satisfy that craving for intellectual beauty which is their highest aim».[19]

Architecture, it soon becomes clear, cannot be dealt with in any one division, as it partakes of all the Anthropic arts – the Technic, the Aesthetic and the Phonetic. He does, however, manage to list it in yet another subsidiary diagram of the fine arts, along with jewelry, ceramics, landscape-gardening, gastronomy, tailoring, embroidery, driving and yachting. Fergusson himself is a bit dubious as to these last two. The common feature of all though is that in the proper performance of their

19 Ibid., p. 78.

inherent function, some attraction should arise which might be termed a sense of beauty. Fergusson should be allowed to explain himself; even if at length.

«... there is attached to the exercise of every function a certain gratification or inducement to its exercise, which, properly cultivated, converts that which is a task and burden into a source of pleasure and enjoyment; and with man, at least, the inducement that attracts him to the healthful exercise of his faculties may, in most cases be greater than the force that goads him to it.

It would be vain to attempt to enumerate the various names that have been given to this attraction or inducement, but the most common and the most generic name is that of 'beauty' or 'sense of beauty', which means really nothing more than the gratification which we are able to extract out of every useful function we perform, and which is necessarily attached to the proper performance of all these functions».[20]

Architecture, being the expression of so many categories of the arts and sciences, pops up all over the place in the summaries Fergusson provides. In the analysis of the Technic arts, we are told that «ornament can change a utilitarian building into architecture».[21] Naked engineering can be redeemed of its common-place vulgarity. «Not only, however», he allows, «are the permanent works of the engineer capable of being elevated into objects of art, but both ships and carriages are, to a certain extent, capable of such cultivation. To my mind all ships are more or less objects of beauty».[22]

Having dealt with the Phonetic arts – Sculpture, Painting, Engraving, Symbolism, Poetry and Eloquence – something more of the possibilities of architecture are suggested:

«Architecture», he writes, «can repeat no narrative, illustrate no book – it imitates nothing, illustrates nothing: it tells no tale, and barely manages to express an emotion of joy or sorrow with the same distinctness with which they can be expressed by the unphonetic brutes. It is true that by the addition of sculpture and painting, a building may become phonetic, but we must not here confound two distinct modes of utterance: the voice is in the last-named arts, not in the technic; but combined together, they form one of the noblest compounds that man has yet put together».[23]

And here he adduces the cathedrals of Chartres and Rheims. Somehow though, despite all such specifics, architecture seems to slip through the extraordi-

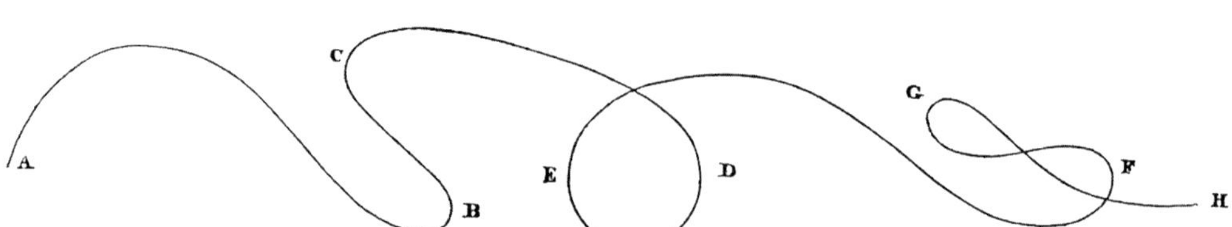

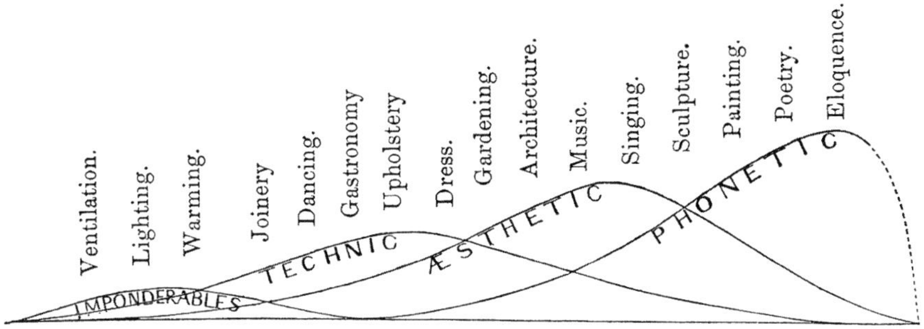

The line of progress, in: J. Fergusson, *An historical enquiry…*, London 1849, p. 69.
The composition of the arts, in: J. Fergusson, *An historical enquiry…*, London 1849, p. 143.

nary mesh of categories and definitions, as yet undefined. Fergusson thus tackles the problem in a totally new section «On beauty in art», with its expected subdivisions, Technic, Aesthetic and Phonetic Beauty. He contrives a table in which the various aspects of architecture can be measured in each division or subdivision, and a total score attained. The various divisions do not, of course, have equal rank or value, so individual scores have to be multiplied by 1, 2 or 3, depending on the division, to obtain a quotient. The highest score is 35, Cologne cathedral gets 22, Rheims, 23, the Parthenon 24, despite having done rather badly in the Heating and Ventilation table. «The Parthenon at Athens», Fergusson concludes, «is perhaps the most perfect building we posess».[24]

We are offered more on beauty and sublimity, reaching back to Burke and sex (despite this last not being intellectual), but in the end Fergusson returns to the issue with which he began, how to achieve a contemporary architecture of distinction. There are three requisites.

«The first is to restore to art its progressive vitality, or, in other words, to give up all imitation of past styles.

The second is to enlist a higher order of minds in their practice.

The third is to fit them with some highter aim than merely to please the dilettanti or the connoisseur; for they must teach and elevate …».[25]

It is this moral purpose, parallel to Ruskin's, that he thus upholds as the only hope of redemption. But by 1862, this high purpose had faded, at the end of his *History of the Modern Styles of Architecture*, he offers the same lame panacea as Leeds, and in almost the exact same terms: «There is yet one other style within whose limits progress still seems possible», he wrote, «The Renaissance Italian is by no means worked out».[26]

20 Ibid., p. 95.
21 Ibid., p. 102.
22 Ibid., p. 105.
23 Ibid., p. 121.
24 Ibid., p. 144.
25 Ibid., p. 155.
26 Fergusson 1862, «Conclusion».

Little is known of the third of these architectural expositors, Edward Lacy Garbett, but his book was to run into a great many editions. It is sharp and intelligent and, appearing in 1850, it provided the first response to *The Seven Lamps*. Garbett was, in fact, surprisingly responsive to many of Ruskin's ideas – he took over entirely (with full acknowledgment) Ruskin's notion of the picturesque as the «parasitical sublime»; he approved his remarks on breadth in architecture and those on deception in the use of surface coverings; he agreed with him entirely as to the falling off in late Gothic traceries, the emphasis moving from mass and void to linear abstraction, but on the matter of ornament itself he was in constant disagreement – «some,» he remarked, «mistake ornament for beauty»,[27] there was no question in his mind but that ornament could not make architecture and that it was all too easy to have too much of it, no matter if it was good or bad, but the most erroneous of all Ruskin's beliefs, Garbett thought, was that the value of ornament might be related to the degree of manual labour involved. Garbett somewhat distorted Ruskin's propositions. But the real divide between them was Garbett's rejection not only of Greek as a basis of renewal, but also Gothic (of the two, he preferred Greek), and his lame acceptance at the end of his first edition of some sort of Renaissance revival – «On the whole», he wrote, «the Florentine may be called the *common sense* school, and its importation into this country by Barry is a benefit that should atone, perhaps, for its many failures».[28]

But there is a lot more to Garbett's analysis of architecture than this. He rejected the idea that utilitarian design could, of itself, be beautiful – look, he said, at the hideous backs of all London terrace houses – if there was beauty to be found in utilitarian architecture, it was because a designer had been involved, and that designer had exerted his mind.

The first half of Garbett's book was an attempt to isolate the principles of design that might produce beauty in architecture – he aimed at beauty and politeness (Emerson) – beginning with a narrow range of qualities, moving on to broader themes. He would have nothing of what he termed Vitruvian humbug – no primitive huts, no proportional systems derived from human forms, no Corinthian capitals from baskets and flowers. He was well-versed in aesthetic theory, that of Alison in particular. He knew Hay well too. He began his presentation with colour –

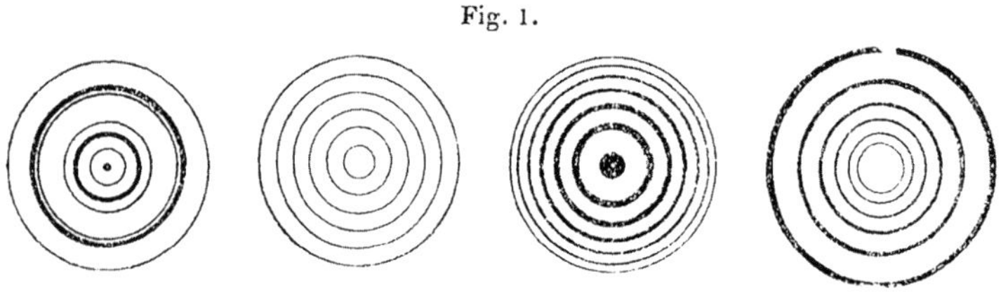

Varity with unity, in: E.L. Garbett, *Rudimentary treatise ... on design*, London 1850, p. 55.

for the response to colour, he thought, alone of all aesthetic responses, might be susceptible of measurement. John Herschel had measured vibrations in the pupils of eyes that might account for our preferences of colour. But even here, association and mental constructs could change all. Children and savages liked different ranges of colours to culivated individuals. As to other forms of beauty, there was no question but that they had to be discovered by the mind, not by mere sensation. Thus he dealt with repetition, symmetry, and straight and curved lines, alone and in varying combinations, to arrive at the principles of Unity and Variety, and the role within them of gradation and contrast (Hogarth and Hutcheson are here introduced). Garbett is, as might be imagined, keen throughout to establish something of scientific certainty in the human reaction to these characteristics, but he concedes sadly that he cannot. However, he believes firmly that there are consistent, underlying preferences. He sets up a small test at one point, four targets made up of concentric circles, variously spaced and with varying thicknesses of line. That with lines of even thickness, evenly spaced he finds the least interesting. That with an even gradation of spacing and a contrary gradation in thickness of line he likes best. And he assumes this to be the taste of all educated people. Though many would today scarcely agree. He moves on then to different kinds of beauty – the sublime and the picturesque. He refers to Burke, Alison again, and others, but, more significantly, he makes an attempt of his own to analyze the effects of angles and curves and their combinations in nature – he looks to the rhinoceros, the ox and the bulldog for lines of force.

«Forms may be divided», he concludes, «as regards their inherent or essential expression (apart from association) into at least five classes, according to their degree of contrast or gradation; from the most grand, severe, and forcible, to the most elegant, fanciful and delicate».[29]

He then lists the five combinations:

«1. Rectilinear and rectangular forms

2. Rectilinear but oblique angled forms

3. Curvilinear forms without contrary flexures

4. Curvilinear forms with artificial contrary flexures

5. Curvilinear forms with natural contrary flexures».[30]

«It may be taken then», he concludes, «as a principle hardly admitting of question, that, as in nature, so in art, the graver and more forcible varieties of form should in every case prevail most in the ruling and structural part of a work, and that the more elegant varieties should find their place chiefly in the ornamental details».[31]

27 Garbett 1850, p. 12.
28 Ibid., p. 244.
29 Ibid., p. 84.
30 Ibid., p. 85.
31 Ibid., p. 86.

From here he moves to the matter of constructive truth as it derives from nature: «It is by a particular application of this principle that we discover *angularity* to be an important part of Nature's mode of expressing *force* – and *reflexed curvature* to be part of her mode of expressing *delicacy*. The same method must be applied to every variety of character ...».[32]

Some idea of what he intends is illustrated in a grotesque diagram showing forces acting on a beam in three forms – through an elephant's foot, from above; through a brawny arm, from the side; and from a Doric columns, from below. All are shown to taper from the fixed to the unfixed end, and all have similar curves.

From Constructive Truth he moves to Constructive Unity, and we are now provided with a long, long analysis of the two styles of architecture in which both have been embodied – the Greek trabeated system, and the Gothic arcuated system. Both declined, the Gothic more precipitously: «... the fall of the Gothic architecture perhaps differed from that of the Classic», he writes, «and was more complete. It was a fall out of which nothing could be expected to arise, – a fall not of a style or system merely, but in a certain sense, of the entire art».[33] Constructive Unity had been lost. But, in any event, both systems were past and dead: «we can never revive them».[34] A third constructive system, the tensile system, the truss, had not yet been elaborated as a style, but it was nonetheless, he reassured, «the destined architecture of the future» (cf. Bartholemew).[35]

However, this architecture would never be, he was convinced, an architecture of a pure taste, like Greek and Gothic, for a pure taste could be produced only by the few, the thinking and truth-seeking few, and there were few enough of them, the best one might hope for is that they might fight for something new.
«There *is* a class of buildings», he concluded, «tending towards a new style of construction, – becoming less mixed in this respect, – and approaching a consistent use of tensile covering to the exclusion of every other. To this third system of constructive unity, there is NO old style adapted. None was invented for it. It is a new thing and its treatment must be NEW, –».[36]

He had no real solution to offer. But by the time his next edition was printed he had the Crystal Palace to hand, almost all made of a new material at least, and he grasped hard at that.

Ruskin showed surprising interest in this critical farrago. To Leeds he did not deign to reply. Though Leeds responded angrily enough to Ruskin. In the second edition of *The Orders*, of 1851, Leeds rounded against Ruskin's dismissal of the Ionic and rejection of the Renaissance as semi-pagan and lascivious. Ruskin's similes he termed «sentimental twaddle», – in particular the conceit of the Greek scroll representing the sea – «who more than once plunges into arrant nonsense in his will-o'-the-wisp chase after peregrine, fantastical phrases, and alembicated double dis-

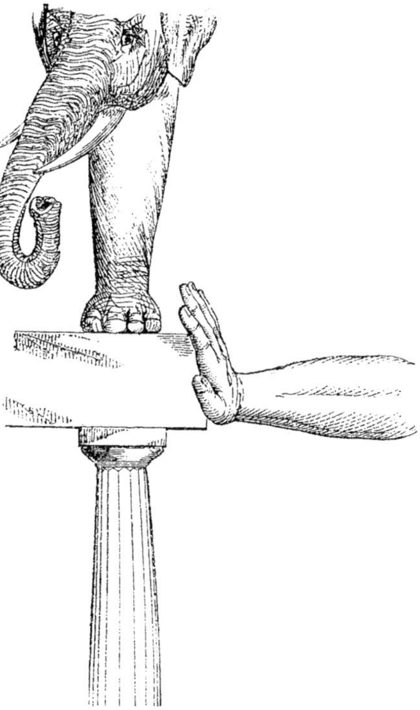

Three forces acting in relation to a beam, in: E.L. Garbett, *Rudimentary treatise … on design*, London 1850, p. 116.

tilled conceits».[37] However, Leeds did approve Ruskin's recommendation to «Think in shadow». Fergusson likewise, was mocked by Leeds for his suggestion that the Ionic emerged from the volutes at Persepolis – to Leeds this was monstrous.

Ruskin confessed (in six and a half pages) to astonishment at Fergusson's system – «he must disentangle himself from his system, or he will be strangled by it», he advised, later judging, «It is a perfect entanglement of gun-cotton, and explodes into vacuity wherever one holds a light to it».[38] This was in the first edition of *The Stones of Venice*. He removed this appendix from the subsequent editions. But he retained his mocking comment on Fergusson's views on ships – «Mr. Fergusson says, somewhat doubtfully, that he perceives a '*kind* of beauty' in ships: I say, without any manner of doubt, that a ship is one of the loveliest things man ever made, and one of the noblest; nor do I know any lines, out of divine work, so lovely as those of the head of a ship, or even as the sweep of the timbers of a small boat, not a race boat, a mere floating chisel, but a broad, strong, sea-boat, able to breast a wave and break it: and yet, with all this beauty, ships cannot be made subjects of sculpture.»[39] That was all – nothing on fitness and form.

32 Ibid., p. 114.
33 Ibid., p. 236.
34 Ibid., p. 135.
35 Ibid., p. 135.
36 Ibid., p. 262.
37 Leeds 1848, 1851 edition, p. 135.
38 Ruskin 1851–1853, I, 1851, Appendix 13, quotations from p. 375 and 377.
39 Ruskin 1851–1853, 1858 edition, I, p. 209.

To Garbett, Ruskin had more to say. He found his approval of the Tudor arch quite unacceptable,[40] his analogy between the Doric column and the elephant's foot arrant rubbish,[41] even more unmeaning was the claim that natural forms were not, inevitably, beautiful. Ruskin quoted Garbett at some length on this, before condemning him utterly.[42] But his real scorn was reserved for Garbett's later approval of the Crystal Palace: «The quantity of bodily energy which that Crystal Palace expresses is very great», he wrote, «So far it is good. The quantity of thought it expresses is, I suppose, a single and very admirable thought of Sir Joseph Paxton's, probably not a bit brighter than thousands of thoughts which pass through his active and intelligent brain every hour, – that it might be possible to build a greenhouse larger than any greenhouse that was built before. This thought, and some very ordinary algebra, are as much as all that glass can represent of human intellect».[43] Ruskin had struggled in the *Seven lamps* – in the lamp of Truth – with the issue of iron construction in architecture. «Abstractly», he wrote, «there appears no reason why iron should not be used as well as wood; and the time is probably near when a new system of architectural laws will be developed, adapted entirely to metallic construction».[44] He was inclined, at first, to admit its use, but as the chapter progressed his natural feelings began to assert themselves. Iron was not really acceptable because it broke with received notions of size, proportion and decoration based on the use of traditional materials of construction. In architecture, Ruskin responded only to the past: «true architecture», he concluded, «does not admit iron as a constructive material».[45]

Fergusson too, thought the Crystal Palace lacking in a sense of solidity and mass, that could not, as he said, «be elevated to the class of the Fine Arts».[46] And Viollet-le-Duc, himself, would have agreed.

Pugin, for all his bigotry, had been more open-minded. He did not like iron construction. But in *An apology for the revival of Christian architecture in England*, of 1843, he felt forced to approve iron as a structural material, though he felt thus free to denounce it as «a meagre substitute for the mason's skill».[47] He could applaud the introduction of the steam engine as a source of power for lifting and moving things. He could even conceive that railway architecture might be impressive. He concluded his assessment of the modern condition with two simple and surprising statements – «Any modern invention which conduces to comfort, cleanliness or durability, should be adopted by the consistent architect; *to copy a thing merely because it is old, is just as absurd as the imitations of the modern pagans*»[48] and «There is no reason in the world why noble cities combining all possible convenience of drainage, water-closets, and conveyance of gas may not be erected in the most consistent and yet Christian character. *Every building that is treated naturally without disguise or concealment, cannot fail to look well*».[49]

Pugin seems to have been trying harder than his successors to come to terms with the nineteenth century – and that, however much one might enjoy Ruskin's ruminations, was the real task of these architectural critics. Ruskin might be said to have failed in that.

40 Ibid., 1858 edition, I, p. 144.
41 Ibid., 1858 edition, I, p. 74.
42 Ibid., 1858 edition, I, p. 340.
43 Ibid., 1858 edition, I, p. 381.
44 Ruskin 1849, p. 36.
45 Ruskin 1849, p. 37.
46 Fergusson 1862, Book XI: «Ferro-vitreous art».
47 Pugin 1843, p. 41.
48 Ibid., p. 38.
49 Ibid., p. 39.

James Fergusson's only known building: North Gallery, Royal Botanic Gardens, Kew, London.

Viollet-le-Duc's own house: 68 rue Condorcet, Paris, 1862–1863.

«Traceries from Caen, Bayeux, Rouen, and Beauvais», Taf. III in:
John Ruskin, *The Seven Lamps of Architecture*, London 1849

Claus Uhlig

Nostalgia for Organicism. Art and Society in Ruskin and Pater

In times of dramatic change, not to speak of cultural crisis, people tend to look to history for redress of their grievances or in search of orientation in their everyday lives. Now, according to the consensus of scholarly opinion, the Victorian age is just one such period of change in British history, a period that frequently turned to the past in order to illuminate the present. Therefore a brief characterization of 'Victorianism' as contemporary context should precede the paper's attempt to examine the largely retrospective and often antithetical modes of thought of the two prominent nineteenth-century critics of art and society in question, namely John Ruskin (1819–1900) and Walter Pater (1839–1894), at once so similar to and yet so different from each other. A concluding section will then try to relate the historical assumptions as well as the aesthetic and moral convictions of the two great Victorians under discussion to the wider context of a psychology and sociology of nostalgia which yearns for organic unity in all spheres of life the moment it is deemed lost for good.

I.

To be sure, more than any other generation before their time, the Victorians had to cope with unprecedented changes indeed, and these above all due to the massive advance of technology and industrialization, which was visibly reshaping both the landscape and the social structure of the whole country. So widespread and so rapid were the changes brought about by the nineteenth century in the material conditions of living that no one could escape a sense of bewilderment rushing in upon him. Politics, when not alone summarized with the fears of revolution and the questions of social reforms, can be seen as the vehicle which brought new transportation systems into being, illustrated by the steamship and the railroads. Further impressive inventions of this period include: the telegraph and telephone, photography, the gas burner and electric light, the tipewriter and later the automobile. Owing to rapid communication and transportation the farthest corners of the British Isles became easier of access, while the spread of the factory system virtually destroyed England's agricultural economy and transformed the way of life of the working class. In addition to that, the population multiplied at an alarming rate, whereby London especially grew out of all proportion within the century, until it had developed into the world's largest city.[1]

All this is tantamount to saying that the democratic-industrial society resulting from these changes could no longer be a society in the traditional sense. With the breakup of a long-established order and the concomitant fragmentation of life, men and classes were no longer integral parts of a Christian-feudal organism where everyone had his recognized place and function and was united to Church and State by established rights and duties. Symbol of the new liberal-industrial society was the city, drawing men and women away from the country, thus severing their ties to the ancestral village and destroying the ancient sense of community. Small wonder therefore that this experience of loss, if ever so full of promise with regard to personal liberty in theory, provoked feelings of isolation, loneliness, and above all nostalgia – nostalgia for an earlier time of mental peace and unifying belief, to be associated for ever with the country in opposition to the city.[2]

In this connection, then, it becomes clear that loss of home could have a spiritual dimension, too. Poets like Tennyson and Arnold in particular were nostalgic for a lost age of faith. The former poet's *In Memoriam* (1850), antedating Darwin's controversial *Origin of Species* (1859) by nine years, tried to ward off the dangers of atheism, risen in the wake of scientific advance, by honestly spelling out all the doubts with regard to Christianity, providence, immortality, indeed man's special place in the universe – doubts which threatened to dissolve the social order of 'Victorianism'.[3] So, if the period under discussion was in fact an age of multiple tensions and dualities, the opposition between agnosticism and belief certainly belonged to its most dominant traits.[4] And in view of such dualistic modes of thought, it is likewise easy to understand why Victorian writers, no longer able to satisfy their intellectual needs in the present, turned to the past in their yearning for oneness, wholeness, or totality. Even if, as has been well said, «the use of history is to learn from the study of it and not to carry preconceived notions or external objectives into it»,[5] most of the «Victorian Sages»[6] did precisely that, thereby possibly misusing their much-vaunted «historical sense»[7] to provide foils of contrast from the remote past to set off the 'Zeitgeist' of their own present.

Not least for this reason should one be careful here in introducing Hegelian notions of the philosophy of history and avoid talking about dialectics when the concept of mediation is lacking,[8] because what was at issue on the part of Victorian «historical mindedness» was in fact contrast in the sense of contradiction. Take for example Augustus Welby Pugin's most persuasive book *Contrasts* whose full title: *A Parallel between the Noble Edifices of the Middle Ages and the Corresponding Buildings of the Present Day; Showing the Present Decay of Taste* (1836) unmistakably announced its theme, not to mention the accompanying illustrations.[9] The theme of historical opposition could further be exemplified by Thomas Carlyle's *Past and Present*

(1843), exposing as it did the blatant deficiencies of nineteenth-century industrialism by contrast with selected aspects of the bygone feudal civilization of the Middle Ages. Written in outraged sympathy with England's proletarian work force, harassed by a capitalist minority, it was emphatic in its prediction of a «Chivalry of Labour» that must nevertheless have appeared anachronistic to many a contemporary.[10] But not so to the Scottish sage who wanted to see the well-ordered past of medieval England as an antidote to the dreadful and squalid present of the nineteenth century. Thus we can only agree with John Stuart Mill who during the 1830s had already, in tune with Carlyle, noticed the pre-emincence of Clio and uttered the then prophetic verdict: «The idea of comparing one's own age with former ages» had occurred to philosophers in the past, «but it never before was itself the dominant idea» of the age.[11]

II.

Ruskin with his voluminous writings now fits squarely into this Victorian context, emphatically taking his stand, and that despite his period's «state of doubt and ignorance», as he put it in *The Seven Lamps of Architecture* (1849),[12] on all questions of art and society. But it should be noticed from the start that Ruskin, due to his multi-faceted genius and the great variety of his interests, can always be quoted on either side of an argument. His mind lacked tidy compartments and ranged freely over many areas of thought, so that one must beware of misprisions arising from neglecting the wholeness of the Ruskinian universe.[13] For wholeness both of life and work was, as his recent biographers have justly reaffirmed, his constant concern; and it likewise accounted for the «over-arching coherence» of all his seemingly disparate activities from the art criticism of the 1840s to the social criticism of the 1870s and 1880s.[14] They bear witness to his belief in the autonomy of the

1 See Buckley 1966, pp. 1–13, esp. p. 9; Altick 1974, pp. 96–106; as well as Newsome 1997, pp. 1–12, esp. p. 3.
2 See Houghton 1957, pp. 54–89, esp. pp. 77–79; and Williams 1973, pp. 153–164, 182–196.
3 See Young 1936, p. 86; Houghton 1957, pp. 58–60; as well as Miller 1963.
4 See also, in addition to Young 1936, p. 86, Ulke 1980.
5 Handlin 1979, p. 414.
6 The term is owing to Holloway 1953.
7 See Dale, 1977, pp. 1–12.
8 This could perhaps be criticized with regard to Culler 1985, pp. 152–184, esp. p. 171, in his otherwise brilliant treatment of Ruskin's medievalim; whereas Altick 1974, pp. 105–106, sees the period's «most favored artistic device» of chronological contrasts for what it was, i.e., contrast.
9 See Clark 1928, pp. 122–149, esp. p. 145.
10 Carlyle 1904–1905, «Past and Present», IV, v, viii; III, 233, 249. Hereafter referred to as *Works*. See also Tillotson 1978, p. 69.
11 Mill 1965, p. 28; quoted from Dale 1977, p. 3, n. 4 (p. 257).
12 John Ruskin, *The Seven Lamps of Architecture*, ch. vii, § 8, aph. 33; in Cook/Wedderburn 1903–1912, VIII, p. 259. Henceforth cited only as *Works*.
13 See, on this score, already Rosenberg 1963, pp. 34, 41–42; cf. also Shrimpton 1999), pp. 131–151.
14 See Hunt 1982, pp. 2, 5, 6, 412; and Batchelor 2000, pp. 331–333.

workman, the centrality of nature in human experience, the dignity of man, the wickedness of industrial capitalism, and the hope for a better society than the one he had to live in.[15] And in view of this manifest unity of Ruskin's thought it will not be ill-advised, I suppose, to trace the idea of organicism through both his major and minor works, giving special attention to its nostalgic overtones in the process.[16]

Taken in their chronological sequence, his writings reveal the concept of organic unity throughout, evolving as it does from Romantic origins into a central motif of both his art and social criticism. In this respect, *Modern Painters* I (1843) which despite its title «Of General Principles, and of Truth» may still be called the empirical volume, contains already adumbrations of our concept – thus when, in discussing landscape painting of the old school in contradistinction to Turner's art, Ruskin insists on «generalization» as fulfilling the requirements of «unity»,[17] or when later, in connection with the «Truth of Vegetation», he remarks upon the «unison of parts» in nature's foliage;[18] all this leading up to the definition of a «complete picture» as possessing «both the general wholeness and effect of nature, and the inexhaustible perfection of nature's details».[19] The full exposition of his theoretical assumptions, however, comes three years later in *Modern Painters* II (1846) when he proposes his special bifurcated aesthetics, of which one part, «Typical Beauty», is symbolic of the order that is the nature of God, and the second, «Vital Beauty», is created by moral order, the ordinance of God.[20] Of course, the two categories of beauty belong together, as we may learn from Ruskin's own clarification in his much later autobiography *Praeterita* (1885–1889) where he states his purpose in writing the second volume of *Modern Painters* as having been «to explain ... the nature of that quality of beauty which I now saw to exist through all the happy conditions of living organism; and down to the minutest detail and finished material structure naturally produced».[21] But the occasional nostalgic note is primarily struck when, with regard to «Typical Beauty», i.e., especially its «repose», he does not disguise his own yearning for peace and permanence in view of the restlessness and changefulness of his times,[22] whereas under the head of «Vital Beauty», whose manifestations are pursued from plants via animals to man, references to organicism, and that – small wonder in regard to Ruskin's latter-day Romanticism – in constant opposition to mechanistic modes of thought,[23] are more than frequent. «Organic creation» here finds itself correlated to «loveliness», «sympathy», «happiness», and «moral dispositions or principles»;[24] it is forever opposed to «mechanical contrivance» and ultimately consists in the «felicitous fulfilment of function in living things».[25] This much one could have expected from an admirer of Romantic poetry, yet when it comes to «Vital Beauty in Man», Ruskin is anything but enthusiastic about Humanism's former «paragon of animals» (*Hamlet*, II.ii.307), deploring instead man's «degradation» and the loss of «equality or likeness», due to «evil diversity», and writes: «Wrecked we are, and nearly all to pieces ...»,[26] thus adding his version to the Victorian fragmentation of man alluded to in the opening section. Well might one relate this pessimistic diagnosis to the religious, i.e., Evangelical world-view of his youth that had to come to terms with the «Adamite curse», but it sounds a bit strange in the development of an aesthetics to account for 'modern' art to find notions of «authority» or «a perfect state» – «... it is appointed for some to be in authority and others in obedience» – linked to considerations of beauty.[27] At this point already, it seems to me, Ruskin's art theory, in conjunction with morality from the outset,[28] shades off into the concerns of his social criticism that interrupted work on *Modern Painters* for ten years or, rather, sees itself carried over into another field of study, namely, architecture.

By definition suited to point up the interrelationships of art and society, architecture, a «distinctively political art» according to Ruskin's introduction to *The Seven Lamps of Architecture*, comprises all the laws necessary for understanding the «close analogy» between «human work» and the «moral world».[29] Written as a somewhat belated contribution to the controversy surrounding the Gothic Revival in England,[30] the book nevertheless contains «the germ» of his subsequent writings,[31] brought forward in thirty-three aphorisms that embody his basic convictions. With regard to the theme of organicism, they assert the association of «all most lovely forms and thoughts» with «natural objects»;[32] liken man's «true life» to «that of lower organic beings», his «false life» to «one of the conditions of death»;[33] oppose «free handwork» to «machine-work»;[34] praise – in true historicist

15 Batchelor 2000, p. xi.
16 For this idea, although with a different emphasis, i.e., on Ruskin's use of analogical and metaphorical modes of expression, see Neville 1958, p. 291.
17 *Modern Painters* I, Pt. II, sec. II, ch. v, § 10; *Works*, III, 334.
18 *Modern Painters* I, Pt. II, sec. VI, ch. i, §§ 20–21; *Works*, III, 592.
19 *Modern Painters* I, Pt. II, sec. VI, ch. iii, § 18; *Works*, III, 622.
20 *Modern Painters* II, Pt. III, sec. I, ch. iii, § 16; *Works*, IV, 64. See also Wellek 1965, pp. 136–149; Landow 1971, pp. 110–179, esp. p. 109; as well as Hewison 1976, pp. 54–64.
21 *Praeterita*, II, ch. x, § 183; *Works*, XXXV, 413.
22 *Modern Painters* II, Pt. III, sec. I, ch. vii, §§ 1–7; *Works*, IV, 113–124. See also Landow 1971, pp. 139–140.
23 As for Ruskin's Romanticism in general and the said contrast in particular, see Hough 1947, pp. 1–39; Abrams 1953, pp. 167–177, 186, 218–225; and Wellek 1965, pp. 138–139.
24 *Modern Painters* II, Pt. III, sec. I, ch. xii, § 1; *Works*, IV, 146–147.
25 *Modern Painters* II, Pt. III, sec. I, ch. xii, § 1; *Works*, IV, 146. Cf. also ibid., Pt. III, sec. I, ch. iii, § 16; *Works*, IV, 64.
26 *Modern Painters* II, Pt. III, sec. I, ch. xiv, §§ 1–2; *Works*, IV, 176–178.
27 *Modern Painters* II, Pt. III, sec. I, ch. xiv, §§ 8–9; *Works*, IV, 182–184. Cf. Landow 1971, p. 167.
28 See *Modern Painters* I, Pt. II, sec. I, ch. iv, § 5; *Works*, III, 157 («The duty of the painter is the same as that of a preacher»); as well as ibid. II, Pt. III, sec. I, ch. xii, § 8; *Works*, IV, 156 («There is not any organic creature but ... will exemplify or illustrate to us some moral excellence or deficiency ...»).
29 *The Seven Lamps of Architecture*, introd., § 4, aph. 2; *Works*, VIII, 22; cf. ibid., § 2, p. 20: «the distinctively political art of Architecture».
30 See Rosenberg 1963, pp. 47–58; and Hewison 1976, pp. 128–132.
31 According to the «Preface» to the edition of 1880, § 1, see *The Seven Lamps of Architecture*, in *Works*, VIII, 15.
32 *The Seven Lamps of Architecture*, ch. iv, § 3, aph. 19; *Works*, VIII, 141.
33 *The Seven Lamps of Architecture*, ch. v, § 3; *Works*, VIII, 191–192.
34 *The Seven Lamps of Architecture*, ch. v, § 21, aph. 25; *Works*, VIII, 214; cf. ibid., ch. v, § 24, aph. 26; *Works*, VIII, 219–220.

manner – landscapes and buildings saturated with memories of the past;[35] and finally inveigh against «liberty» plus «idleness»[36] – but not before having listed his favourite four styles of architecture among which the «Gothic» is of paramount importance, of course.[37]

This brings us to Ruskin's justly famous two volumes on *The Stones of Venice* (1851–1853), where all the motifs of thought alluded to so far find their full elaboration. Broadly speaking, Ruskin here traces in great detail the rise and fall of Venice as documented through her main buildings, thus at the same time providing a moral object-lesson for Europe in general and Great Britain in particular.[38] And since this case history depends on a transition in architectural style from the Gothic to the «pestilent art of the Renaissance»,[39] the second volume's celebrated and influential chapter on «The Nature of Gothic» now merits special attention for being the clearest evidence of the medieval extension of Ruskin's organicism.[40] In this context, his singling out of the six «characteristic or moral elements of Gothic» is intimately connected with the free and individual contribution of the medieval workman, as yet spared the fate of alienation (Marx) or «division of labour» (Victorian fragmentation) and therefore able to represent «the Naturalism of the Gothic», above all «the forms of Vegetation», in the spirit of «Vital Beauty» (*Modern Painters* II).[41] Yet, as is well known, all this soon came to naught, and that on account of the stylistic corruptions of the Renaissance, especially its «unwholesome demand for perfection» at the cost of the workman's creative freedom and of the wholeness of life and work.[42] Add to these «immoral» elements their religious dimension, i.e. «Pride and Infidelity», coupled with the «pursuit of pleasure», and you have grasped the reasons for the fall of Venice – in Ruskin's moralistic terms, that is to say, manifest primarily in the debasement of the city's art and architecture.[43] How about the change of trade routes by sea, one feels tempted to ask.[44] But this might be a pointless question, for Ruskin's moralistic and holistic vision at this point in time, i.e. in the early 1850s, is such that he apparently wishes to rely on an all too familiar historiographic rise-and-decline pattern, notwithstanding the fact that years later, in a letter of 1877 written for *Fors Clavigera* (1871–1884), he is to warn his readers against easy acceptance in these matters: «All evidences of progress or decline have ... to be collected in mass, – then analyzed with extreme care, – then weighed in the balance of the Ages, before we can judge of the meaning of any one ...».[45]

Here as elsewhere, it becomes obvious that Ruskinian positions always require qualification in the light of his whole œuvre. Returning with the author to *Modern Painters* III (1856), we thus see him there, as if oblivious of his own medievalism in *Stones*, castigate his age for its infatuation with history, especially with the «ages of chivalry», risen as it is «out of the contrast of the beautiful past with the frightful and monotonous present», but ultimately only being harmful for the present.[46] This is not only a striking anticipation of Bakhtin's principle of «historical inversion», whereby the bygone is enriched at the expense of both the present and the future,[47] but also a pointer in the direction of his own time whose urgent needs he is soon to address in *Unto this Last* (1860, 1862), his passionate intervention in Political Economy, and that in the name of justice and humanity – with its closing statement: «There is no Wealth but Life».[48] In between, there are quite a few passages throughout his writings that betray his abiding concern with «Organic Form».[49] They range from the «socialized tree», exemplifying, in its disciplined growth, the laws of nature, as we may read in *The Elements of Drawing* (1857),[50] pass, in search of an organic social system, through a paternalistic, nay, even authoritarian phase in his two Manchester lectures of 1857, published in the same year as *«A Joy for Ever» (and its Price in the Market)*, with their proposition of «the farm and its servants» as model for «a wholesome national organization»,[51] and continue, in *The Two Paths* (1859), his five lectures on applied art, the apotheosis of the «vital law» of «Organic Form» by transforming its feudal-agrarian implications into almost an ideology of «the plough and the needle» for the benefit of an «orderly function» of society.[52] No matter how this assertion may sound to modern ears, it is at least compensated for, I think, by his insistence that «Fine Art», as distinct from «Manufacture», involves «the whole man».[53] The cumulative statement of Ruskin's holistic organicism finally comes in *Modern Painters* V (1860), itself the

35 *The Seven Lamps of Architecture*, ch. vi, §§ 1–2, esp. aph. 27; *Works*, VIII, 221–225; cf. *Modern Painters* III, Pt. IV, ch. xvii, § 21; *Works*, V, 369 (on the contrast between European and American landscape).

36 *The Seven Lamps of Architecture*, ch. vii, §§ 1–2, esp. aph. 32; as well as § 8, aph. 33; *Works*, VIII, 248–250, 259–263.

37 *The Seven Lamps of Architecture*, ch. vii, § 7; *Works*, VIII, 258–259.

38 See Hunt 1982, pp. 195–220.

39 *The Stones of Venice* I, ch. i, §§ 38–39; *Works*, IX, 46–47.

40 *The Stones of Venice* II, Pt. II, ch. vi; *Works*, X, 180–269. Although unthinkable without Pugin's influence, Ruskin always denied it when writing on Gothic architecture. Cf. *Modern Painters* III, App. iii: «Plagiarism»; *Works*, V, 427–430. See also Hough 1947, p. 90; Rosenberg 1963, pp. 79–105; as well as Culler 1985, pp. 161–170.

41 *The Stones of Venice* II, Pt. II, ch. vi, esp. §§ 6–18, 41, 64–65, 68; *Works*, X, 184–198, 215, 231–233, 235–236. See also Unrau 1981, pp. 33–50.

42 *The Stones of Venice* III, Pt. III, ch. i, esp. §§ 2–5, 16, 20; *Works*, XI, 3–42, esp. pp. 4–6, 14, 17–18; cf. ibid., Pt. III, ch. iv, § 21; *Works*, XI, 212–213.

43 *The Stones of Venice* III, Pt. III, ch. ii, § 5; cf. ibid., Pt. III, ch. iii, §§ 1–2; *Works*, XI, 46, 135–136.

44 See, on this point, Rosenberg 1963, p. 85.

45 *Fors Clavigera*, Letter 82: «Heavenly Choirs» (October 1877); *Works*, XXIX, 220–256, esp. § 5, p. 224. Cf. Buckley 1966, p. 33, n. 38 (p. 161).

46 *Modern Painters* III, Pt. IV, ch. xvi, §§ 15–17; and ch. xvii, § 21; *Works*, V, 325–327, 369.

47 Bakhtin 1981, pp. 146–151, esp. p. 147.

48 *Unto this Last: Four Essays on the First Principles of Political Economy*, Essay iv: «Ad Valorem», § 77; *Works*, XVII, 105. See also Lee 1981, pp. 68–88; and Ruskin 1985, pp. 19–30.

49 See also Rosenberg 1963, pp. 71–75, esp. p. 73 (n. p. 234), pointing to the importance of Ruskin for Frank Lloyd Wright's concept of «Organic Architecture». Cf. further, on the motif of the «Organic Body» in Ruskin, Sawyer 1985, pp. 171–175.

50 *The Elements of Drawing*, Letter iii, § 215; *Works*, XV, 187. For the «socialized tree» see Clark 1964, pp. 89, 93 (no. 85).

51 «A Joy for Ever» (and its Price in the Market), Lecture i, §§ 13–15; *Works*, XVI, 24–26.

52 *The Two Paths*, «Preface to the First Edition», and Lecture v, §§ 174, 191; *Works*, XVI, 251, 395–396, 407–408.

53 *The Two Paths*, Lecture ii, §§ 52–55; *Works*, XVI, 294–295.

result of a long tree-like growth,[54] when, in his idiosyncratic Biblical terminology, he explains what he means by «the Law of Help»: «A pure or holy state of anything ... is that in which all its parts are helpful or consistent»; in the same context spelling out the «first law of the universe» with the sentence: «The highest or organic purities are composed of many elements in an entirely helpful state».[55]

Manifold indeed are the ramifications of Ruskin's fundamental belief in organic unity throughout the writings following upon the completion of *Modern Painters*: if only glimpsed at in *Munera Pulveris* (1863), a further contribution to Political Economy in the manner of Carlyle,[56] it is openly deployed in *Sesame and Lilies* (1864), his most popular book, where, especially in the lecture «Of Queens' Gardens», he treats the theme of social cohesion in medievalizing and poetic terms.[57] A more peremptory variant of our motif is then to be found in his affirmative lectures on «Work, Traffic, and War», gathered in *The Crown of Wild Olive* (1866) where he seeks to mediate between his earlier ideas on architecture and his more recently formulated social views, speaking once more of «knightly example» or in praise of «husbandman» and «shepherd»,[58] a line of reasoning he immediately afterwards pursues in *Time and Tide* (1867), a series of letters to a «Working Man of Sunderland», ranging from «Co-operation» to «Submission to Authority».[59] So, in short, Ruskin always remains true to himself with regard to the concept of organicism, extending as it does from nature and art to society. Thus it does not really matter if later, in *Fors Clavigera*, his rather radical monthly letters to British workers, he calls himself in one of them a Communist and in the other a Tory,[60] because this apparent contradiction is dissolved through yet another letter's Arcadian Utopianism that is the social pendant to his aesthetic yearning for «Organic Form».[61] And if he could experience the «ennui» of his «sadder ages» of «doubt and misery» as any of his fellow «unbelievers» and yearn, like them, for beauty lost,[62] then he at least did not sit back in idle melancholy but tried to put his principles into practice – witness only his involvement with the Working Men's College, his endowment of the Oxford School of Drawing or his foundation of the Guild of St. George[63] – thereby giving sanction to his beliefs and setting an example to his contemporaries as well as to posterity.

III.

Ruskin set in fact an example now to Pater, the most prominent exponent of British fin-de-siècle Aestheticism, although, as the label indicates, not yet in social matters. What is more, Pater did not suffer Ruskin's influence gladly and all his life felt he had to oppose, if ever so indirectly, the overwhelming rhetoric of his famous precursor in art criticism.[64] Already his first essay, devoted to Coleridge (1866) and commenting on 'Modern thought' as distinguished from ancient by its cultivation of the 'relative' spirit in place of the 'absolute' willingly resigns itself to the determination of «man's physical organism» by «remote laws of inheritance», and consequently goes on to criticize Coleridge's – and by implication Ruskin's – Romantic organicism as on its part «mechanical».[65] Pater here quite ostensively bows to the 'new' science of the age, being represented by men such as Darwin, Huxley or Spencer, and thus, with his relativism, also to the spirit of evolution and 'flux',[66] which is so alien to Ruskin's pantheistic notion of organicism, refusing as it does to see man descended from the mollusc.[67] Toward the close of the same essay, Pater then speaks of Coleridge's – or his own? – hunger for eternity, his being «a true flower of the ennuyé», and finally as representing «that inexhaustible discontent, languor, and home-sickness, that endless regret, the chords of which ring all through our modern literature»,[68] thereby alluding to the other motif of our argu-

54 *Modern Painters* V, «Preface», § 8; *Works*, VII, 10.

55 *Modern Painters* V, Pt. VIII, ch. i, § 6; *Works*, VII, 207. For a summary of Ruskin's convictions concerning the nature of art, see Clark 1964, pp. 133–134.

56 *Munera Pulveris*, «Preface», § 22; ch. v, § 135; *Works*, XVII, 145, 260–261 (his tribute to Carlyle).

57 *Sesame and Lilies*, Lecture ii, esp. §§ 64, 86; *Works*, XVIII, 119–120, 136–137. See Sawyer 1990, pp. 129 –141.

58 *The Crown of Wild Olive*, Lectures iii, § 85, and iv, § 152; *Works*, XVIII, 459, 508.

59 *Time and Tide, by Weare and Tyne*, Letters i («Co-operation»), and xxv («Hyssop»); *Works*, XVII, 315–318, 455–464.

60 *Fors Clavigera*, Letters 7: «Charitas» (July 1871), on Communism, and 10: «The Baron's Gate» (October 1871), on Toryism; *Works*, XXVII, 115–131 and 165–180. Cf. also *Praeterita* I, ch. i, § 1: «I am, and my father was before me, a violent Tory of the old school; – Walter Scott's school, that is to say, and Homer's.» *Works*, XXXV, 13. There is, by the way, a tendency to revalue *Fors* on the part of modern scholarship; see esp. Hilton 2000, pp. 629f. (Index s.v. *Fors Clavigera*).

61 *Fors Clavigera*, Letter 5: «The White-Thorn Blossom» (May 1871); *Works*, XXVII, 79–97, esp. §§ 10–11, pp. 87–89.

62 *Modern Painters* III, Pt. IV, ch. xvi, §§ 9–10, 15; *Works*, V, 321–323, 325–326. As to the problem of Ruskin's belief(s), see Wheeler 1999; and for beauty lost, see also *The Two Paths*, Lecture iii, §§ 91–92 (on the contrast between Rochdale and Pisa); *Works*, XVI, 338–341.

63 Ruskin always spoke up against «idleness»; see, e.g., *Modern Painters* III, Pt. IV, ch. xvi, § 32; *Works*, V, 336; or *Fors Clavigera*, Letter 5, § 10; *Works*, XXVII, 87. As to the benefactions mentioned, see, instead of many, Rosenberg 1963, pp. 104, 178, 188f., 195 ff.; and Batchelor 2000, pp. 137–144, 228 f., 254–258.

64 See Bloom 1985, «Introduction», pp. 1–21, esp. pp. 4, 8–9.

65 «Coleridge», in Pater 1910, V, 65–104, esp. pp. 66–67, 79–81. All subsequent references to the individual works of Pater are likewise to the *New Library Edition* of 1910.

66 See Toulmin/Goodfield 1965, pp. 232–246; Buckley 1966, pp. 47–48; and Monsman 1977, «Preface», p. [ii].

67 *Modern Painters* II, Pt. III, sec. I, ch. xi, § 1; *Works*, IV, 142–143; and ibid. III, Pt. IV, ch. xvii, §41; *Works*, V, 385–386: «... the simplest forms of nature are strangely animated by the sense of the Divine presence; the trees and flowers seem all, in a sort, children of God [...]».

68 *Appreciations*, p. 104.

ment, i.e. nostalgia, whose note is, by the way, struck more often throughout Pater's works than in Ruskin's writings.

A second veering away from Ruskin's impact must further be seen in Pater's critique of nineteenth-century medievalism, significantly brought forward in his review of *Poems by William Morris* (1868), Ruskin's closest disciple and «the most incurably nostalgic of all Victorian thinkers»,[69] and being in particular addressed to the poems' «delicate inconsistencies», aggravated for Pater by the fact that the «monastic religion of the Middle Ages» was nothing but a beautiful disease or disorder of the senses in the first place.[70] Clearly, then, Pater's favourite historical epoch is the Renaissance. Yet with the publication of his famous *Studies in the History of the Renaissance* in 1873, it became all too obvious that he himself was prone to read the Victorian malaise nostalgically into his subject. Hence, after yet another dig at the Slade Professor of Fine Art for having attempted «to define beauty in the abstract» and the exposition of his own diametrically opposed principles of 'impressionist' criticism,[71] Pater embarks on the presentation of his chosen epoch's «unity of spirit».[72] It appears surprisingly modern, though. Read for instance only his description of Leonardo's *Gioconda*, that is, of her «beauty, into which the soul with all its maladies has passed!»[73] More revealing still, and that not least with regard to Pater's own aesthetic aspiration and nostalgic temperament, is his essay on the life of Winckelmann, written earlier (1867) and then included in the later volume for representing, on account of his subject's «Hellenism», «the last fruit of the Renaissance»,[74] where we hear not only of his hero's «wistful sense of something lost to be regained», his «weariness of the North» and hence life-long yearning for the Greek culture's «breadth, centrality, with blitheness and repose», and ideal dimmed, however, by «the gaudy, perplexed light of modern life», but also of the «home-sickness» and the «thought of death» of the «pagan sentiment» itself, soon to pass into «the mournful maturity» of later times.[75] Leaving by the way Du Bellay's «ennui» and «longing for rest, nostalgia, home-sickness» as expressed in his *Regrets* while at Rome,[76] we find, in «The School of Giorgione», Pater's clearest confession of his faith in the privileged moment, absorbing as it does «past and future in an intense consciousness of the present» – «ideal instants» like these being «exquisite pauses in time», containing «the fullness of existence» as well as the «quintessence of life».[77] That we, as lovers of «art for its own sake», should now live for «those moments' sake» and thus make the best of the Heraclitean 'flux of things', is then, as formulated in the abstract, the injunction of Pater's much-quoted and very controversial «Conclusion» to *The Renaissance*, the frank hedonism of which marks the highest point of his aestheticism in the 1870s.[78]

But seeing that dedication to the intense and wholly individual moment could in fact be a very isolated and solitary experience, let alone the danger of misunderstanding Pater had to concede himself,[79] further clarification, if not even atonement, proved necessary. They came in 1885 with his novel *Marius the Epicurean*, almost autobiographically describing the «Sensations and Ideas» of a young Roman born in the second century A.D., i.e. the time of the Antonines, when Christianity was tolerated, thus making it possible for the contemplative hero on his «intellectual pilgrimage»[80] to compare the spiritual options open to him, extending from the religion of Numa, his childhood faith, via Epicureanism and Stoicism, to the very threshold of Christianity which he does not quite cross, though. And in this context, Pater now seizes the opportunity to revise, nay, correct the hedonism of the «Conclusion»,[81] by alternately subjecting Marius to the influences of both Heraclitus of Ionia and Aristippus of Cyrene, the predecessor of Epicurus, that way trying to counter the «perpetual flux» of things and the search for pleasure with visions of the «general completeness of life», in short: «... it was thus his (scil. Marius') longing defined itself for something to hold by amid the 'perpetual flux'».[82] This yearning for stability is then linked to a desire for companionship, reinforced by his moment of «Beatific Vision» in the Campagna,[83] and all but fulfilled through his friendship with the Christian Cornelius and his introduction to «the Church in Cecilia's House».[84] By and large, as Marius tends in the direction of the early Christians, Pater himself leaves behind his own earlier sceptical relativism and begins to use the language of holistic organicism, starting with Cecilia's «well-ordered precincts» and ending with «the aesthetic charm of the catholic church»,[85] while the note of nostalgia, in the sense of yearning for «the lost Golden Age» associated

69 According to Newsome 1997, p. 186.
70 Pater's essay «Aesthetic Poetry» was first published as part of «Poems by William Morris», in: *Westminster Review*, 1868. It then appeared in *Appreciations* (1889), but was omitted from the second and later editions. Yet see Walter Pater, «Essays on Literature and Art» in: Uglow 1973, pp. 95–102, esp. pp. 97, 101; and p. 152.
71 See, under the title of the second (1877) and third (1888) edition, Walter Pater, *The Renaissance: Studies in Art and Poetry*, «Preface», pp. vii–xv, esp. pp. vii, viii. See also Hough 1947, pp. 157–166; as well as Culler 1985, pp. 244 f.
72 *The Renaissance*, «Preface», p. xiv.
73 Ibid., p. 125; see Culler 1985, p. 256: Modernity is certainly the keynote of *The Renaissance*». As to Pater's abiding interest in 'modernity' within history, see also his posthumous (1896) *Gaston de Latour. An Unfinished Romance*, ed. Charles L. Shadwell, ch. iii: «Modernity», pp. 48–72; cf. Bann 1984, p. 158, n. 51 (p. 191).
74 *The Renaissance*, «Preface», p. xv. As to Pater's throughgoing aestheticization of the Renaissance, see Chai 1990, pp. 88–93.
75 *The Renaissance*, pp. 177–232, esp. pp. 179, 196, 227, 201, 209.
76 Ibid., pp. 155–176, esp. p. 173; cf. Rehm 1960, pp. 87–119, esp. p. 119.
77 *The Renaissance*, pp. 130–154, esp. p. 150.
78 Ibid., pp. 233–239, esp. p. 239. As to the problems surrounding the contemporary reception of the «Conclusion» to *The Renaissance*, see, instead of many, only Benson 1906, pp. 45–48; Monsman 1977, pp. 54–57; and Levey 1978, pp. 141–144.
79 *The Renaissance*, p. 235 (on «the individual in his isolation, each mind keeping as a solitary prisoner its own dream of a world»), and p. 233, n. 1 (on the «Conclusion», the possible danger of misleading young readers, and the promised clarification in *Marius the Epicurean*).
80 *Marius the Epicurean: His Sensations and Ideas* II, Pt. III, ch. xix, p. 64; cf. ibid., I, Pt. II, ch. viii, p. 134; and II, Pt. IV, ch. xxiv, p. 171.
81 On the 'corrective' aspect of *Marius*, see Monsman 1977, p. 80; Fletcher 1985, pp. 41–73, esp. pp. 61–65; as well as Culler 1985, p. 262.
82 *Marius the Epicurean* I, Pt. II, ch. viii: «Animula Vagula», pp. 123–143, esp. pp. 128, 131, 134–136, 142; and ibid. I, Pt. II, ch. ix: «New Cyrenaicism», pp. 144–157, esp. pp. 151f, 155.
83 *Marius* II, Pt. III, ch. xix: «The Will as Vision», pp. 57–72.
84 *Marius* II, Pt. IV, ch. xxi, pp. 92–108.
85 *Marius* II, Pt. IV, ch. xxi, p. 95; and ibid. II, Pt. IV, ch. xxii, pp. 109–127, esp. p. 123.

with the religious usage of the time of Numa, is most strongly sounded in the Weltschmerz-chapter preceding the hero's death as a martyr.[86] Through this self-sacrifice undertaken in order to save his Christian friend – thus Pater's crowning if ironic intimation – Marius in the end perhaps attains the goal of his longing, i.e. «... some ampler vision, which should take up into itself and explain this world's delightful shows, as the scattered fragments of a poetry, till then but half-understood, might be taken up into the text of a lost epic, recovered at last».[87]

What is so discreetly tentative in *Marius the Epicurean* acquires a more definite voice, as Pater, mainly in the 1890s, goes back beyond not only the Renaissance but Roman Antiquity, too, and turns his attention to the culture of ancient Greece. It is as if, delving deeper into history now, he wanted to get at the origins of his youthful assumptions, in an attempt to reconcile aesthetics with ethics, even with politics. To buttress this effort theoretically, he operated with a philosophy of history that rested on an unmediated conflict between two antithetical tendencies throughout the ages, called by him the «centrifugal» and the «centripetal». Pater here was both in keeping with Victorian habits of thought, that is, the period's fondness for speculative historical contrasts, as discussed already with reference to Pugin and Ruskin, and at the same time dependent on Continental philosophies of history that had fallen on fruitful soil in England. Take for instance Carlyle's recurrent distinction between «Epochs of Belief» and «Epochs of Unbelief»,[88] Mill's admiration for the French Saint-Simonians with their division of all history into «organic periods and critical periods»,[89] or Arnold's famous dichotomy between Hebraism and Hellenism, indebted as it is to Börne and Heine,[90] in order to note the undialectical see-saw rhythm of Victorian writing on history. Nearer at hand, Pater's immediate source background would be Nietzsche's familiar opposition between Apollo and Dionysus, a «duplicity», as is explained in *The Birth of Tragedy from the Spirit of Music* (1872), bearing upon a contrast between serenity or Dorian sternness on the one hand and ecstatic or mystic passion on the other.[91] To be sure, Pater is not content with this basic contrast but enriches it with further amplifications, as they are adumbrated already in his seminal essay on Winckelmann[92] but fully explicated only in *The Marbles of Ægina* (1880), a much later text that was to be included in his posthumous *Greek Studies* (1895). According to this mature interpretation, the centrifugal tendency is Ionian, Asiatic in origin, whereas the centripetal tendency is Dorian, generally European and embodied in the religion of Apollo. The one emphasizes variety, change, individualism; the other unity, stability, order. Heraclitus of Ephesus, the philosopher of becoming or 'perpetual flux', whose doctrine seemed to have prevailed in the time-dominated 'new' evolutionary science of Pater's own day,[93] was representative of the one, Parmenides of Elea, the philosopher of being or «abstractness and calm», of the other, in a word, of Apollonian «sanity, its proportion, its knowledge of itself».[94]

Historical convictions like these now inform Pater's philosophical chef-d'œuvre, the late lectures *Plato and Platonism* (1893). Trying to expound «the leading principles of Plato's doctrine», he sees in them «relics of an earlier organic life» and is anxious, in opposition to the Heraclitean 'flux' or centrifugal tendency going with it, to display Plato as an «advocate of the immutable» and to align him with Parmenides, the head of the Eleatic School, whose assertion «of the nullity of all that is but phenomenal» symbolizes the centripetal principle that only recognizes «The One».[95] In view of the fact that «metaphysical formulae» always have their «practical equivalents», let alone their «ethical alliances»,[96] Pater, after yet one more elaboration of the Ionian-Dorian contrast, this time with reference not only to the notorious rivalry between Athens and Sparta but also, somewhat unexpectedly, to an opposition between «inorganic» and «organic growth»,[97] carries his favourite dichotomy over into the sphere of society and politics, using its heuristic potential for a detailed interpretation of Plato's *Republic*. This major dialogue of the Greek philosopher treats of the theme of justice, best to be seen in a perfect city-state and, if discovered there, to be found by analogy in man. Concomitant with this, the ideal state, consisting of three classes, and its forms of political organization, which may degenerate, once social harmony is disturbed, from aristocracy via democracy into tyranny, comes under scrutiny by Socrates.[98] Pater now, on his part, reads all this in the light of his historiographical terms, i.e. praises the Dorian military discipline of Sparta and opposes it – with Plato – to the «laxer» Ionian ways of Athens which are condemned as «evil». And in this context we come across Pater's most Ruskinian passage: «Organic unity with one's self, body and soul, is the well-being, the rightness, or righteousness, or justice of the individual, of the microcosm; but is the ideal also, it supplies the true definition, of the well-being of the

86 *Marius* II, Pt. IV, ch. xxv: «Sunt Lacrimae Rerum», pp. 172–185, esp. pp. 178–180.
87 *Marius* II, Pt. IV, ch. xxviii: «Anima naturaliter Christiana», pp. 208–224, esp. pp. 219 f.
88 See Kedenburg 1960, pp. 27–68.
89 John Stuart Mill, *Autobiography* (begun in 1853, but published only posthumously in 1873), in: Stillinger 1971, pp. 98–99; cf. Houghton 1957, p. 30.
90 Matthew Arnold, *Culture and Anarchy* (1869), chs. iv, v; in Super 1960–1976, V, pp. 163–191, esp. pp. 165, 176. DeLaura 1969, pp. 165–170, Arnold's dichotomy is not «dialectical» but points to mutual exclusion. See also Uhlig 1986, pp. 218–233, esp. pp. 224–226, on Arnold. The same holds true with regard to Pater's antitheses (DeLaura 1969, pp. 253, 298).
91 Friedrich Nietzsche, *Die Geburt der Tragödie aus dem Geiste der Musik* (1872), secs. 1–4; in: Schlechta 1960, I, pp. 21–35; cf. Uhlig 1986, pp. 226–228, on Nietzsche and Pater.
92 Walter Pater, «Winckelmann», in *The Renaissance*, pp. 177–232, esp. p. 204.
93 See Toulmin/Goodfield 1965, p. 245; Buckley 1966, p. 6; and, quite generally, Burrow 1966.
94 Walter Pater, «The Marbles of Ægina», in: *Greek Studies: A Series of Essays*, pp. 251–268, esp. pp. 251–255. See also Culler 1985, pp. 275 f.; as well as McGrath 1986, pp. 217–221, and pp. 221–225, carrying the contrast into a discussion of Pater's essay on «Style» (1888).
95 *Plato and Platonism: A Series of Lectures*, ch. i: «Plato and the Doctrine of Motion», pp. 5–26; and ch. ii: «Plato and the Doctrine of Rest», pp. 27–50, esp. pp. 7, 12–22, 24, 33–41, 48.
96 *Plato and Platonism*, p. 48.
97 Ibid., ch. v: «Plato and the Sophists», pp. 99–123, esp. pp. 103–105.
98 For Plato's *Republic* see, instead of many, Jaeger 1959, II, pp. 270–360; III, pp. 1–104.

macrocosm, of the social organism, the state».[99] – This is a far cry indeed from the essay on «Coleridge» and the «Conclusion» to *The Renaissance*, especially in view of the fact that the last lecture, dedicated as it is to Plato's aesthetics, sees them as «ever in close connexion with Plato's ethics»,[100] and thus would appear to show Pater as both having come full circle and at the same time satisfied his yearning for wholeness in the end.

IV.

Let us now, by way of conclusion, try to ponder the historical and theoretical implications of what has been brought forward so far in regard to Ruskin's as well as Pater's nostalgia for organicism.

To start with the first notion, 'nostalgia', the word itself is derived from the Greek νόστος, to return home, plus ἄλγος, a painful condition; it thus signifies a painful yearning to return home. Medically diagnosed as an illness and coined as a term in 1688 by the Swiss physician Johannes Hofer, nostalgia was intended to designate a familiar condition of extreme homesickness among Swiss mercenaries fighting all over Europe far away from their native land. Hofer saw the illness as a «continuous vibration of animal spirits through those fibres of the middle brain in which the impressed traces of ideas of the Fatherland still cling».[101] Passing in due course from physical denotations to mental connotations, nostalgia could include among its symptoms not only melancholia or despondency but also, in all sorts of complicated ways, moods mixing present discontents with yearnings for the past, joys clouded with sadness, or feelings of paradises lost. Not so much as a physical malady than rather as a state of mind, nostalgia further entertains a special relationship with the past, its reminiscences – one calls to mind Marius' habit of living «much, and as it were by system, in reminiscence»[102] – being infused with imputations of beauty, joy, happiness, or love, and being, above all, never oblivious of the usually sharp contrast between «the good past and the bad present».[103] While all this holds true for the subjective or individual side of nostalgia, fashioned as it is from the alternating continuities and discontinuities of our lives, the sentiment has a collective side, too. Most notably in moments of an identity crisis for whole communities or societies, nostalgia may become the dominant temper of an entire historical period.[104] Needless to say in our context, Victorian Britain did experience just that: a collective identity crisis unprecedented in history that of its own accord, and by way of reaction, triggered off a pervasive nostalgia for forms of life felt to be forever lost. Hence, as outlined already in my introduction, the need of the Victorians to have recourse to past epochs of history, be they Classical Antiquity, the Middle Ages, or the Renaissance for that matter, in order to create and construct the alternatives they wanted for their psychological equilibrium.[105] In a broader perspective, the nostalgic sentiment of the Victorian age only partook of one of the great and abiding processes of European civilization: the ceaseless tension of change versus stability, innovation versus restoration, new versus old, or Utopia versus Arcadia.[106] It is especially this last opposition which sustains the life of one of Europe's most constant literary modes of expression, namely, pastoral poetry, where poets from Theocritus and Virgil to Stevens and Frost have, as representatives of man, longed for the lost unity of primitive society and, as individuals, for their – and our – lost childhood.[107] Yet even the said contrast is not absolute, seeing that Utopias may at times be Arcadian, hence nostalgic, retreats and, as is the case with William Morris' *News from Nowhere* (1890), by harking back to the medieval past lead to a reforestation of the pastoral[108] – ultimately a yearning for an Edenic agrarianism that is the concomitant reaction to industrialism's crowded cities and spoilt countryside,[109] albeit regardless of the problem of how to feed and clothe growing populations in a machineless paradise. Still, even the weather, according to Ruskin's uncannily prophetic lecture «The Storm-Cloud of the Nineteenth Century» (1884), was no longer what it used to be.[110]

The goal of nostalgia, organicism, the second notion discussed so far, likewise belongs to the invariant hypotheses of man's interpretation of the world, and that in constant opposition to mechanism with its root metaphor of the machine. Over against this, organicism with its root metaphor of the biological process always aims at an integration of conflicting fragments.[111] Historically considered, the ancient Greek philosophers already worked with these or similar categories of thought when attempting to establish organic wholes or coherent totalities. More often than not conceived in anthropomorphic terms, their cosmological theories in particular made comparisons between the world as a whole and the single living organism of man. Especially Plato, in more than one passage of his dialogues, notably the *Republic*, the *Timaeus*, or in *Laws*, stressed the connection between order in man

99 *Plato and Platonism*, ch. viii: «Lacedaemon», pp. 197–234; and ch. ix: «The Republic», pp. 235–266, esp. pp. 207, 238, 239 (quot.), 240f., 249, 255. See also Stein 1975, pp. 287–293, esp. p. 288.
100 *Plato and Platonism*, ch. x: «Plato's Æsthetics», pp. 267–283, esp. p. 282.
101 Johannes Hofer, *Medical Dissertation on Nostalgia* (1688), quoted both in Davis 1979, p. 1, n. 1; and in Lowenthal 1985, p. 10, n. 38.
102 Walter Pater, *Marius the Epicurean* I, Pt. II, ch. ix, p. 154.
103 Davis 1979, pp. 13–16, 29.
104 Ibid., pp. 97–117, esp. pp. 101, 107 f., 110.
105 See, in addition to the references in my introductory section, Lowenthal 1985, pp. 96–105.
106 Thus, appositely, Davis 1979, p. 116.
107 See, quite generally, Toliver 1971; and, in particular, Lerner 1972, ch. ii: «On Nostalgia», pp. 41–62; and ch. iii: «Arcadia and Utopia», pp. 63–80, esp. pp. 61–62.
108 See Levin 1970, App. B: «Some Paradoxes of Utopia», pp. 187–193, esp. p. 191.
109 See also Williams 1973, pp. 289–306; as well as Rosenberg 1963, p. 199.
110 See Ruskin, *Works*, XXXIV, 7–80; cf. also Rosenberg 1963, pp. 212–216; Kemp 1983, pp. 383–392; Batchelor 2000, pp. 288 f.; as well as Hewison/Warrel/Wildman 2000, pp. 245–269.
111 See Pepper 1942, Pt. II, ch. ix: «Mechanism», pp. 186–231, esp. p. 186; and ch. xi: «Organicism», pp. 280–314, esp. pp. 280 f., 283, 291, 298.

himself or in society and order in the cosmos as a whole. Owing to this interdependence of human and divine order, Plato could also articulate his ideas of social and political organization, anti-democratic and authoritarian as they admittedly were in the last resort (*Republic*, 555b–565a). But one should see them in relation to his desire for holism, whereby ideas derived from the spheres of politics, biology, and even technology (the world as work of a craftsman-god) were used to explain the universe as a single whole, by human analogy a living organism obeying the principles of natural growth or evolution, and in its macrocosmic structure providing the pattern of the microcosmic order of society and politics, envisaged by Plato in his ideal state.[112] Through the centuries of Western thought, Plato's anthropomorphic and cosmological vision of the commonwealth, closely tied as it is to an organic conception of the state, has had a most impressive afterlife, perhaps never more so than in the medieval and Renaissance doctrine of the 'body politic' with its hierarchic and holistic implications.[113] Yet in the course of its own complex semantic history, the concept of organicism could not be confined to the realm of politics alone and had acquired, thanks to the Romantic era above all, quite a variety of additional senses by the nineteenth century, the age of the 'new sciences' – primarily evolutionary biology – which were all sciences 'in time', governed by temporal methodologies.[114] Darwin himself employs a striking organicist simile when, in summing up the central thesis of the *Origin of Species* in a long paragraph, he likens «the affinities of all the beings of the same class» to «a great tree», i.e. «the great Tree of Life, which fills with its dead and broken branches the crust of the earth, and covers the surface with its ever-branching and beautiful ramifications».[115] A parallel image, albeit in a different field of study, occurs in Carlyle's *Past and Present* when historical continuity is at issue, exemplified for him in the «Life-Tree Igdrasil» of the old Norse Edda, rooted down deep in the past, but with its boughs reaching «always beyond the stars»[116] – a metaphoric way of expression that is to recur in Ruskin's reference (mentioned already in a preceding section) to the long gradual growth of *Modern Painters*.[117] And what to the lover of nature is the «tree», to the lover of art and aesthetic diction, namely Pater in his theoretical essay on «Style» (1888), which seems to recant his youthful critique of «organic form», is enshrined in «the original unity, the vital wholeness and identity» of «good writing».[118] All these quotations bear once more evidence of the sway of organicist notions in nineteenth century discourse.

As for the twentieth century, to complete the story briefly, organicism would appear to have fallen on evil days, at least during the first half of the period. Attacks now came from the political camp furthest removed from any kind of Toryism, that is, from authors writing under the impact of European Fascism and from the perspective of either a sociology of knowledge or a general theory of society and politics. For the former approach, one has to instance Karl Mannheim's anti-traditionalist *Ideology and Utopia* (1929), trying to establish sociological correlations between organicist thinking and interpretations of history and, in an almost revolutionary drive, aiming at breaking up the morphological categories of conservative thought into smaller independent units for the sake of renewed analysis – a criticism of totalities, «characteristic of the parties of the left», as he avows.[119] But, of course, the main onslaught against political organicism in the sense of Plato came with Karl R. Popper's *The Open Society and its Enemies* (1945), where the Greek philosopher is focused upon as the chief target of attack, and that because it is «the so-called organic or biological theory of the state» which can precisely be applied to «a closed society», ruled by «taboos» and fearful of individuals capable of making their own decision, who by contrast would be the members of an «open society».[120] What is more, Plato's «holism» is, according to Popper, closely related to a «longing for the lost unity of tribal life», a longing that could ultimately degenerate into «totalitarianism», with its accompanying «principle of leadership», Popper's real enemies.[121] Yet before all is said and done, and Plato condemned outright, one should remember that as a young man he had witnessed the defeat of Athens by Sparta (405 B.C.); so why should he not yearn for law and order, or, put differently, choose to reject democracy, of the Athenian type at least?[122]

This was well understood by Pater when demonstrating Plato as taking Lacedaemon as model for his *Republic*;[123] and Ruskin, too, avid reader of Plato that he was and full of admiration for him as «thinker and seer»,[124] would have had problems with Popper's critique. Be that as it may, the two eminent Victorians here discussed – 'eminent' in spite of not having been written about by Lytton Strachey – were pivotal figures of their time and stood at the crossroads of cultural issues and debates of abiding concern. Their roots, as I have tried to show, go deeper than only into the Romantic era, just as the ramifications of their thoughts are likely to spread out, through our present, into the future. Each in his own way was both nostalgic for the beauty of order as well as an order of beauty that one day, perhaps not so far from the present moment, might well be beyond recovery for even the most earnest of our yearnings.

112 See Lloyd 1966, Pt. II, ch. iv: «Metaphor and Imagery in Greek Cosmological Theories», pp. 210–309, esp. pp. 232–272, 294–296.
113 See Barkan 1975, ch. ii: «The Human Body and the Commonwealth», pp. 61–115, esp. pp. 62, 71.
114 See above, n. 93; as well as Williams 1958, pp. 263 f.
115 Darwin 1872, ch. iv, pp. 104 f.; cf. Toulmin/Goodfield 1965, p. 209.
116 Thomas Carlyle, *Past and Present*, I, vi; *Works*, III, 32.
117 See above, n. 54.
118 Walter Pater, «Style», in *Appreciations*, pp. 5–38, esp. p. 22.
119 Mannheim 1936, pp. 126, 246.
120 Popper 1962, I: «The Spell of Plato», ch. x, pp. 169–201, esp. p. 173.
121 Ibid., I, 80; and ch. vi: «Totalitarian Justice», pp. 86–119, esp. p. 87; plus ch. vii: «The Principle of Leadership», pp. 120–137.
122 Although Popper admits the need to contextualize Plato (ibid., I, 195), the Greek philosopher still requires defence along the lines indicated; cf. De Crescenzo 1985, pp. 318–320.
123 *Plato and Platonism*, pp. 200, 202.
124 *Modern Painters* III, Pt. IV, ch. xvi, § 28; *Works*, V, 333–334; cf. Clark 1964, p. 269.

«Cornice Decoration», Taf. XVI in:
John Ruskin, *The Stones of Venice*, I, London 1851

Wolfgang Kemp

«*The Stones of …*» – «Materialistische» Architekturästhetik bei Ruskin und Stokes

I.

Die beiden Bücher, die im Mittelpunkt meines Beitrags stehen, *The Stones of Venice* (1851 ff.) und *The Stones of Rimini* (1934) sind die bekanntesten Exemplare einer kleinen Literaturgattung, die man «Stadtgeologien» nennen könnte. Sie ragen aus einer Zahl ähnlicher Publikationen heraus, die etwa heissen *Was uns in Zürich die Steine erzählen* von Leo Wehrli 1897, *Bau- und Ornamentsteine an öffentlichen und privaten Bauten der Stadt St. Gallen* von G. Allenspach 1906, *The Stones of London* von J.V. Elsden und J.H. Howe 1923, *Dekorationssteine am Boulevard Pérolles, Freiburg* von Erwin Nickel 1981, und die gründlichste Aufnahme dieser Art: *Die Steine der Wiener Ringstraße* von Alois Kieslinger, erschienen 1972.

Diese Publikationen sind nötig und möglich, weil es etwas zu erklären gibt, und das ist das Ende der Selbstverständlichkeit, dass Architektur sich materiell wie konzeptionell aus lokalen Baustoffen erklärt und dass sich deren Formgebung der menschlichen Hand verdankt. Der Schweizer Geologe Leo Wehrli schreibt 1897: «Wie wir heute paradoxe Lagerungsverhältnisse mit hypothetischen, versunkenen Randgebieten, Überschiebungstheorien und Gletscherverfrachtung erklären, so wird für die Archäologen und Geologen späterer Generationen einst 'Eisenbahntransport!' das Schlagwort sein».[1] In diesem Sinne konnte er an der 1889–1891 erstellten Unionbank am Oberen Graben in Zürich nachweisen: Eingangssäulen aus rotem schwedischem Granit, 27 Pfeiler von grauweissem Granit aus dem Fichtelgebirge im Vestibül, 18 Säulen im Schalterraum aus norwegischem Labrador-Granit sowie deren Postamente aus Karstmarmor von Santa Croce bei Triest.

Die Bewertung des Steintourismus fiel je nach ästhetischer und politischer Einstellung sehr unterschiedlich aus: Der Stein war für Wehrli «ein stummes Glied einer wunderlich bunten Gesellschaft, in der das Einheimische mit dem entlegensten Fremden zeitlich und örtlich sich mischt». Er diene als «wahrer Kosmopolit» dem Ganzen und damit dem «Aufbau der Fremdenstadt».[2] Diesem weltoffenen Multimaterialismus gesellte sich eine provinzielle oder nationale Variante bei, die etwa auf der Ausstellung der Baumaterialien der Schweiz am Bahnhof Olten 1865 zu studieren ist: über dem zentralen Triumphtor, das aus Quadern von 18 Kanto-

1 Zitiert nach Röllin 1982, S. 422.
2 Ebd.

nen zusammengesetzt wurde, stand die lange und anspruchsvolle Inschrift: «Ein geordneter Bau ist das Bild eines geordneten Staates, Massen müssen das Ganze stützen, ein Gedanke das Ganze durchweben».[3] Nach diesem Muster paradierten auch einzelne Kantone, etwa das St. Gallische «Mineralreich», das seine 155 Steinsorten zu einem dorischen Torbogen verbaute.[4] Dieses Abbildungsverhältnis von politischem Reich und Mineralreich wird man in vielen Demonstrativbauten der jungen Nationen und aufbegehrenden Teilreichen antreffen; in Prag, um nur ein Beispiel zu nennen, kommen Nationalmuseum und Nationaltheater geologischen Mustermessen gleich, aber auch den Dritten Hof des Hradschin pflasterte Josip Plečnik in den 20-er Jahren des 20. Jahrhunderts mit Platten, die er aus zahlreichen Steinbrüchen des Landes zusammengeholt hatte, um an ihrem höchsten Platz die neue Republik flächendeckend zu repräsentieren. Die Gewinnung und Verlegung dieser Steine, vor allem aber der Transport des ebenda aufgerichteten Obelisken, waren Gegenstände nationaler Aufmerksamkeit und wurden in Zeitungen und Wochenschaufilmen fortlaufend kommentiert. Womit wir wieder zu unserem Eingangsakzent zurückgekehrt sind: das Steinreich im Zeitalter seiner Transportierbarkeit.

II.

John Ruskin, der die Buchreihe *Die Steine von...* mit seinem Venedig-Buch 1851 eröffnete, im Jahr der ersten Weltausstellung, nahm sich vor, alle byzantinischen und gotischen Bauwerke auf den fünf Quadratmeilen der Lagunenstadt zeichnen und vermessen zu wollen: «stone by stone, to eat it all up into my mind, touch by touch».[5] Sein Gegenstand ist die schlechthin nicht selbstverständliche Stadt, das amphibische Venedig, das jede seiner Entscheidungen auf die Gefahr von Überleben oder Untergehen hin auf das genaueste abwägen muss: Das betrifft wörtlich die Gründung der Stadt, die exakte Höhe des steinernen Niveaus über dem wässrigen, die Wahl der Baumaterialien hinsichtlich der Kriterien Resistenz und Gewicht. Ruskin hat vor Darwin Venedigs Geschichte mit Darwinistischen Kriterien beschrieben. Venedig ist ein Gemeinwesen unter hohem Dauerstress, eine Art Grossversuch, deswegen kann man an ihm «the history of all men, not in a 'nutshell' but in a nautilus shell» studieren.[6]

Aus unserer Perspektive ist die Nichtexistenz ortsgegebener Baumaterialien die Ausgangslage. Bauen in Venedig heisst Einsatz vielfältiger Materialien: Holz im Untergrund, Packsteine als Lage über den Holzrosten, Ziegel (weil leichter) für das Mauerwerk und Dach, istrischer Marmor für die Bewehrung, für die Stufen, Kanten und die Dekore. Die venezianische Baukunst erklärt ihren konstitutiv synthetischen und materialreichen Charakter auch oberflächlich durch ihren Zierstil.

Was Ruskin in Venedig und Oberitalien als Eigenart der romanischen und gotischen Baukunst schätzen lernte, verabsolutierte er zum Massstab aller Architektur, deren Wert sich bei Ruskin durch ihre Verzierungen bestimmt. Diese können sich, so weit sie wollen, von funktionalen Aufgaben oder Reminiszenzen entfernen. So hat die venezianische Baukunst auch keine Säulenordnung, sondern eine Ordnung der Inkrustation hervorgebracht, sie besitzt das System einer «vollkommenen und beständigen chromatischen Dekoration».

Natürlich entstand diese Sitte, flach geschnittene Steinverkleidungen vor Ziegelwänden anzubringen, aus den lokalen Bedingungen, aber entscheidend ist das Bekenntnis zur Farbe, zum heiligsten Wert im Reich der Künste, der in der Baukunst am sträflichsten misshandelt wird. Und natürlich ist der reichliche Einsatz von Spolien ein Nebeneffekt der Seefahrt, aber auch er verkörpert einen vitalen Wert des Bauens, den Ruskin «vitality of assimilation» oder «anpassende Umwertung» nennt, für ihn ein besonders starkes Indiz für eine grossherzig unbekümmerte, nicht systemhaft bornierte Baukunst. Von daher gesehen schenkt Ruskin mit den *Stones of Venice* dem Zeitalter des Materialmix seine Architekturästhetik, die als Lehre von den Oberflächenverzierungen mit dünnen Plattenfurnieren rechnet. Eine ironische Volte. Der Feind von Eisenbahn und maschineller Steinbearbeitung stösst theoretisch und nicht ohne praktische Folgen die Tore zum internationalen Steingrosshandel auf. Aber – und das Aber, der Einspruch, ist wie immer bei Ruskin grösser als der Zuspruch: zu haben sind Farbe, Vielfalt, Reichtum nur unter den Auflagen der Echtheit, Handarbeit, Freiheit.

Hinter diesen Postulaten steht eine vollausgearbeitete «Politische Ökonomie der Künste», auf die ich nicht eingehe.

Zu einer der hier interessierenden Kernfragen, das Problem der (billigen) Nachahmung edler Materialien betreffend, ein längeres, sehr ergiebiges Zitat: «Die Farben des Marmors sind für uns ganz wie auf einer vorbereiteten Palette gemischt. Alle Schatten und Farbtöne (mit Ausnahme der schlechten) sind vorhanden, manche vereint und glatt, andere gebrochen, vermischt, und unterbrochen, um so weit als möglich die Hand des Malers zu ersetzen, der die Farben mit dem Pinsel vertreibt und mischt. Aber es liegt in den Farben noch mehr als diese Zartheit der Anpassung. Es liegt Geschichte drin. «There is history in it». Durch die Art, wie sie in jedem Marmorstückchen angeordnet sind, erinnern sie an die Herstellungsart dieses Marmors und an die stufenweisen Veränderungen, die er durchgemacht hat. Und in all seinen Adern und Kreisen und geflammten Flecken, oder

3 Ebd., S. 423.
4 Ebd., S. 423.
5 John Ruskin in: Cook/Wedderburn 1903–1912, Bd. 10, S. XXVI.
6 Ebd., Bd. 19, S. LIV.

seinen abgebrochenen und unzusammenhängenden Linien, stehen die verschiedensten, niemals unwahren Sagen geschrieben von dem früheren politischen Zustande des Bergreiches, zu dem er gehörte, von seinen Schwächen und Stärken, Zuckungen und Verdichtungen vom Anbeginn der Zeit her. Wenn wir nun nie daran gewöhnt worden wären, etwas anderes als wirklichen Marmor zu sehen, dann würden wir seine Sprache bald verstanden haben, d.h. auch der unaufmerksamste Beobachter unter uns würde erkennen, daß gewisse Steine eine besondere Klasse bilden, und würde sich die Frage vorlegen, woher sie kommen und schließlich ein schwaches Interesse für die Hauptfrage zeigen, warum sie nur an diesem oder jenem Orte gefunden werden, und woher sie zu diesem Berge gehören und nicht zu jenem. Und nach einiger Zeit würde man sich nicht einen Augenblick gegen die Säulen einer Ladentür lehnen können, ohne sich an etwas zu erinnern, oder nach etwas zu forschen, was wohl des Erinnerns und Erforschens wert ist und das die Hügel von Italien, Griechenland, Afrika oder Spanien betrifft; und wir würden von Wissen zu Wissen geführt werden, bis die bildwerklosen Wände unserer Straßen so kostbare Bände für uns darstellen würden, wie die unserer Bibliotheken. Aber von dem Augenblick an, wo wir Marmornachahmung zulassen, ist diese Quelle des Wissens zerstört».[7]

Die «historische Sprache der Steine» wird durch die falsche Rede der Imitate genauso zum Verstummen gebracht wie der Einsatz von Maschinen und von Materialien wie Eisen und Glas, die dem craftsman keine individuellen Ausdrucksmöglichkeiten lassen und beim Rezipienten die Empfänglichkeit für lebendige Handarbeit abtöten: «The modern city intrudes upon the plenitude and legibility of the natural world. It undermines the confidence of our gaze».[8]

Hervorzuheben ist an dem langen Zitat neben der Leitunterscheidung wahr – falsch der Satz: «Es liegt Geschichte darin» und das weiterreichende Analogisieren, das etwa vom «früheren politischen Zustand des Bergreichs» spricht. Für Ruskin ist alles politisch, und alles Politische hat für ihn seine Legitimation und Inspiration in der Geschichte, einer Geschichte, die wenn sie richtig war, auch schön war, und die alles zusammengenommen, die schlimmen und die guten Zeiten, für die Gegenwart immer noch darin vorbildhaft ist, dass sie reich war. Wenn alle Steine vermessen und bestimmt sind, ist es in letzter Instanz diese Idee von Reichtum, welche die starren Materien zur lebendigen Vision, zum Ineins von Kunst und Natur transformiert. Hier ist der letzte Satz von Ruskins berühmter Beschreibung der Fassade von San Marco, er ist jetzt schon ziemlich hoch geklettert: «... und über diesen eine neue Reihe glitzernder Spitztürme, untermischt mit weißen, von scharlachfarbenen Blumen eingefaßten Bogen, ein wonnevolles Durcheinander ... bis zuletzt, wie in Ekstase, die Kronen der Bogen in marmornem Schaum sich brechen, und weit hinein in den blauen Himmel Ringel und Sprühregen marmornen Gischtes schleudern, als ob die Brandung am Lidostrande zu Eis erstarrt wäre, ehe sie niedersank, und die Meeresnymphen sie mit Korallen und Amethysten geschmückt hätten».[9]

Venedig ist nicht nur die Stadt im Meer und nicht nur die ehemalige Herrscherin der Meere – in ihren grossen Werken und in ihren charakteristischen Bauten ist sie wie das Meer: eine Gischt aus Marmor, eine Perle in geöffneter Muschel, eine Ansammlung von überraschendem Treibgut am Strand.

III.

85 Jahre später schrieb ein anderer Engländer über Venedig: «It is the sea that thus stands petrified, sharp and continuous till up near the sky. ... Amid the sea Venice is built from the essence of the sea. ... Venice herself, is an incrustation».[10] Dies ist der Übergang zu Adrian Stokes und zu seinem Buch *The Stones of Rimini*, das 1934 als zweiter Band einer auf drei Teile geplanten Reihe zur Kunst des Quattrocento erschien.

Einige Worte zu Stokes, der im deutschen Sprachraum so gut wie unbekannt ist: 1902 geboren, gestorben 1972.[11] Kunstschriftsteller, Lyriker, Erzähler, Maler; für die wenigen englischen Kollegen, die nicht den kontinentalen Weg der Ikonologie und Sozialgeschichte gehen, sondern die englische Tradition des 'Criticism' im Sinne von Ruskin und Pater fortsetzen, also für Richard Wollheim, Lawrence Gowing, Stephen Bann ist er eine inspirierende Präsenz geblieben, ohne wirkliches Gegenstück in Deutschland: Manches erinnert an Rudolf Borchardt, der damals ebenfalls in Oberitalien lebte und schrieb. Auf jeden Fall erwähnt werden muss noch, dass Stokes 1930 eine siebenjährige Analyse bei Melanie Klein begann und dass er in seinen Nachkriegsschriften, aber auch erst dann zu einem der wichtigsten psychoanalytisch orientierten Kunstschriftsteller Englands wurde: *Inside Out* (1947), *Smooth and Rough* (1951), *Michelangelo*, *Painting and the Inner World* sind wichtige Titel. Sein Verhältnis zu Ruskin ist in vieler Hinsicht bemerkenswert. Am bemerkenswertesten ist, dass er überhaupt eines hatte, denn in der Zeit nach 1918 war Ruskin schlicht und einfach passé, oder – wie Stokes selbst in *The Quattrocento* (1932) schreibt: «we ... have learned the anti-Ruskin lesson well».[12] Als angehender Schriftsteller sich gleichwohl mit ihm auseinanderzusetzen und gar im Titel eines Werks auf ihn anzuspielen, nicht ironisch, sondern wie ein bescheidener Fortset-

7 Ruskin 1903 ff., Bd. 3, S. 31 f.
8 Mallett 1995, S. 50.
9 Ruskin 1903 ff., Bd. 2, S. 80.
10 Stokes 1978, Bd. 1, S. 185.
11 Zu Stokes 1978 vgl. das Vorwort der *Critical Writings* von Lawrence Gowing. Vor allem aber die vorbildliche gestaltete Website, die Richard Head Stokes gewidmet hat: www.pstokes.demon.co.uk. Zu Ruskin und Stokes siehe Casillo 1986, S. 1 ff.
12 Stokes 1978, S. 127.

zer, das ist bis zur Selbstaufgabe kühn. «I think Ruskin must have been an eunuch although a great man», schreibt Stokes am 9. Mai 1925 in sein Tagebuch – der Ort ist Venedig –, «he lashes me daily, hurls at me Stones of Venice».[13] Womit ein Verhältnis beschrieben sein dürfte, das mehr als die Ablösung vom Vertreter einer älteren Epoche zum Gegenstand hat.

«This book», lesen wir in der Einleitung zu den *Stones of Rimini*, «is concerned with the imaginative meanings that we attach to stone and water in relation». Anders gesagt, die beiden Protagonisten dieses Buches heissen: Limestone and the Mediterranean, wobei der eine sich der Wirkung des anderen verdankt und beide zusammen, in ihrer natürlichen Koexistenz und Koevolution den Kulturraum Mittelmeer ausmachen. Es ist laut Stokes die grosse Leistung des Quattrocento, diese Genealogie und Verwandtschaft von Stein und Wasser offenzulegen und «imaginativ» auszudeuten. Die menschlichen Agenten sind in diesem Fall Sigismondo Malatesta und sein Bildhauer Agostino di Duccio, der in den Annalen der Kunstgeschichte zu Stokes Zeiten keinen Spitzenplatz besetzte und danach auch nicht; nur in Hamburg hatten die Liebhaber «bewegten Beiwerks» und schwieriger astrologischer Programme ihm ein freundliches Gedenken bewahrt – freilich könnte die Distanz zwischen der Warburg-Schule und der Materialästhetik von Stokes nicht grösser gedacht werden. So lautet also das volle Programm der *Stones of Rimini*: «This book is concerned with the imaginative meanings that we attach to stone and water in relation, so far as an emphasis put upon those meanings is essential to the interpretation of Agostino's Tempio sculpture. Diesen Weg wählend, entdecken oder wieder-entdecken wir das Leben und die Kunst des Mittelmeerraums, den Charakter des Kalksteins, die Unterschiede zwischen Skulptur und Plastik, die antike Astrologie. Agostinos Skulpturen stellen die Verwandtschaftsbeziehungen zwischen diesen Elementen heraus».[14]

Zum Kalkstein also, über dessen «pleasures» Stokes folgendes zu sagen hat: «Kalkstein, der zu größtem Teil aus organischen Ablagerungen besteht, ist das Bindeglied zwischen der organischen und der anorganischen Welt». Gleichzeitig ist er das Bindeglied zwischen der Naturgeschichte und der Menschengeschichte, denn, so Stokes: «Kalkstein repräsentiert in mumifiziertem Zustand das Leben, das in der Silurischen und in anderen vergangenen Epochen herrschte und vergangen ist, so wie die aus Istrischem Stein gefertigten Paläste Venedigs in räumlicher Ausdehnung die aufgehäuften Schätze des alten Unternehmens Venedig darstellen». Fazit: «The very substance of limestone suggests concreted Time».[15] Vergleiche Ruskin: «There is history in it». Ohne dass sie sich dieser Grundtatsachen immer bewusst sein mussten, haben laut Stokes «die unbewußten Phantasien vieler Völker ihre Künstler dahin gelenkt», die Natur dieses Steins kongenial zu erfassen. Das reicht bis ins Abbildliche: Die Quattrocento-Skulptur, findet Stokes, habe in Meeresmotiven geschwelgt; Delphine, Meeresungeheuer, Fische finde man überall, und die

Muschel, «the first geological concretion in the history of marble», sei ihr Emblem. «The metamorphosed structure of marble encouraged an extreme anthropomorphic interpretation of its original life».[16]

Einen Bau wie den Tempio Malatestiano, der in einer dem alten Ziegelbau von San Francesco innen und aussen übergezogenen Marmorhülle vor uns steht, beschreibt Stokes als «an ideal quarry whose original organic substances were renewed by the hand of the carver to express the abundant seas collected into solid stone».[17] Um zu begreifen, dass dies nicht nur poetisch im Sinne des Redeschmucks, sondern poetisch im Sinne einer Engführung von Poesis, der schaffenden und nachschaffenden Arbeit von Natur und Kunst, gemeint ist, reicht ein Blick auf Agostinos Relief mit der Darstellung des Einflusses, den der (wässrige) Mond auf die Welt hat. Das Wasser bewegt sich in Wirbeln («vortex») – es war übrigens der Erz-Vortizist Ezra Pound, der Stokes zu diesem Buch über Rimini angeregt hat –, und aus den Wirbeln steigen pyramidenförmige Inselwelten. «Die Pyramide, der neue Kalkstein, der aus den Wassern und ihrem Leben entsteht, wird mit den konzentrierten Kräften des whirlpools zusammengebracht. ... Hier wird in einer unbewussten Parabelform die ganze Anmutung des Kalksteins und durch sie die grundlegende Mythologie des mittelmeerischen Kunstschaffens veranschaulicht».[18] Agostino ist wie gesagt Stokes Vorzeigekünstler, was die Obsession mit amphibischen und aquarischen Welten angeht; alles was er anfasst, gerät ihm fliessend: «Agostino's root preoccupation was with water forms and water movement».[19] «Agostino was the master of undulation in the stone».[20] «In the Tempio reliefs Mediterranean life has complete expression: there, water is stone».[21]

Agostinos «Reliefs haben die Wirkung von Marmorgliedern, die wir unter Wasser liegen sehen. Das Zusammenspiel so vieler Oberflächen, wie sie in diesen Reliefs ausgeformt wurden, ihre übertriebene Perspektive, die Wiedergabe des Vollrunden durch merkwürdige Auslängungen des Runden, diese schwangereren Erhebungen und Ausläufer ins Flache, diese wandelbaren Verkürzungen, sie erinnern an die Wahrnehmung von Steinen, die im Wasser liegen, von Marmorfußböden in Bädern. ... Aber anders als der Stein, den wir aus der Flut nehmen oder der Fußboden, den wir betreten, um seine wahre Beschaffenheit kennenzulernen, hören Agostinos Formen niemals auf, beides zu sein: Möglichkeit und Wirklichkeit.» – «They never cease to be potential as well as actual».[22]

Wie Ruskin ist Stokes sich seines Standorts in der Geschichte der Materialverwendung bewusst. Die «homogenous marble sheets» an den zeitgenössischen

13 Zitiert bei Bann 1988, S. 138.
14 Stokes 1978, S. 187.
15 Ebd., S. 196.
16 Ebd., S. 197.
17 Ebd., S. 261.
18 Ebd., S. 254.
19 Ebd., S. 229.
20 Ebd., S. 249.
21 Ebd., S. 214.
22 Ebd., S. 225.

Lyons Corner Houses lehnt er ab, da klingt er wie Ruskin: «Nowhere upon them is the human impress. ... They were sheared from their blocks by impervious machines».[23] Aber nicht deswegen fühlt sich Stokes aufgefordert, sein Buch «a symptom of altered culture» zu nennen: «Today, and not before, do we commence to emerge from the Stone Age: that is to say, for the first time on so vast a scale throughout Europe does hewn stone give place to plastic materials».[24] Das Thema ist also nicht mehr die freie Verfügbarkeit der Steine dank Eisenbahn, Dampfschiff und Dampfsäge. Das Thema ist jetzt der Ersatz des Natursteins durch «Kunststoffe» – ein fundamentaler Ablösungsvorgang, der die Frage Ruskins nach wahr oder falsch überflüssig macht, aber neue Probleme mit sich bringt, wie Stokes ausführt: «An attitude to material, an attitude conceived in this book as being far more than the visual-aesthetic basis of Western civilization, can hardly survive long. The use in building of quarried stone must, we shall argue, increasingly diminish, and with it one nucleus of those dominant fantasies which have coloured the European perception of the visual world».[25] Und damit steuert Stokes die Leitunterscheidung von «carving» und «modelling», von Skulptur und Plastik an, die für ihn die Herangehensweise von Künstlern, von Kunstepochen, von ganzen Kulturen unterscheidbar macht: «In the work of men, manufacture, the process of fashioning or moulding, supersedes, whereever it is possible, the process of enhancing or carving material, the process that imitates thoses gradual forces that vivify and destroy Nature before our eyes».[26] Die Formulierung macht deutlich, wo Stokes Sympathien liegen: «carving» ist «enhancing», ist die Qualität des Materials herausarbeiten, die Kräfte der Natur freimachen oder lesbar machen, «carving» ist materialgerechtes Arbeiten, «modelling» ist bildgerechtes Formen. «A figure carved in stone is fine carving when one feels that not the figure, but the Stone through the medium of the figure, has come to life. Plastic conception, on the other hand, is uppermost when the material with which, or from which, a figure has been made appears no more than as so much suitable stuff for this creation».[27] Die Moderne tendiere unaufhaltsam zum Plastischen. Das habe Folgen für das Gesamtsystem der Künste, auch und vor allem für die Architektur, «the mother art of stone». «Building becomes a plastic activity pure and simple». Während in der Vergangenheit die Steinbaukunst im besten Fall nicht Formgebung, «moulding of shape» bedeutete, sondern Steinblöcken eine Ordnung auferlegte, die einer Hervorhebung des räumlichen Charakters des Steins gleichkam – «an order imposed on blocks from which there results an exaltation of the spatial character of stone». Man erkennt, wie Stokes hier im Kräftefeld jenes Prinzips operiert, das Ruskin und die Architekturästhetik seiner Zeit unbekannt war – ich spreche von der Kategorie Raum, die Stokes offenbar auf unterster, mineralogischer Ebene vorgegeben sieht – deutlicher erklärt er sich nicht – er ist kein Mann der Architektur.

Einige zusammenfassende Bemerkungen zum Schluss: Das die Zwischenkriegsjahrzehnte verpflichtende Axiom der Materialgerechtigkeit wird von Stokes weniger aus Physik und Chemie, als aus Naturgeschichte abgeleitet: einer Naturgeschichte, deren weitere Ablagerung («accretion») die sich in ihrer naturalen Vorgeschichte wiedererkennende Kulturgeschichte ist.[28] Das ist ein genuin romantisches Argument: Noch einmal wird Wordworths Gedanke vom «ennobling interchange», von der Einheit von Natur und Kultur als wesensgemäss für einander bestimmter Aspekte der Schöpfung angestimmt. Und künstlerische Arbeit wird gleichgesetzt mit der Aufdeckung und imaginativen Ausdeutung dieser Geschichte als Struktur; sie ist ein Akt der «deep imaginative communion» mit diesen ebenso physikalischen wie geschichtlichen Strukturgesetzlichkeiten.

In der Durchführung dieses Gedankens ist Stokes genauer als Ruskin, der das ja nicht anders gesehen hat. Darin liegt eine gewisse Ironie. Ruskin war neben vielem anderem Geologe und verstand unendlich viel mehr von Steinen als Stokes, der sich die wichtigsten Daten aus zwei, drei Büchern zusammengestellt hatte. Ruskin, der Naturwissenschaftler und Empirist, baute zwischen Erd- und Kunstgeschichte, organischer and anorganischer Welt, Vergangenheit und Gegenwart poetische Brücken. Die Moral lebte von der Kraft der Vision.

Und ein weiterer Unterschied: Stokes ist kein Mann der programmatischen Rede. Wo Ruskin predigt, kämpft, und teilweise praktischen Erfolg hat, will Stokes nur noch den Vorteil des Nachrufschreibers einheimsen. Was tot ist, lässt sich besser erkennen, sagt er. «Nothing in writing is easier than to raise the dead». To «raise the dead» ist natürlich die sprechende Metapher überhaupt für die Entstehung des Kalksteins und nicht nur seiner Kultur, der mediterranen.

23 Ebd., S. 184.
24 Ebd., S. 188.
25 Ebd.
26 Ebd.
27 Ebd., S. 230.

28 Zu dieser Sichtweise siehe generell Böhme 1989, S. 129 ff. und zuletzt Böhme 2000, S. 129: «Es hat einen für die Ökologie der Kultur augenöffnenden Effekt, der Tatsache eingedenk zu sein, daß einer der Grundakte der Kultur, nämlich Bauen, aufruft auf der jahrmillionenlangen Arbeit von Organismen».

J. Ruskin　　J. C. Armytage

66. Light in the West, Beauvais.

«Light in the West, Beauvais», Taf. 66 in: John Ruskin, *Modern Painters*, vol. V, London 1860

Francis O'Gorman

Ruskin, and writing history from home

«There certainly *is* a special fate in getting this house»
John Ruskin to Joan Severn, 14 September 1871[1]

'The sermon' lay deeply behind Ruskin's literary project throughout his life. Whether writing pamphlets, lectures, public letters, or complete books, the sound of the preacher, to whom he had listened from his earliest childhood years, did not leave him, and it remained in various ways a continuous, characteristic, though changing, inflection of his public voice.[2] The most ample work from the first half of Ruskin's career governed by this sense of himself as speaking from a pulpit was *The Stones of Venice* (1851–1853). This text, a bedrock of his public reputation as an authority on the moral identity of architecture, and more generally as a cultural critic avant la lettre, was shaped by the mode of the sermon – the sermon that was at root a warning, and a national warning at that. Ruskin, at the beginning of the 1850s in the pages of his Venetian history and cultural diagnosis, understood himself as preaching to England as a whole, conceiving her as a nation on the verge of ruin, a state perilously close to repeating the story of Venice, slipping from great prosperity and spiritual health into degradation, decay, «less pitied destruction»,[3] and entire ruin.

Telling history at this point in Ruskin's career was inseparable from admonishment. And history as he conceived it here was of huge dimensions. The important and unignorable lessons, whose value was «difficult to overrate» which could be learned from «a faithful study of the history of this strange and mighty city» (IX.18), were, as Ruskin fathomed them, the grand lessons of an (implied)[4] grand narrative. His terms, and his conclusions, were vast. Studying history in *The Stones of Venice* was to reveal cultural movements, key currents of the past, and shifts of national temper – centrally, of course, the movement from the Gothic and its reverent spirit to the debased energies of the Venetian Renaissance. The micro-details

1 Ruskin Foundation, University of Lancaster (hereafter RF), BEM L 36, italic original.
2 The influence of some of the actual sermons Ruskin heard as a child is usefully discussed in the Introduction of Wheeler 1999, pp. 3–26.
3 Cook/Wedderburn 1903–1912, IX, p. 17. Subsequent references are given in the text, by volume and page number.
4 It is a curious kind of history, of course. Ruskin assumes his reader's familiarity which much of his narrative and often gives little factual information or chronological detail. Tanner 1992, p. 81, thinking about this aspect of *The Stones*, appropriately calls it «a history with the history left out».

of the forms of capitals, tracery, roofs, door mouldings, and lintels served as matter for the germination of a macro-history, which grew through the three volumes, of a culture's rise and fall. And shaping this implied grand narrative, and its inquiry into the causality of degeneration, was the underlying myth that amplified its grand terms yet further: the story of the city was framed in the universal language of the fall from Eden and the loss of paradise.[5]

In the central chapter of the central volume, Ruskin refocused his interest for a moment, on a subject destined to develop in scope as Ruskin's thinking matured. In that chapter, «The Nature of Gothic», he reflected on some of the conditions of ordinary men at work during the apogee of Venice's health in words which, when separated from their context, would in due course become part of the common linguistic currency of reformist thought in the mid-century. The labourers of whom he spoke were not individualized, and their identity was always treated as inseparable from their labour. But their conditions mattered, and their contentment was celebrated as a living part of a Christian state. They were written without discrete human identity, but they were fundamental within Ruskin's broader economy of signification in *The Stones*. And as a subject of history, the lives of ordinary men and women and the conditions of their existence would develop markedly, and come, at the point of greatest maturation in Ruskin's thought, to assume a new role.

The Stones of Venice grew from Ruskin's assured conception of himself in the early 1850s as a Christian critic of English spiritual identity, and history was the form in which he cast a prophet's sermon and statement of national chastisement. Loss and destruction were inextricable parts of his theme. This history of grievous loss troubled him, and at the Christian core of *The Stones* was the acknowledgement of a theological mystery to which Ruskin could find no satisfactory answer: why was it that God had permitted Venice's fall? Why did God give so much, and then allow even this, the «best (of) gifts» (X.178) to be trampled under foot? It was an inscrutable act of divinity that seemed to Ruskin, already experiencing some restlessness with the Evangelical faith he had learned at home, to constitute one of the veritable curses of the world. «There is no subject of thought more melancholy», he wrote in volume II of the fate of the spectral city he called «the ghost upon the sands of the sea» (IX.17),

«more wonderful, than the way in which God permits so often His best gifts to be trodden under foot of men, His richest treasures to be wasted by the moth, and the mightiest influences of His Spirit, given but once in the world's history, to be quenched and shortened by miseries of chance and guilt. I do not wonder at what men Suffer, but I wonder often at what they Lose ... The fruit struck to the earth before its ripeness; the glowing life and goodly purpose dissolved away in sudden death; the words, half spoken, choked upon the lip with clay for ever; or, stranger than all, the whole majesty of humanity raised to its fullness, and every gift and power necessary for a given purpose, at a given moment, centred in one man, and all this perfected blessing permitted to be refused, perverted, crushed, cast aside by those who need it most, – the city which is Not set on a hill, the candle that giveth light to None that are in the house; – these are the heaviest mysteries of this strange world, and, it seems to me, those which mark its curse the most» (X.178).

Ruskin conceived himself in *The Stones* as bringing to public consciousness divinely appointed truths inscribed in the story of Venice. Those truths involved the contemplation of a mystery that fastened to the heart of his historical project an acknowledgement of loss and the defeat of great purposes, and the acceptance of a troubling inexplicability about God's dealings with the world.

The Stones of Venice was sermonic, and anchored in decline. It was not Carlylean in its focus on architecture and the lessons of stones, and in its general eschewal of individual heroic biography, but it was certainly sustained by Ruskin's new enthusiasm for Carlyle in other ways. Like Carlyle, Ruskin here understood the practice of writing history as a literary mode for the instruction of the present, and he shared with the man whom he would much later – from December 1873 – start to call «Papa Carlyle», a belief that writing history was a form of cultural diagnosis and a way of giving expression to the moral and spiritual shifts of a nation's life. Shortly after publishing the last volumes of his Venetian history, Ruskin would revealingly say in public that he «owed more (to Carlyle) than any other English writer» (XII.507). He had in mind partly the indebtedness of *The Stones of Venice*.[6]

Writing history, after *The Stones of Venice*, was set aside for many years. Ruskin's literary identity was developing along other paths, and, indeed, with the completion

5 The personal dimensions to Ruskin's configuration of Venice in terms of the Edenic are suggestively discussed by Bullen 1995, pp. 502–520. Ruskin makes a link between Eden and Venice in the very first page of volume I of *The Stones*, see IX.17. The whole notion of Ruskin and Paradise is a guiding idea of Spear 1984. Tanner 1992, pp. 155–156 compares Ruskin's writing of Venice as Paradise with Pound's related inscription of the city in *Venice Desired*.

6 Carlyle, correspondingly, liked the book himself – and also recognized its indebtedness to the pulpit. Beginning to read the first volume of *The Stones* in 1851, he wrote to Ruskin to say that it was «A strange, unexpected, and I believe, most true and excellent *Sermon* in Stones ... The spirit and purport of these critical studies of yours are a singular sign of the times to me, and a very gratifying one» (IX.xlvi, italic original). Ruskin's relationship with Carlyle is best approached from Cate 1982. There was a thought-provoking re-assessment of the relationship in Coreau 1974, pp. 15–19.

of volume V of *Modern Painters* in May 1860, he would not begin any new major multi-volume study, of history or of any other subject, in book form again. Certainly, the ambitious cultural history of the sort explored in *The Stones* would never entice him in the future. Many years would pass, after Smith and Elder issued the last volume of *The Stones of Venice*, on 2 October 1853, before Ruskin turned back to history as a fruitful practice of writing and serviceable mode for his teaching. The work of the turbulent and troubled 1860s began with what he later referred to as the «central work» of his life,[7] the four articles comprising *Unto this Last* (1860), and were followed by other important works: *Sesame and Lilies* (published 1865 from lectures of 1864), *The Ethics of the Dust* («1866» but actually 1865), the articles that would later form *Munera Pulveris* in 1872, the letters of *Time and Tide* (1868), and the major climax of Ruskin's interest in Greek myth, *The Queen of the Air* (1869). Ruskin's thought in those works was enriched by a continuous contemplation of the past, but there was no sustained engagement with history as a specific practice of writing. The intellectual developments – in political economy, the proper duties and characters of the sexes, the uses of Greek mythology, the ethical lessons of crystallography, and children's education more generally – took his writing in other directions.

It was increasingly urgent meditation on this last question, the matter of children's education within schemes for the rejuvenation of English society, that would be the first major step in taking Ruskin back to the consideration of, and in due course, the writing of history after the 1860s. Thinking about the nature of true education, the training of an admirable English citizenry, and, in more specific terms, about the content of the educational curricula for the schools of the Guild of St George, in the early years of the 1870s, brought history as a discipline and literary practice back into the forefront of Ruskin's mind. Outlining the details of his school curriculum for the St George's Schools in *Fors Clavigera*, his monthly letters to the workingmen and labourers of Great Britain, he declared history an essential element. A «little, well known», he had said in March 1871, «will serve you much» (XXVII.45). He did not believe a good and moral adult could be ignorant of the lessons of the past. Specifically, he told his readers in the *Fors* letter for August 1871, the most ample discussion of the projected curriculum, that the children of the Schools were to study in detail the histories of five cities (for history as a subject of writing throughout Ruskin's career was almost always deeply associated with the histories of particular cities): Athens, Rome, Venice, Florence, and London. From these they would learn essential elements of the story of European civilization, what «has been beautifully and bravely done» (XXVII.157), and of the culture that gave shape to, respectively, Virgil, Plato, Carpaccio, Dante, and Shakespeare, men from whom Ruskin believed the modern world could and should learn. Carlylean historiography with its accent on heroic biography exerted its pressure here still.

But 'writing' history was only resumed well after Ruskin's first thoughts on the St George's Schools. *St. Mark's Rest* (1877–1884), which took Ruskin back to the story of Venice, partly reflected some of his frustrations with the ignorance and indifference towards the cultural heritage of Europe he had found among his undergraduates at Oxford where he had been Slade Professor of Fine Art since 1870. He considered he was writing, as he expressed it in his subtitle, «the history of Venice, for the help of the few travellers who still care about her monuments» (XXIV.193), and such words revealed the disillusion that was the product of that professorial experience. But it was in writing not of the real Venice but of a French Gothic city, the «Venice of France» (XXXIII.25), Amiens, that Ruskin found most satisfaction. In *The Bible of Amiens*, he was more ambitious and wide-ranging than in his second project on Venetian history, and here he expressed the conclusions of his thinking about historiography, the uses of narration, and the proper focus of historical narrative. *The Bible of Amiens*, incomplete, uneven, inaccurate, and written irregularly over four difficult years, is, hardly surprisingly, little read today, remembered if at all for its impact upon Marcel Proust.[8] But there is significance to this initially unpromising text, the first of the planned but never realized series, *Our Fathers Have Told Us*. Uneven and unfinished, *The Bible of Amiens* is also revealing of the last phase of Ruskin's literary endeavour, a significant document in Victorian cultural history, and in the history of the writing of history.

Ruskin was a different man from the author of *The Stones of Venice* when he began *The Bible of Amiens*. He was, in the first place, no longer an Evangelical protestant: his faith was broader, more eclectic, more generous, and, at an important level, he now believed sincerely in the value and virtue of a life well lived whatever the exact condition of religious faith or the nature of denominational affiliation. Ruskin was partly using *The Bible* as a way of textually signifying to his readers, and to himself, exactly this theological distance from his earlier self: he was commemorating the movement of his mind through thirty years. *The Bible of Amiens* was a volume, in this respect, of oblique autobiographical reflection and silent self-assessment of personal history. And within this particular theological dimension of the book, St. Martin of Amiens stood as a tutelary figure. He was a saint whose great and

7 Cook 1912, II. 2.

8 Ruskin 1986. Also, Autret 1955; Macksey 1982, pp. [172]–197; Gamble 1993, pp. 270–286; and Gamble 1997, pp. 31–42.

defining act of charity in dividing his cloak for a freezing beggar was made while he was not a Christian: he was the gentle, good-mannered man of God who well knew that 'undipped people may be as good as dipped if their hearts are clean' (XXXIII.44). Ruskin recognized in him something of his own conclusions about human virtue, community responsibility, and religious broadmindedness.

But the shifts in Ruskin's critical identity and his understanding of his intellectual purpose were more than this. *The Bible of Amiens* made particularly visible other substantial developments away from earlier convictions. And nowhere was this more true, or more interesting, than in Ruskin's understanding of the task of writing history, which had by this stage intersected with a development in his beliefs about the use of narrative as a literary form.

The Bible of Amiens presented the task of writing history in sharply different terms to the sermonic impulse of the early 1850s. At a key level, Ruskin was not warning or admonishing in this text, but celebrating. History as he understood it here taught not the path which English society should avoid at all costs, but presented admirable narratives of virtuous men and women whose lives were exemplary in their goodness and faithfulness. Lessons were taught now not from the testimony of stones, the book of architecture, but from the stories and myths of human endeavour. And these ancient human narratives – Ruskin dwelt much, for instance, on the stories of St Martin, and his saintly kindnesses to the poor – were of admirable behaviour and good works, of the establishment of meaningful human relationships, and the fulfilment of communal responsibilities. History now, for Ruskin, was not shaped to outline or imply a great narrative of a culture's rise and fall, nor was it configured to accent loss and decline, nor was it drawn in the shape of a warning. History was now about the celebration of good lives. In the Preface to *The Bible* Ruskin gave this dramatic shape in ascribing to history the same essential role as he had, throughout his life, given to the visual arts. «It has been told (to readers) in *The Laws of Fésole*», he said, «that all great Art is Praise». Now, expressing the spirit of *The Bible of Amiens* in crisply simple terms, he made the crucial addition: «so is all faithful History».

The Bible of Amiens and its faithful history of praise contained no dispiriting theological mystery about God's action in the world. It was instead an acknowledgement that history, properly told, spoke of two positive, clearly discernible forces: the «virtue of men» and the «Providence of heaven» (XXXIII.38). These were, Ruskin said, the «only powers of which history has ever to tell any profitable truth» (XXXIII.38). The action of divinity in history seemed more confidently legible to Ruskin, who no longer contemplated the loss of Venice, or, as he had done in *Modern Painters* IV the disturbing enigma of God's acceptance of human misery (see «The Mountain Gloom», VI.385–417), as great mysteries and signs of a curse alive within the world. Narrating the virtue of men and women, and the benign ways of Providence, Ruskin revised his own person as teacher and cultural prophet, assuming a fresh voice of acclaim that textually privileged human actions of goodness over the theology of the Fall.

The Stones of Venice had included Ruskin's long survey of the defining characteristics of the Gothic in stone, which had described the joyful worker, the ordinary Venetian craftsman, as an indication of, as well as a necessity for, great architecture. In *The Bible*, Ruskin thought about ordinary lives in a different way. He placed them not as central to the healthiness of architecture, and all that that implied about a well-regulated Christian state, but as the real focus of all important history. He proclaimed the centrality of what was customarily absent from most «recognised world history» (XXXIII.59) that typically comprised narratives of the triumph, defeat, and «wandering» (XXXIII.59) of armies, the expansion of empires, the advance of invasion forces, the reorganization of political alliances. This material was only the «apparent» matter of history: «the real history», he said, «is underneath» (XXXIII.59). And this «real history» was that of hidden, obscure bodies, the distant ancestors of the ordinary lives on which he had meditated in «The Nature of Gothic», whose stories were almost unrecoverable and whose voiceless presences were the most meaningful absences in all efforts to retell and draw meaning from the past, and he orientated his own account of history towards this hidden voice of the «Suffering Life»,

«the rooted heart of native humanity, growing up in eternal gentleness, howsoever wasted, forgotten, or spoiled, – itself neither wasting, nor wandering, nor slaying, but unconquerable by grief or death ... Of this low-nestling, speechless, harmless, infinitely submissive, infinitely serviceable order of being, no Historian ever takes the smallest notice, except when it is robbed, or slain. I can give you no picture of it, bring to your ears no murmur of it, nor cry. I can only show you the absolute 'must have been' of its unrewarded past, and the way in which all we have thought of, or been told, is founded on the deeper facts of its history, unthought of, and untold» (XXXIII.59–60).

This untold history was a major modification of Ruskin's Carlylean historiography: he was declaring biography, albeit unrepresentable biographies, as a practice central to the telling of history, but celebrating now the lost lives of the underside of official history. George Eliot had begun her career in fiction with a story of humble clerical life, and brought it to a close with the more ample canvas of *Daniel Deronda* (1876). Ruskin, as a historian, moved, mutatis mutandis, in the opposite direction, away from the spacious ambitions of *The Stones of Venice* towards the acknowledgement of the centrality of ordinary stories, involving the «unhistoric» life,[9] as Eliot had once it at the conclusion of *Middlemarch* (1871–1872), the «unthought» lives of unofficial history. Ruskin suggestively pointed towards the future, moving towards rather than, like Eliot, away from what would become in due course the next century's more radical engagement with lost narratives and hidden histories, and with, so to speak, the recovery of the annals of the poor, and the recuperation of those on the margins of official history.

Actual narratives of the unheroic life that Ruskin proclaimed as the true subject of history in *The Bible of Amiens* had begun to fascinate him the decade before, and the spirit that is reflected in that book had its origins partly in the 1870s and a particular literary mode Ruskin had explored there. One key moment in Ruskin's writing, I think, without which *The Bible* could not have been written, occurred in the *Fors Clavigera* letter for June 1873. *Fors* was an experimental mode of expression and thought in many ways, and boldly innovative. But Ruskin's exploration of narrative form – borrowed stories, not invented ones – proved especially enabling to him.

In that letter for June 1873, Ruskin's first subject was the issue of class. He was commenting on what he called, with the hyperbole which characterized the letters generally, the «frantic fear of the ordinary British public» about falling «below their proper 'station in life'», and consequently with their «passionate belief in the propriety of keeping up an appearance» (XXVII.548). This was a disliked feature of English life he had criticized earlier in the lecture «Of King's Treasuries» from *Sesame and Lilies* (published 1865; see XVIII.54–5). In *Fors*, he remarked that his «young lady readers» in particular would be infinitely better off endeavouring to find out not where they thought they belonged, but for which «station» God intended them. That station might require of them «some menial service», he said, such as a housemaid's. Would they be able to do such work without feeling «aggrieved at being made lower housemaid instead of upper» (XXVII.548)? Ruskin's strong sense of individual duty and responsibility (for both men and women), about finding one's own work and doing it, was always central to the politics of *Fors*.[10]

But this particular critique of social expectations and preserving one's «station» in life, resolved unexpectedly, on this occasion, into a narrative, a story of use, Ruskin said, to those who would do God's work either as, symbolically, upper or as lower housemaids. A narrative of ordinary daily life functioned here, for the first but by no means the last time in Ruskin's later work, as a vehicle for the easy transmission of a politics of duty, well-directed and content labour, and well-managed family life. Ruskin's story – he called it *The Broom Merchant* – was a translation (actually a double translation, because he could not read German so used a French version initially) of *Der Besenbinder von Rychiswyl*, by Albert Bitzius («Jeremias Gotthelf»), the original first published in 1852. The tale was set in a mythic time of social stability in which family life was central, and, echoing the ideal society described in *Unto this Last* (1860), where the merchant was honoured as a man of faith and duty in whom his customers placed their trust. Ruskin's retelling of this story of Hansli, the young broom maker, his apprenticeship, romance, home economy, and eventual success, his coming to «take good heart in his work» (XXVII.552), accented esteemable domestic values and the dignity of well-managed daily life and personal relations. It gave appealingly simple narrative form to a life made an exemplum, just as Richter, Ruskin later said in the Oxford lectures published as *The Art of England* (1884), gave visual form to related virtues.[11]

The tale of Hansli, and his «superb» brooms (XXVII.552), which he continued sporadically until July 1875,[12] was significant in the articulation of Ruskin's thinking about the proper subjects of political economy but also, as *The Bible of Amiens* later testified, in the development of his ideas about the subjects of good history. After *The Bible*, Ruskin's preoccupation with similar narratives of humble lives grew, revealing the extent to which he perceived his own duties in the last years of his working life as guiding his readers with ordinary human histories worthy of praise. Thus came his edition of Francesca Alexander's *The Story of Ida* (1883), the Italian story of the death of a good child, a year before the completion of *The Bible* and, later, another tale from «Gotthelf», «one of his great novels», he said in *Fors* for January 1876, «great as Walter Scott's, in the truth and vitality of it» (XXVIII. 492): *Ulric the Farm Servant* (1886–1888). This text, translated by Julia Firth and edited by Ruskin, was included in the Standard Library or *Bibliotheca Pastorum* (1876–1885),[13] and was the story of the moral reformation of a servant partly thanks to the understanding of a kind master; it was related to *The Broom Maker* as a further Protestant narrative of good work and healthy content, «exquisite in its

9 Eliot 1871–1872 in: Carroll 1986, p. 825.
10 See, for instance, the injunction in October 1872, where Ruskin tells his readers that «you, for your part, will do good work, whether you live by it, or die» (XXVII.379). This is part of Proposition III, general principles for St George's Company.
11 Ruskin says that Richter's illustrations «are enough, in themselves, to show that whatever its errors, whatever its backslidings, this century of ours has in its heart understood and fostered, more than any former one, the joys of family affection, and of household piety» (XXXIII.285).
12 Ruskin said, in concluding his narration that July, that he could return to discuss some of the «debatable matters in this story» (XXVIII.373), but he did not, in the end, find space to do so.
13 The *Bibliotheca Pastorum* was Ruskin's «cottage library» planned for the members of the Guild of St. George. As it stands, it comprises four volumes: I. *The Economist of Xenophon* (1876); II. *Rock Honeycomb: Broken Pieces of Sir Philip Sidney's Psalter. Laid up in Store for English Homes* (1877); *Elements of English Prosody* (1880) – originally intended to be another instalment of Sidney; and IV. *A Knight's Faith: Passages in the Life of Sir Herbert Edwardes* (1885). Maidment considers the *Bibliotheca* in Hunt/Holland 1982, pp. 159–171, esp. pp. 162–163; the *Bibliotheca* as an effort to form a national canon is discussed by Stoddart 1998, pp. 141–142.

sympathy» (XXXII.345). In presenting the narrative of another (contemporary) author, moreover, Ruskin could continue to stress that living, healthy art was indeed still being created in modern Europe, and that this was a sign of real hope for the future.

Ruskin's privileging of the unheroic life in his later literary work was, to be sure, part of that general movement in the second half of his career of increasing concern for the conditions of daily existence, and the sufferings of ordinary men and women in contemporary England. It was part of a more general refocusing of energies. But Ruskin's increasing political investment in the lives of ordinary men and women, which came even to be reflected in his interpretations of modern British painting,[14] was given additional momentum as the 1870s moved on by his increasing dissatisfaction with what he could achieve at Oxford as Slade Professor, the discontent he registered, as I said earlier, in the pointed subtitle of *St Mark's Rest*. Ruskin, as the first Professor of Fine Art in the ancient universities, had, while acknowledging the limits imposed on him by what he perceived to be his failing energies, hoped to achieve much at Oxford. «I shall», he told William Cowper-Temple in September 1869, «set things, as far as, with the help of the many good men who, I know, are ready to help me there, I can put them in right train, and say as much, in the course, of the year, as any one is likely to remember» (XXXVI.589–90). Always a teacher, he perceived the appointment, announced in 1869, as a welcome opportunity for effecting good in a nationally significant arena. Principally, he believed it gave him the occasion to address directly the upper classes in what seemed to Ruskin the all-important period immediately after the 1867 Second Reform Act, and to urge them to take energetic action to maintain, as best they could, what he saw as their natural – and now imperilled – right to rule. But what the Oxford Ruskin had once found unrewarding as an undergraduate, he found more so as a Professor. He felt irritatingly constrained by the authorities, even, he later claimed, from the day of his Inaugural lecture in February 1870,[15] and became increasingly aware that his students were neither as spirited nor as dutiful as he had hoped. He would lament, indeed, at the end of his final tenure that, though he had announced in the Inaugural lectures plans for his undergraduates, they had not heard him: to not «one word» of those lectures, he would say with frustration and disappointment to the University in December 1884, have «any of you ... practically attended» (XXXIII.536).

It was early in his professorship that Ruskin began to perceive a troubling disparity between this unhappily ineffective labour in the University, and the pressing tasks of social rejuvenation outside it. He had been sceptical about the utility of teaching Art at the University in the heart of the nineteenth century before he began, but he came increasingly certain as his tenure moved on that he could achieve more elsewhere.

Walking to the University galleries to give the last of the «Val d'Arno»-lectures in November 1873, Ruskin saw someone who, he thought, made his anxieties plain. He was, he said later in *Fors*, «hindered for a moment» on his way, «by a nice little girl», whose efforts to play with a whipping top on the pavement were being drastically hindered by her shoes, «a large and dilapidated pair of woman's shoes», he observed, «which projected the full length of her own little foot behind it and before» (XXVIII.14). This impoverished girl, in the heart of the prosperous academic city, lodged in his mind so deeply because she was associated precisely with his gnawing doubts about the professorial role, and his sense that there were more pressing matters to which he should promptly attend. She gave his inner disquiet a distinct and literal focus. «There were some worthy people at my lecture», he continued, relating the event in *Fors* for January 1874:

«and I think the lecture was one of my best. It gave some really trustworthy information about art in Florence six hundred years ago. But all the time I was speaking, I knew nothing spoken about art, either by myself or other people, could be of the least use to anybody there. For their primary business, and mine, was with art in Oxford, now; not with art in Florence, then; and art in Oxford now was absolutely dependent on our power of solving the question – which I knew that my audience would not even allow to be proposed for solution – 'Why have our little girls large shoes?'» (XXVIII.14)

The plight of this vulnerable, nameless girl crystallized for Ruskin the fact that social questions about the conditions of ordinary life, in England, on the streets of her cities now, needed answering more urgently than the academic and historical matters his polite University audience was expecting him to address.

Ruskin's investment in narratives of ordinary life, the championing of a historiography of the «untold», connected as it was with his political engagement with the «suffering life», as he would express it in *The Bible of Amiens*, was also given mo-

14 See O'Gorman 2000, pp. 185–203.
15 In *Fors Clavigera* for June 1874, Ruskin remarked that at the end of his Inaugural lecture, «my University friends came to me, with grave faces, to remonstrate against irrelevant and Utopian topics of that nature being introduced in lectures on art» (XXVIII.92). Birch 1988, pp. [132]–157, discusses some of Ruskin's disillusionment with Oxford in chapter 6 of her *Ruskin's Myths*. Hewison 1976, pp. 179–180, also considers this *Fors* letter as focussing Ruskin's belief that «his [Oxford] duties seemed a hindrance to his social work». The letter provides Harris 1985 with the title for his consideration of the whole of the Guild of St George: *Why have our little girls large shoes? Ruskin and the Guild of St. George*.

mentum by another factor. This distinct pattern in his thought was partly enhanced by a change in Ruskin's material circumstances, a deliberate decision made in the summer of 1871 that was to have consequences not only on his practical life but also on his intellectual purposes, as well as, and by no means irrelevantly, on the constitution of his circle of friends and acquaintances. The implications to Ruskin of life as a Londoner, at Herne Hill and Denmark Hill, were searchingly analysed by Dinah Birch in 1997.[16] Ruskin's critique of England's condition, his perception of her decay through his own lifetime, was sustained by his changing experience of the capital and her fragile environs. But there has been no discussion about the significance of Ruskin's move to the north-west of England, the purchase of what seemed at first the crumbling, «small, old, damp, and smoky-chimneyed» (XXXVI.35) villa Brantwood from the republican W.J. Linton, on the eastern bank of Coniston Water in the Lake District, in the late summer of 1871, and his taking up residence there in 1872.[17] Once restored and expanded, Brantwood was to become Ruskin's home, increasingly and then exclusively his only home, until his death there on 20 January 1900. His relocation from the metropolitan centre, home since childhood, to the Lakes, and his subsequent involvement in the shore side village of Coniston, were matters of consequence, and not only for understanding the shape of Ruskin's important later work, but also for a consideration of his cultural legacy more generally.

Ruskin had been a celebrator of home well before he bought his own. In *Unto this Last*, he had promoted the good home as a model for the national economy;[18] «Of Queen's Gardens» had framed an eloquent tribute to ideal home life and the division of duties between the sexes which secured it. And in the Inaugural lectures at Oxford, Ruskin had been more plainly prescriptive about the necessity of a home, telling his audience that all men, «at some not very advanced period of life ... should desire to have a home, which they do not wish to quit any more, suited to their habits of life, and likely to be more and more suitable to them until their death» (XX.112). Home to him was a moral centre. In a relatively short time after these words, Margaret Ruskin, Ruskin's mother, had died, and thus he was freed from the necessity of staying close to Denmark Hill. In fact, at the time of her death he had already bought the new house for himself. He relished Brantwood immediately as a real home, his first purchase of domestic property for his own use. «Here», he told Charles Eliot Norton excitedly on his first visit, «I have rocks, streams, fresh air, and, for the first time in my life, the rest of the purposed *home*». He had, he added, «no intention of seeking ever again for [another]» (XXXVI.35, italic original).

Ruskin's intellectual and emotional outlay on the idea of home gave the purchase of Brantwood significance. And both as a naturally sociable man and a believer in the primacy of community and mutual responsibility, he was quick to become involved in the networks of Coniston life, and to explore the social possibilities this lakeside community provided. Now without the guiding direction of John James (who had died in 1864) or of Margaret, Ruskin began to form friendships and associations with men and women of a kind new to him, even if, at some level, these had to be negotiated through Joan and Arthur Severn who were particularly watchful of his friendships with single women. There were many friendships, some more substantially recorded than others. The most documented was with Susan Beever (1806–1893), who caused the Severns no anxiety, and Ruskin valued her – they became friends from the autumn of 1873 – especially. Miss Beever, who lived at Thwaite House, diagonally across «the entirely pastoral and pure» (IV.8) Coniston Water from Brantwood, cherished her garden, and this was the subject that first brought them together. Ruskin rowed across the Water to see her regularly (XXXIII.xxii), and she helped him practically by gathering selections from *Modern Painters* that he published as *Frondes Agrestes* in 1875.[19] Ruskin called Susan and her sister, Mary, «at once the sources and loadstones of all good to the village in which they had their home, and to all loving people who cared for the village and its vale and secluded lake, and whatever remained in them or around of the former peace, beauty, and pride of English Shepherd Land» (XXXVII.79). They were associated here (the Preface to their published letters *Hortus Inclusus: Messages from the Wood to the Garden, Sent in Happy Days to the Sister Ladies of the Thwaite, Coniston*, 1887),[20] in a suggestively pan-European model of ideal rural citizenship, with the naturally good men and women of Italy and Switzerland to be commemorated later in *The Story of Ida*, *Ulric the Farm Servant*, and *Christ's Folk in the Apennines*. Susan Beever

16 See Birch 1997, pp. [234]–249.

17 Ruskin was thoughtful about the previous owner of Brantwood, seeing a suggestive link between his work and Ruskin's own. He wrote to Joan Severn on 14 September 1871, two days after his first visit to Brantwood as its new owner, that «There certainly *is* a special fate in getting this house». He continued: «The man from who I buy it ... Linton – wanted to found a 'republic' – Printed a certain number of 'the Republic' – like my Fors Clavigera! ... Well – it won't be a 'republican centre' now – but whether the landed men round will like my Toryism better than his Republicanism, remains to be seen», in: RF, BEM L 36, italic original.

18 See, for instance, where Ruskin describes the employer, merchant, or manufacturer, as invested with «distinctly paternal authority and responsibility» (XVII.41).

19 She is also the «aged friend» remembered in the Preface to the Small Edition of *Sesame and Lilies* (1882), who requested the reissue (XVIII.49).

20 The letters of *Hortus Inclusus* were collected and arranged by Albert Fleming, a Ruskin follower who revived the Langdale Linen Industry in 1883 and later established a similar concern at Keswick. In the *Library Edition*, Cook/Wedderburn 1903–1912, following the first edition of the book, print the *Hortus* Preface with Ruskin's description of Fleming as «my Master of the Rural Industries at Loughrigg» (XXXVII.80). But the ms. of the Preface indicates that this line includes a textual change made by Fleming. Ruskin actually wrote (the emphasis is mine) that «she [Susie Beever] has permitted *her* Master of the rural industries and Loughrigg, Albert Fleming ...». Fleming's change of «her» to «his» implies to the reader that he was actually working as *Ruskin's* «Master»: a rather more ambitious claim. RF, MS 91. *Hortus* was very much a local production, stressing the productivity of rural communities.

lies buried, as testimony to the importance of their friendship, close to Ruskin in Coniston churchyard.

Ruskin, Slade Professor of Fine Art at the University of Oxford, also worked hard for what he called «my Coniston parish school» (XXVI.298). He was often «planning lessons, arranging pictures, and giving treats», said his later biographer and editor E.T. Cook after his death.[21] In *Deucalion*, Ruskin's textbook of geology, he outlined what astronomical knowledge the Coniston children should have (see XXVI.298–299), and wrote them a few pages of «Children's Botany» in the old-fashioned dialogue form he had used for *The Ethics of the Dust* (see XXV.l) as part of his work on *Proserpina*, though these did not make it into the Library Edition.[22] He invented a large globe for the children to climb inside, painted with the constellations. He also formed friendships with some whose political views he did not share; his argument, remembered by W.G. Collingwood in *Ruskin Relics* (1902), with William Bell of Haws Bank (who was the master builder for Ruskin's boat, the «Jumping Jenny»), remains in Coniston lore today. Though in due course good friends (see *Deucalion*, XXVI.309 for a public declaration of this), a dispute with Ruskin behind closed doors, on their first meeting, included Bell's much-quoted declaration «Ye're wrong to rags, Mr Ruskin!»[23]

Ruskin's friendship with Kate Smith, later Kate Raven, his «indoors Stewardess» (XXVIII.531) at Brantwood, as he called her in *Fors Clavigera* in 1876, indicated something else of the new freedom of human relationships he experienced there.[24] He donated a window to the Roman Catholic chapel (he knew Fr. Gibson, the priest), and lectured in 1883 – badly, he said – to the Coniston Mechanics Institute with material that would later be included in *A Knight's Faith* (1885).[25] He was always careful to provide as best he could for local men and women with fewer resources than himself. Hardwicke Drummond Rawnsley, in his personal *Ruskin and the English Lakes* (1901), recalled meeting a Coniston hill worker shortly after Ruskin's death who gave expression to this quality. The shepherd praised the «Professor's» generosity as a Coniston resident. He «was terble humble-minded», Rawnsley remembered him saying, «heddn't a bit o'pride aboot him, I tell ye; he tret poor and rich alike, it wadn't a mattered a pin whedder it was a lord or a sarvin'man, if he could hev' deun owt for ever he wad a deun it».[26] He might have been a Professor, said Rawnsley's companion, but there was no doubt that «ivery shepherd for miles round kenned him an aw».[27]

In *Fors Clavigera* for February 1875, Ruskin gave a public account of an example of the new affiliations he was enjoying at Brantwood, a narrative that usefully compares with the account of the little girl with large shoes in the *Fors* letter thirteen months previously. «Yesterday», Ruskin told his readers informally in the letter 'Agnes' Book', «in the course of my walk, I went into a shepherd-farmer's cottage, to wish whoever might be in the house a happy new year. His wife was at home, of course, and his little daughter, Agnes, nine years old; both as good as gold, in their way» (XXVIII.256). This informal encounter is swiftly assimilated into Ruskin's political discourse. He remarks that the cottage – it belonged to the Stalker family with their eleven children[28] – is «nearly a model of those which I shall expect the tenants of St. George's Company, and its active members, to live in», and that Agnes Stalker[29] is an ideal child for the education programme planned for the Company. Agnes should be taught good, rhythmic verses (especially Herrick's), Ruskin said, obedience to her father and mother's words, «order and cleanliness in her own departments and person; ... gentleness to all inoffensive creatures» (XXVIII.265), and, in a properly regulated national economy, she should be given her own small plot of land to cultivate, and a beehive to tend. In managing her own ground and in making honey, contributing to the sustenance of bodily life, Agnes would have been fulfilling cardinal principles of the Guild.

Agnes Stalker, whom Ruskin translates into the language of Catholic sainthood as the «little Agnes of the hill-side» (XXVIII.264), does not serve in *Fors* to indicate

21 Cook 1912, II.433. Ruskin came to know some of the school children individually quite well. See, for instance, Evans/Whitehouse 1953–1956, p. 1105. Hereafter *D*. See also the letter about schoolgirls being allowed to play on the Brantwood lawns that Ruskin sent to Sydney Cockerell on 3 April 1887 (Meynell 1940), p.29), and the account from *The Girls' Realm* for April 1900 given in Cook 1912, II.372. James S. Dearden adds more about Ruskin's activities at the school, including the dinner for 315 children in the schoolroom, in Dearden/Thorne 1971, pp. 15–16.

22 See also the plans for another (unfinished) textbook, noted in the diary for 29 April 1885, «yesterday at Infant school, very happy and after perfectly sound sleep planned "Grammation" – and am eager to set about it», in: *D*, p. 1107.

23 Collingwood 1903, p. 24. The whole story, with details of Bell, are given on pp. 23–24. The same tale is also given in Dawson 1988, p. 10, along with other local stories about Ruskin at Coniston.

24 For some information about Kate Raven's role in Ruskin's life, especially at a time of crisis, see Hilton 2000, p. 539. I give some of the Ruskin-Kate Raven [Smith] correspondence in my «I am often thinking of you»: Ruskin, Brantwood, and Kate Raven, forthcoming in *Notes and Queries*.

25 «The Battle of Kineyree» was the title of a lecture given to the Mechanics' Institute at Coniston on 22 December 1883. The *Yorkshire Post* had a note about it on Christmas Eve. *A Knight's Faith: Passages in the Life of Sir Herbert Edwardes* grew from this interest in an ideal modern Christian hero. The battle of Kineyree was part of Edwardes's Punjab campaign in the winter of 1848–1849. The Mechanics Institute and Literary Society at Coniston was certainly established by 1852. Nearly half the population of Coniston by that time worked in copper mining, and the Institute was intended to expand educational opportunities for the villagers. See Dearden 1975.

26 Rawnsley 1901, p. 71.

27 Ibid., p. 67. There is more on the specific topic of Ruskin's friends and acquaintances in Coniston in Dearden/Thorne 1971, esp. pp. 17–20.

28 Ruskin helped the Stalker family practically in a number of ways. He employed Isabella, another of the children, at Brantwood, while he employed Hannah, a further daughter, to take over Kate Smith's work when Kate married Thomas Raven, a Coniston tailor. Helen Gill Viljoen notes that the name 'Stalker' appears often in the record of Ruskin's personal expenses (the white 'bankbooks' in the F.J. Sharp Collection in the Pierpont Morgan Library) during the 1885–96 period. Evidently, Ruskin was continuing to support them financially. See Viljoen 1971, p. 608. On the land tenanted by the Stalkers, see Dearden/Thorne 1971, p. 13.

29 Remembrance of her later, and her need for good rhythmic poetry, perhaps prompted Ruskin to republish *Dame Wiggins of Lee and her Seven Wonderful Cats* (1885), which he had initially thought of in connection with her in this *Fors* letter (see XXVIII.261).

the poverty of urban children, or the priority of social action in the city. She is not another little girl with large shoes. But her humble life does show what natural goodness and power is being neglected in England's countryside, even the countryside whose uncontaminated beauty was to Ruskin as great as that of Lago Maggiore.[30] She is a living sign of the carelessness of modern life, which does not make the most of what it has. Invest resources in ordinary, potentially helpful lives like those of little Agnes Stalker, Ruskin was saying, and a step will have been taken towards making England a happier nation, a country, in the words of his Oxford Inaugural, «ordered and wide and fair» (XX.43).

Ruskin's shift of attention towards the historiography of humble life was energized by his new geographical placement from 1872, writing not on the margins of the English countryside but in the midst of it, not in the increasingly prosperous suburbs of south London but in the rural north west. This relocation has not seemed of great consequence to some, especially those who view the productions of the later years that I have discussed here as evidence only of Ruskin's apparently declining powers and his drift towards irrelevance. But that relocation is in fact worth noting. It gave focus to some of Ruskin's creative energy in his later years, helping sustain the direction of his politics, as well as his movement away from the persona of *The Stones of Venice* in the 1870s and 1880s. Ruskin remained a preacher in many ways, and the pulpit served him as a model, including in *Fors Clavigera*, for his public authority.[31] But he became also a writer from home, sustained not by the pulpit but, as it were, by the view of Coniston from his study windows in Brantwood, the friends he had made in the village and in the hills around, and, at a more abstract level, by the patterns of living he came increasingly to see were worthy of praise.

30 Ruskin told Joan Severn this on first seeing Brantwood after he had bought it: «Anything so lovely as the view from my rocks was to day – I haven't seen since I was at Lago Maggiore!», RF, BEM L 36, letter of 13 September 1871. He cherished the association between Coniston Water and the Italian lakes partly because it had been his father's opinion too. The «view of the long reach of the lake, with its softly wooded lateral hills, had for my father», Ruskin remembered affectionately much later in *Praeterita*, «a tender charm which excited the same feeling as that with which he afterwards regarded the lakes of Italy» (XXXV.95).

31 There is some useful consideration of the indebtedness of *Fors* to the sermon in Birch 1999, p. 179.

«Pierced Ornaments from Lisieux, Bayeux, Verona, and Padua», Taf. VII in:
John Ruskin, *The Seven Lamps of Architecture*, London 1849

Jurij Zwetkow

John Ruskin in Russland

John Ruskin galt in Russland als bedeutender Vertreter einer neuen Soziallehre und als wichtiger Literatur- und Kunstkritiker des 19. Jahrhunderts. In seinem umfangreichen Schaffen wurden echtes Interesse für die Antike und für die Natur wie auch scharfe Kritik an den sozialen Widersprüchen der modernen Gesellschaft zusammengeflochten. Seine aufklärerischen und romantischen Ideen, seine besondere Gabe für Essays und sein philosophischer Universalismus fanden in Russland breite Anerkennung. Ruskin hatte bedeutende Anhänger unter den russischen Dichtern des Symbolismus (A. Blok, W. Brjussow, O. Mandelstam) sowie in Lev Tolstoj, der ein Vorwort zu Ruskins Buch *Die Erziehung. Das Buch. Die Frau* schrieb.[1]

John Ruskin übte darüber hinaus Einfluss auf die Kunstprogramme einiger russischen Malerschulen aus. Seine ästhetischen Ideen werden noch am Ende des 20. Jahrhunderts weitererforscht. Die gegenwärtige russische Kunst- und Literaturwissenschaft betrachtet vor allem sein ästhetisches Erbe.

In einem Artikel ist es nicht möglich, über alle Aspekte der Ruskin-Rezeption in Russland ausführlich zu schreiben. Es ist hingegen wichtig, grundsätzliche Richtlinien der russischen Rezeption zu skizzieren, einige Problemkreise zu umreissen und der weiteren Forschung Impulse zu geben.

Die russische Ruskin-Rezeption begann ziemlich spät und erfolgte in der Zeit des sogenannten «silbernen Zeitalters» oder der symbolistischen Epoche der russischen Kulturgeschichte an der Jahrhundertwende. Die Spätentwicklung der Ruskin-Rezeption ermöglichte bereits eine Analyse des Gesamtwerkes Ruskins. Die meisten kritischen Materialien stammen aus dieser Zeit – mehr als 70 mir bekannte Publikationen. Die erste stammt aus dem Jahre 1893 und die letzte ist 1915 datiert. Dann ist eine grosse Lücke festzustellen. Eine neue Welle wissenschaftlicher Auseinandersetzung mit Ruskins Kunsttheorie in Russland beginnt in den 60-er Jahren und entwickelt sich bis heute.

Ruskins Primärwerke waren in Russland in den Jahren 1895–1911 geschlossen übersetzt worden. Das erste Buch hiess *Der König des goldenen Flusses*.[2] Im Jahre

1 Tolstoj/Ruskin 1898, S. 3. Die im Original russischen Titel sind transkribiert und hier und im folgenden in deutscher Übersetzung des Autors angegeben.

2 Russkaja mysl' 1895, Bd. 7, S. 347–354.

1902 publizierte man den ersten Band der zweiteiligen Ausgabe von Ruskins Werken unter dem Titel *Ausgewählte Gedanken John Ruskins*,[3] der zweite Band erschien im Jahre 1912. Eine zehnbändige Ausgabe von Ruskins Werken wurde in den Jahren 1900–1904 verwirklicht.[4] Diese kunsthistorischen Werke sollten die erste Reihe der Übersetzungen darstellen. Aus der geplanten zweiten Reihe der gesellschaftskritischen Schriften erschien nur ein Band im Jahre 1905.[5] Die weiteren Bände durften vermutlich wegen der strengen Zensur in der Zeit der Reaktion nach der ersten russischen Revolution 1905 nicht veröffentlicht werden.

Im Todesjahr des englischen Ästhetikers erschienen drei seiner Ausgaben: *Kunst und Wirklichkeit: Ausgewählte Seiten*,[6] *Der Kranz von Olivenzweigen, Vier Abhandlungen über die ersten Grundsätze der Volkswirtschaft*[7] und *Sesam und Lilien*.[8] Die weiteren Werke wurden am Anfang des 20. Jahrhunderts veröffentlicht: *Florenzspaziergänge*,[9] *Der König des goldenen Flusses* (in der neuen Übersetzung),[10] *Für einen Geburtstag: Gedanken für jeden Tag*,[11] *Dem letzten wie dem ersten*.[12] Zweimal wurde *Vorträge über Kunst* verlegt.[13] Das letzte veröffentlichte Originalwerk Ruskins in russischer Übersetzung ist *Moderne Maler*.[14]

Verschiedene Aspekte der Ruskin-Rezeption vor der Revolution 1917 in Russland sind eng mit seiner Ablehnung der maschinellen Zivilisation, der Verneinung des Viktorianischen Fortschritts und dem intensiven humanistischen Suchen verbunden. Lew Tolstoj schrieb: «Zum ersten Mal in der Geschichte der englischen Ästhetik hob Ruskin deutlich die Unvereinbarkeit der Gemeinheit mit der Welt der echten Kunst hervor. Ruskins Stellung der ästhetischen Probleme und die Analyse der Kunstkategorien sind untrennbar mit seiner sozialen Position verbunden, die sehr kritisch bezüglich der modernen Gesellschaft war».[15]

Sehr hoch schätzte Lew Tolstoj diese Eigenart der Ideen Ruskins ein. Bei Tolstoj fanden auch wichtige Grundzüge von Ruskins Ästhetik Erwähnung: die Poetisierung der schöpferischen manuellen Arbeit eines Handwerkers, das Problem des Volksideals, die Idee der moralischen Kraft der Kunst und auch die Idee einer 'christlichen Kunst'. Lew Tolstoj nannte Ruskin «einen der hervorragendsten Menschen unserer Zeit nicht nur Englands, sondern aller Länder und aller Zeiten. Er ist einer der seltenen Menschen, der mit dem Herzen denkt … und darum das denkt und spricht, was er selbst sieht und fühlt und was alle in der Zukunft denken und sprechen werden. … Die Gedankenkraft und ihr Ausdruck bei Ruskin sind so, daß trotz aller einträchtigen Opposition die er hatte und hat, sein Ruhm sich herauszubilden und die Gedanken ins breite Publikum einzudringen beginnen».[16]

Darum ist das zweite Anliegen dieses Artikels, die Beweggründe zu erklären, warum Ruskins Ideen eine grosse Verbreitung in Russland an der Jahrhundertwende hatten. Die pragmatische Entwicklung der Zivilisation in England, dem industriell mächtigsten europäischen Land in der Mitte des 19. Jahrhunderts, war die Ursache der breiten Entwicklung einer ästhetischen Gegenbewegung, die zu dieser Zeit für Russland nicht der Fall war. Nur an der Jahrhundertwende zeigten sich in Russland die Wesenszüge einer raschen ökonomischen Entwicklung. Darum waren Ruskins Ideen um diese Zeit besonders aktuell. Der englische Denker unternahm einen Versuch, den Ästhetizismus zu sozialisieren und der Schönheit einen gesellschaftlichen Charakter zu verleihen.

Die negativen Züge der russischen sozialen Wirklichkeit, vor allem der Leibeigenschaft bis 1861, führten zu einem deutlichen Protest zuerst von der Seite der bedeutendsten russischen Schriftsteller: Nikolaj Gogol, Ivan Turgenev, Nikolaj Tschernyschevskij, Fjodor Dostojevskij und Lew Tolstoj. Besonders verbreitet waren die Ideen Tschernyschevskijs: «Das Schöne ist das Leben» sowie Dostojevskijs: «Die Schönheit rettet die Welt». Der Ausweg aus der gesellschaftlichen Disharmonie, den Dostojevskij zeigte, stellte eine hohe, aber utopische Idee dar. Die Verbindungen zwischen den Theorien von Ruskin und Dostojevskij als auch von Ruskin und Tschernyschevskij zu untersuchen, ist auch ein interessantes Thema für Ästhetiker und Literaturwissenschaftler.

John Ruskin – wie später William Morris – gab nicht nur theoretisch der Kunst im Leben und in der Gesellschaft eine führende Rolle. Dieser Gedanke sollte, nach Ruskins Meinung, eine wichtige Aufgabe in der Zukunft des ganzen Landes sein. Der Weg Ruskins zur Schönheit und zur menschlichen Harmonie führte über ein neues Verhältnis zur Arbeit, wovon auch Lew Tolstoj schrieb. In den Schriften über Präraffaeliten, Architektur und Kunstgewerbe (besonders in den *Steinen von Venedig*) behauptete Ruskin, dass jede manuelle und schöpferische Arbeit des Menschen zur Entfaltung der Schönheit und der Freude beitragen kann, und der Künstler zu einem Muster für jeden arbeitenden Menschen sein wird.

In den besonderen russischen Verhältnissen des ausgehenden 19. Jahrhunderts waren Ruskins Ansichten aber auch als Soziallehre wichtig. Im Dialog mehrerer Parteien in Russland nahm eine friedliche und harmonisierende Soziallehre vor allem unter den einzelnen Gruppen der Intellektuellen und der russischen Symbolisten ihren Platz ein. Darum konnte man in den russischen Zeitschriften, die vor dem ersten Weltkrieg erschienen waren, die Anerkennung von Ruskins Gesellschaftskritik finden, wovon Artikel wie «Der soziale Ästhetiker»,[17] «John Ruskin und seine Theorie»,[18] «John Ruskin und seine Ideen des Humanis-

3 Ruskin 1902–1912.
4 Ruskin 1900–1904.
5 Ruskin 1905a.
6 Ruskin 1900a.
7 Ruskin 1900b.
8 Ruskin 1900c.
9 Ruskin 1902.
10 Ruskin 1904.
11 Ruskin 1905b.
12 Ruskin 1906b.
13 Ruskin 1900 / 1905.
14 Ruskin 1911.
15 Tolstoj 1928–1958, Bd. 31 (1954), S. 96.
16 Ebd.
17 N.W. 1898, 7, S. 5–28; 8, S. 45–70.
18 Nadeždin 1900, S. 51–53.

mus in der Sphäre der wirtschaftlichen Beziehungen»,[19] und «Soziale Anschauungen John Ruskins»[20] zeugen.

Die russischen Kritiker erklärten die gesellschaftliche Position Ruskins als eine Alternative der historischen Entwicklung. Zugleich erschienen Arbeiten, die den utopischen Charakter von Ruskins Ansichten scharf kritisierten. Die Kritik erfolgte sowohl von der Seite der liberalen Literaten mit Artikeln wie «Idealist des praktischen Jahrhunderts»,[21] «Technische Romantik wie eine Utopie von John Ruskin»,[22] als auch von der Seite der Soziologen mit «Philosoph des schönen Lebens»,[23] «John Ruskin und die politische Ökonomie»,[24] sowie «Die Freude für alle Zeiten und ihr Marktplatz oder die politische Ökonomie der Kunst».[25]

Andere Aufsätze in den russischen Zeitschriften betrafen Ruskins Kunsttheorie und Kunstästhetik, wo er «die Kunst aller Epochen vor den Richterstuhl der Mimesis (zieht)».[26] Man betrachtete Ruskin in Russland als einen grossen Kunsttheoretiker. Die besondere Neigung der russischen Kunst zum Realismus wird historisch begründet. Die bedeutendsten Maler des 19. Jahrhunderts (von Alexej Wenezianov angefangen) entwickelten sich unter der Einwirkung der russischen Religion und Literatur mit ihrem grossen moralischen Pathos. Die siebziger und neunziger Jahre waren die Blütezeit der Tätigkeit der Malerschule «Die Wanderer» mit Wassilij Perov, Nikolaj Kramskoj, Ilja Repin u.a. Die realistische Kunsttheorie in Russland (vertreten von Wladimir Stassov), die die Malerei aus der Enge des akademischen Kanons befreien wollte, hatte die Aufgabe, die Vielfalt der gegenwärtigen sozialen Erscheinungen wahr darzustellen.

Darum hatten Ruskins kunsttheoretische Werke einen grossen Erfolg. Der englische Ästhetiker fordert die Naturwahrheit, die zuallererst Nachahmung des Unnachahmlichen sein sollte. Das bedeutet in seiner Theorie, dass «die oberste Qualität der Natur eine Unendlichkeit (ist), die sich in der großen Zahl und Vielfalt der natürlichen Erscheinungen äußert, in ihren Nuancen und Übergängen, im schnellen Wechsel der Formen und in den Phänomenen der Tiefe».[27] Die Vielfalt, die Fülle und die Tiefe der Wirklichkeitserscheinungen in der Kunstästhetik Ruskins entsprach den Bestrebungen der russischen Malerschule «Die Wanderer», die ähnliche Ziele und Aufgaben hatte. Darum war Ruskin als Kunstkritiker auch hoch geschätzt. Im Artikel von Umanov-Kaplunovskij ist ein interessanter Vergleich der ästhetischen Ansichten von Ruskin und Ilja Repin unternommen.[28] In der Zeitschrift *Der Bote der ausländischen Literatur* erörtert der Kritiker A.L. Pogodin Ruskins Kunstideal.[29] Im *Russischen Boten* erschien der Artikel «John Ruskin und seine Lehre».[30] *Die malerische Rundschau* brachte einen Aufsatz des Titels: «Ruskin über die Kunst».[31]

Mehrere Rezensionen aus der westlichen Presse trugen zu Ruskins Rezeption in Russland bei. Die bekanntesten russischen Zeitschriften der Jahrhundertwende publizierten Übersetzungen aus englischer und deutscher Presse: *Review of Reviews*, *Contemporary review*, *Literary digest*, *Athenäum* und *Zeit*. Im Jahre 1893 waren die *Erinnerungen an Tennyson, Ruskin und Browning* veröffentlicht.[32] Zwei Artikel aus der *Review of Reviews* brachte die Zeitschrift *Der Bote der ausländischen Literatur*: «Ein englischer Kunstkritiker, Moralist und Dichter: John Ruskin» und «John Ruskin: Dichter, Maler und Reformer».[33] Die «Erinnerungen an Ruskin» publizierte die Zeitschrift *Gotteswelt*.[34] Dieselbe Zeitschrift veröffentlichte weitere Aufsätze aus der englischen Presse.[35]

Die meisten Artikel der einheimischen Kritiker erschienen im Todesjahr des englischen Ästhetikers. Über die Bedeutung Ruskins in der Entwicklung der Kunsttheorie und der Gesellschaftskritik schrieben in diesem Jahr die Zeitschriften *Gotteswelt*, *Die Flur*, *Der historische Bote* und *Die neue Zeit*.[36]

Mehrere Monographien ausländischer Autoren wurden in Russland übersetzt: Ch.E. Tourneur, *Das Leben und die Lehre John Ruskins*,[37] J.A. Hobson, *John Ruskin als Sozialreformer*[38] sowie derselbe, *Gesellschaftliche Ideale Ruskins*,[39] Robert de la Sizéranne, *Ruskin und die Schönheitsreligion*,[40] und M. Ol'den-Uard, *John Ruskin als Gesellschaftsreformer*.[41]

Eine Reihe von Ruskins Biographien schrieben russische Kritiker. L.P. Nikiforov veröffentlichte eine biographische Skizze mit dem Titel *John Ruskin: sein Leben, seine Ideen und seine Tätigkeit*.[42] L.A. Bogdanovič publizierte eine Broschüre des Titels *John Ruskin: Religions- und Schönheitsapostel*.[43] G.J. Brjunges widmete sein Buch dem religiösen Thema *Ruskin und die Bibel*.[44] M.F. Bunzen gab die Broschüre *Ruskin, sein Leben und seine Tätigkeit* heraus.[45]

Die prominentesten Literaturkritiker der damaligen Zeit, Sinaida Vengerova und Jurij Ajchenval'd, machten regelmässig russische Leser mit dem literarischen Schaffen ausländischer Schriftsteller bekannt. Sinaida Vengerova, eine aktive Mit-

19 Svjatlovskij 1900, Bd. 2, S. 56–69.
20 Bulgakov 1909, Bd. 100, S. 395–436.
21 Dubinskij 1901, S. 137–147.
22 I.M. 1901, S. 201–203.
23 Kogan 1902, S. 233–241.
24 Rykačev 1903a, 10, S. 91–109; 11, S. 82–97; 12, S. 80–102.
25 Rykačev 1903b, 2, S. 103–106.
26 Kemp 1998, S 679.
27 Ebd.
28 Umanov-Kaplunovskij 1901, 18, S. 567–572.
29 Pogodin 1898, 9, S. 3–22.
30 E.G. 1900a, März 1900, S. 155–173; April 1900, S. 523–529.
31 E.G. 1900b, 1, A. 18–20.
32 Ritchy 1893, 4, S. 235.
33 Vestnik 1898, 3, S. 329–333; Tavener 1898, 5, S. 416–420.
34 Wedgwood 1900, 4, S. 56–57.
35 Mooter 1900, 2, S. 55–58.
36 Mir bozij 1900, 2, S. 54; Niva 1900a, 5, S. 101–102; Istoričeskij vestnik 1900, S. 1205–1207; Novoe vremja 1900, S. 2–3.
37 Tourneur 1898, 7, S. 1–11; 8, S. 118–130; 9, S. 210–217.
38 Hobson 1899a.
39 Hobson 1899b.
40 Sizéranne, 1, S. 62–86; 2, S. 91–115; 3, S. 189–216; 9, S. 164–182; 10, S. 73–96; 11, S. 54–73; 12, S. 177–195.
41 Ol'den-Uard 1900, S. 60–94.
42 Nikiforov 1896.
43 Bogdanovič 1900.
44 Brjunges 1902.
45 Bunzen 1904.

arbeiterin der Zeitschrift *Europas Bote*, veröffentlichte einen auch vom heutigen Standpunkt aus scharfsinnigen Artikel «John Ruskin».[46] Jurij Ajchenval'd erzählte den Lesern über Ruskins Buch *Sesam und Lilien*[47] und in einem anderen Artikel über Ruskins Schaffen im Allgemeinen.[48]

In der Zeitschrift *Gotteswelt* erschienen regelmässig Rezensionen des Kritikers Eugen Degen. Die erste betraf Ruskins Kunstvorstellungen.[49] Die zweite Rezension stellte den Lesern Ruskins Werk *Moderne Maler* vor.[50] Die dritte Rezension war dem Begriff 'Volkskunst' bei Ruskin, Tolstoj und Morris gewidmet.[51] Viele namenlose Ruskin-Rezensionen erschienen am Anfang des zwanzigsten Jahrhunderts in den Zeitschriften *Die Flur*,[52] *Neue Zeitschrift der ausländischen Literatur*,[53] *Russischer Gedanke*,[54] *Monatliche Werke*,[55] *Russischer Reichtum*,[56] *Russische Berichte*,[57] *Historischer Bote*,[58] und *Die junge Saat*.[59]

Die russische Literaturkritik äusserte grosses Interesse an der Persönlichkeit des englischen Kritikers und Schriftstellers. Eine in der damaligen Zeit verbreitete Methode der Literaturwissenschaft bestand in der festen Verbindung des literarischen Werkes mit der Biographie des Autors. Die meisten Artikel erschienen im Todesjahr des Ästhetikers: ein Artikel von A. Gurevič,[60] Materialien aus dem Briefwechsel Ruskins mit Dante Gabriel Rossetti,[61] eine Biographie[62] und eine Skizze seines Lebens.[63]

Die zweite Etappe der Ruskin-Rezeption in Russland beginnt in den sechziger Jahren des 20. Jahrhunderts. In der Zeit zwischen den beiden Weltkriegen fand Ruskins Werk in der Sowjetunion keine wissenschaftliche Erwähnung. Der erste Weltkrieg, die Revolution und der Bürgerkrieg in Russland lenkten die Bestrebungen der sowjetischen Philosophie, Ästhetik, Literatur- und Kunstwissenschaft in die Richtung des normativen 'sozialistischen Realismus'. Erst ab den sechziger Jahren ist eine Intensivierung der Beschäftigung mit Ruskins Werk an den Universitäten der Sowjetunion festzustellen. Der erste wissenschaftliche Artikel war dem Ideengut von William Morris und John Ruskin gewidmet (Universität Riga).[64] Mit dem literarischen Märchen Englands im 19. Jahrhundert beschäftigte sich eine Wissenschaftlerin aus Moskau.[65] Die literarischen Beziehungen Ruskins und J. Galsworthys ist das Thema einer wissenschaftlichen Arbeit an der Universität Gorkij (zur Zeit Nishnij Novgorod).[66] In der bis jetzt ersten philologischen Dissertation über Ruskin wird seine Literatur- und Kunstkritik analysiert.[67]

In der neugegründeten Zeitschrift *Referatives Journal* (*RŽ*) werden die neuesten Forschungsergebnisse der ausländischen Wissenschaftler referiert: Elizabeth K. Helsingers *Ruskin and the art of the beholder*, Cambridge MA 1982,[68] *The poison sky: Mith and apocalypse in Ruskin* von R.E. Fitch, Athen/London 1982,[69] F. Kirckhoff, *John Ruskin*, Boston 1984, *John Ruskin. The critical heritage*, London 1984,[70] T. Hilton, *John Ruskin: The early years*, New Haven/London 1985,[71] und

M. Hardman, *Ruskin and Bradford: An experiment in Victorian cultural history*, Manchester 1986.[72]

Die grösste russische Ruskin-Monographie der letzten Zeit wurde von Gennadij Anikin, Professor der Moskauer Pädagogischen Universität geschrieben.[73] Sein umfangreiches Buch heisst *John Ruskins Ästhetik und die englische Literatur des XIX. Jahrhunderts* und richtet sich an Literatur- und Kunstwissenschaftler, Philosophen und Ästhetiker. In diesem Forschungswerk werden Grundideen von Ruskins Schaffens erörtert. Die Haupttendenzen der Ästhetik, Literatur und Kunst werden von modernem Standpunkt aus betrachtet. Die ausführliche philosophisch-ästhetische Grundlage der Forschung gab neue Impulse für ein Begreifen der wichtigsten Aspekte der literarischen Entwicklung. Das ist die Dialektik des Übergangs von der Romantik zum Realismus, der Verbindung des realistischen Schaffens mit den kulturologischen und soziologischen Ideen, der Wechselwirkung der Literatur und Malerei. Das Buch von G. Anikin hat folgende Kapitel: «Romantikkonzeption», «Fantasie und Einbildungskraft», «Pathetische Illusion», «Landschaft in der Literatur», «Poesie als Malerei», «Moralisches Ideal: Von W. Scotts Schaffen», «Ruskin und Carlyle», «Sozialpolitische Publizistik Ruskins und Probleme des kritischen Realismus», «Ruskin und die Präraffaeliten», «Ruskin und Morris». Der Autor des Buches dachte an eine Fortsetzung mit dem Titel *Ruskin in Russland*, starb aber im Jahre 1982. Anikin machte einen wichtigen Schritt, damit sein Vorhaben von den anderen Wissenschaftlern verwirklicht werden kann: «In der Möglichkeit dieser Bewegung ist der Sinn der ganzen Arbeit des Forschers», steht im Vorwort seines Buches geschrieben.[74]

46 Vengerova 1900, S. 674–692.
47 Ajchenval'd 1901, 6, S. 37–46.
48 Ajchenval'd 1910, Bd. 2, S. 17–30.
49 Degen 1901a, 2, S. 84–87.
50 Degen 1901b, 9, S. 82–87.
51 Degen 1904, 3, S. 1–28; 4, S. 183–208.
52 Niva 1900b, 2, S. 426.
53 Novyj žurnal 1901, 10, S. 147–148.
54 Russkaja mysl' 1895, 7, S. 347–354; Russkaja mysl' 1901, 7, S. 210; Russkaja mysl' 1905, 3, S. 104.
55 Ježemesjačnye sočinenija 1901, 10, S. 175.
56 Russkoe bogatstvo 1901a, 9, S. 45–50; Russkoe bogatstvo 1901b, 3, S. 17–19.
57 Russkie vedomosti 1902.
58 Istoričeskij vestnik 1902, S. 1145.
59 Vschody 1902, 9, o. S.
60 Gurewič 1900, Bd. 4, S. 347–362.
61 Novyj žurnal 1900a, 5, S. 199–203.
62 Novyj žurnal 1900b, S. 330–335.
63 Kopročewskij 1900, 3, S. 330–341; 4, S. 460–475.
64 Polis 1966, S. 105–135.
65 Demurova 1975, S. 90–167.
66 Rybakova 1976, S. 60–72.
67 Šustova 1981.
68 Novikov 1984, S. 105–109.
69 Parchomenko 1984, S. 105–107.
70 Krasavčenko 1986, S. 108–113.
71 Novikov 1987, S. 94–97.
72 Spicyna 1987, S. 101–103.
73 Anikin 1986.
74 N.P. Michal'skaja in: Anikin 1986, S. 4 (Vorwort).

Die letzten Ruskin-Veröffentlichungen in Russland untersuchen neue Aspekte seiner umfangreichen Tätigkeit. T. Selitrina (Universität Ufa) beschäftigt sich mit den typologischen Ähnlichkeiten der ästhetischen Ansichten von L. Tolstoj und J. Ruskin.[75] A. Taganov (Universität Iwanowo) erforscht die Rolle Ruskins in der Ausbildung von Marcel Prousts Ästhetik.[76] N. Tišunina (Universität Ekaterinburg) schreibt über die Transformation romantischer Ideen in den ästhetischen Anschauungen Ruskins und der Präraffaeliten.[77] E. Bel'kind (Universität Sankt-Petersburg) untersucht die Aufnahme von Ruskins Ideen durch den russischen symbolistischen Dichter Alexander Blok.[78] Und in der Kunstwissenschaft erschien ein interessanter Artikel von T. Savarenskaja über Venedig nach der Auffassung John Ruskins.[79]

Für die gegenwärtige russische Kritik stellt Ruskin einen der bedeutendsten Literatur- und Kunstästhetiker dar. Er übte einen grossen Einfluss auf die Gesamtentwicklung der russischen Kultur aus. Die Geschichte des 20. Jahrhunderts zeigte allerdings entgegengesetzte und tragische Tendenzen im Vergleich zu Ruskins Soziallehre. Der Utopismus seiner gesellschaftlich-wirtschaftlichen Ideenwelt war deutlich. Heute interessiert man sich in Russland vorrangig für Ruskins Kunst- und Literaturtheorie, was noch weiterer und ausführlicher Forschung bedarf. Die neue Kultursituation in Russland nach der Wende gibt dafür neue Perspektiven.

75 Selitrina 1988, S. 61–72.
76 Taganov 1989, Bd. 3, S. 125–139.
77 Tišunina 1990, S. 77–87.
78 Bel'kind 1991, S. 101–124.
79 Savarenskaja 1988, S. 279–287.

«Intersectional Mouldings», Taf. IV in:
John Ruskin, *The Seven Lamps of Architecture*, London 1849

Laurent Stalder

John Ruskin als Erzieher: Muthesius, England und die neue «nationale Tradition»

«Von Morris bis Gropius» – damit war bereits 1936 der historische Werdegang der modernen Architektur vom englischen Vorbild bis zu ihrem deutschen Höhepunkt festgelegt, ihre Endpunkte personifiziert: Morris habe die Grundlagen für den neuen Stil geschaffen, Gropius seinen Charakter begründet, der erste habe das Kunsthandwerk wieder belebt, der zweite seine Synthese mit der Maschinenkunst sowohl in der Theorie als auch in der Praxis endgültig geschaffen.[1] Der Kreis schliesse sich zu einer historischen Einheit, wie Nikolaus Pevsner am Ende des Einführungskapitels seiner *Pioneers of the modern movement* abschliessend bemerkt hatte, die vom englischen Vorbild zur deutschen Moderne, vom Kunsthandwerk zur Industriebaukunst führte. Innerhalb dieser teleologischen Entwicklung musste John Ruskin zwangsläufig den Nebenplatz eines Vordenkers einnehmen.[2]

Doch Walter Gropius selbst hatte bereits 1923 in einem Einführungstext zum Bauhaus, auf den Pevsner seine Thesen stützte, diesen Kurzschluss wenn nicht ganz ausgeschlossen, so doch in dieser Unmittelbarkeit vermieden. Neben Morris hatte er auch Ruskin zu den ersten Reformern Englands gezählt, beide aber gleichberechtigt neben van de Velde in Belgien, Olbrich, Behrens und den Mitgliedern des Werkbunds in Deutschland gereiht.[3] John Ruskin war nicht nur auf die gleiche Stufe wie William Morris gestellt, sondern neben den englischen Quellen ein eigenständiger, gleichberechtigter, deutscher Weg beansprucht worden, dessen Wurzeln fest im Werkbund und im Gedankengut seiner Vertreter verankert waren.

Tatsächlich war die Rolle John Ruskins in Deutschland während der Lehrjahre Gropius' viel umfangreicher als nur die eines Vorläufers. Kurz nach seinem Tod im Jahr 1900 erreichte seine Rezeption, wie auch die von Morris, mit der Publikation zahlreicher Einzelschriften, der systematischen Übersetzung ausgewählter Werke, die bei Diederichs, dem späteren Verleger der Werkbundjahrbücher erschienen, sowie der Herausgabe von nicht weniger als sechs Darstellungen in deutscher Sprache zwischen 1901 bis 1903 einen einzigartigen und umfangreichen Höhepunkt.[4] Doch so populär der Enthusiasmus für Ruskin in Deutschland war, so

1 Pevsner 1936, S. 41–42.
2 Ebd., S. 22.
3 Gropius 1923, S. 8.
4 Vgl. Muthesius 1974, Fussnote 634, S. 227. Vor 1895 waren lediglich zwei Aufsätze, beide 1861, übersetzt worden. – Die bei Stefan Muthesius erwähnten Darstellungen müssen um folgende Beiträge ergänzt werden: Clemen 1900; Steffen 1902; Weichelt 1902.

wurde von Anfang an dem Einfluss seiner Reformen klare Grenzen gesetzt. So hatte Fritz Schumacher am Ende eines begeisterten Textes zu Ruskin vor einer Übertragung «schöner fremder Gewächse auf unseren unvorbereiteten Boden» gewarnt und bereits dort «eher über ein Zuviel als Zuwenig Ruskin» geklagt,[5] Lichtwark an unterschiedlicher Stelle immer wieder den Rückgriff auf eine eigene lokale Tradition empfohlen und van de Velde in seinem Aufsatz «Die englische und die festländische Renaissance im Kunstgewerbe» von 1901 auf die kulturellen Unterschiede zwischen den beiden Bewegungen verwiesen. Auch Hermann Muthesius, von Pevsner als «Bindeglied» zwischen der englischen Bewegung und Deutschland bezeichnet, hatte 1902 in *Stilarchitektur und Baukunst* die Schriften Ruskins zwar für England als «Triebfeder für eine echte volkstümliche Kunst» lobend hervorgehoben, den Beginn der Reformen in Deutschland hingegen auf den Einfluss des «genialen Lehrers Karl Schäfer» zurückgeführt.[6] Keiner war zu solchem Urteil besser berufen als Muthesius, der zugleich begeisterter aber auch kritischer Schäfer-Schüler und unbestrittenermassen der beste Kenner der englischen Architektur und des englischen Kunstgewerbes seiner Zeit war.

Diese ambivalente Haltung prägte ebenfalls den Nachruf auf John Ruskin, den Muthesius im *Centralblatt der Bauverwaltung* kurz nach dessen Tod im Januar 1900 verfasst hatte. Ruskins Verdienste für England waren unbestritten: England verdanke ihm den künstlerischen Aufschwung in der zweiten Hälfte des Jahrhunderts und seine Schriften hätten «ein ganzes Volk für das Schöne, Wahre und Gute» bekehrt. Schwieriger war hingegen die Umschreibung seiner Bedeutung: Der Erfolg Ruskins sei in England mit den politischen Leistungen Bismarcks, der Einfluss seiner Schriften mit denen Winckelmanns und «zum spärlichen Vergleich» mit Julius Langbehns *Rembrandt als Erzieher* zu vergleichen.[7] So scheinbar beliebig in ihrer Auswahl, so präzise waren Muthesius' Vergleiche in ihrer Aussage. Als den «Einiger Deutschlands»[8] hatte er Bismarck an anderer Stelle gelobt und die neue politische Ordnung als seine Leistung gefeiert. Die Überzeugungskraft der Schriften Winckelmanns hatte er immerhin für den «Bankrott» der heimischen Architektur nach 1800 und für den Beginn des so verhassten Historismus verantwortlich gemacht.[9]

Doch viel allgemeiner entsprach die Würdigung Ruskins im Vokabular, in der Hervorhebung der Widerspüche sowie der Betonung seines gesamtheitlichen Anspruchs, der Beurteilung Langbehns, wie sie Muthesius in seiner Werkbundrede 1911 unter dem Titel «Wo stehen wir?» vorgenommen hatte. Mit dem «Rembrandt-Deutschen» hatte er ebenfalls den Beginn einer neuen Epoche, «jener Jahre des Gärens und Aufwallens, die zwischen 1890 und 1895 liegen»[10] in Verbindung gebracht, und vor allem seinem Verdienst zugeschrieben, «die Wichtigkeit der künstlerischen im Gegensatz zu der wissenschaftlichen Kultur ins Gedächtnis» gerufen zu haben.[11] Und was Langbehn, der hier stellvertretend für die gesamte

Reform stand, in Deutschland in den letzten Jahren des neunzehnten Jahrhunderts bewirkt hatte, das hatte Ruskin dreissig Jahre zuvor in England getan.[12] Genauso wie Muthesius 1911 feststellen konnte, dass «die Ideen, die der Rembrandt-Deutsche, damals als ein Prediger in der Wüste, vortrug, einen Siegeslauf zurückgelegt haben», genauso konnte Ruskin im Nachruf von 1900 als «künstlerischer Apostel» für den Aufschwung in England verantwortlich gemacht werden.[13]

Obwohl bei Ruskin eher der soziale, bei Langbehn der nationale Charakter im Vordergrund stand, strebten sie beide in gleicher Weise mit der Reform der Kunst zugleich die des «gesamten Lebens» an, die es durch erzieherische Massnahmen zu fördern galt. Hatte Ruskin diese Aufgabe durch seine unersättliche schriftstellerische Tätigkeit und die grosse Anzahl seiner Vorträge erfüllt, war dieses erzieherische Programm schon im Titel der Schrift Langbehns vorweggenommen. Die Aufgabe war in ihrem ganzheitlichen Anspruch politisch. Auch der deutsche Kaiser hatte sie wahrgenommen, als er mit Muthesius einen Architekten zum technischen Attaché an die deutsche Botschaft nach London geschickt hatte, der in seinen zahlreichen Schriften genauso erzieherisch die allgemeine Aufmerksamkeit auf das Vorbildliche der englischen Kunst und Architektur lenken sollte. Diesem Anspruch entsprach ebenfalls die Berufung Muthesius' durch Handelsminister Möller 1903 zum Leiter des Dezernats für technisches Schul- und Unterrichtswesen, damit es «nicht wie bisher nur von Juristen» geführt werde.[14] Und diesem Ziel sollte sich schliesslich auch der Werkbund, dem Muthesius als zweiter Vorsitzender angehörte, verpflichten und in seinen Statuten neben der «Veredelung der gewerblichen Arbeit im Zusammenwirken von Kunst, Industrie und Handwerk» auch die Notwendigkeit erzieherischer und sogar propagandistischer Massnahmen festschreiben.[15] Die Forderung nach «Synthese»,[16] die sich im Programm des Werkbundes fand und die auch Langbehn gestellt hatte, schien Ruskin in seiner Person bestens zu erfüllen. Nicht zufällig hatte Muthesius im Nachruf dessen Ausbildung zwischen «Bibel und Naturstudium», sowie seinen Werdegang – gleichsam als Personifizierung der Reformbewegung – von der Wissenschaft weg zur Kunst hin hervorgehoben.[17]

5 Schumacher 1902, S. 116ff. Bei Heitz, dem Verleger dieser Aufsatzsammlung, waren die ersten Übersetzungen Ruskins ab 1895 erschienen.
6 Muthesius 1902, S. 33.
7 Muthesius 1900a, S. 43. Der vollständige Nachruf findet sich im Anhang.
8 Dessoir/Muthesius 1912, S. III.
9 Muthesius 1898, S. 446.
10 Muthesius 1912, S. 14.
11 Gurlitts Vorurteile scheinen sich auch hier zu bestätigen: «Aber es ist das erste Buch seit Jahrzehnten, das von Künstlern wirklich gelesen wurde. Vielleicht nicht bis zur letzten Seite, aber sicher bis zur dritten: bis zum Absatze: Individualismus.» (Gurlitt 1899, S. 495). Zur Bedeutung von Langbehn (und für weiterführende Literatur) vgl. Oechslin 1999, S. 116ff.
12 Muthesius 1900, S. 11.
13 Muthesius 1900a, S. 43.
14 *Berliner Börsenkurier*, Nr. 26, 16. 1. 1903, o. S.
15 Muthesius 1912, § 2 (o. S.).
16 Langbehn 1890, S. 2.
17 Muthesius 1900a, S. 43.

Der missionarische Eifer konnte vorerst über die zahlreichen Differenzen hinwegtäuschen. Doch das Verhältnis zu Ruskin war in mehrfacher Hinsicht zwiespältig. Einerseits nahm er in den Schriften Muthesius' über England immer eine zentrale Rolle ein, andererseits erschien seine Bedeutung für den Kontinent und somit sein Vorbildcharakter problematisch. So wurde er in *Das Englische Haus* – Muthesius' wichtigster historischer Darstellung über englische Architektur, als «Prophet einer neuen künstlerischen Kultur» in England gewürdigt, seine Bedeutung für Deutschland aber zugleich – im historischen Blick, wie Muthesius betonte – auf die eines «sonderbaren Denkers»[18] eingeschränkt.[19] Nicht nur würde die Sprache bei der Übersetzung «ihres besten Theiles beraubt», auch stecke im Deutschen «zu viel wissenschaftlicher Geist, zu viel Denkklarheit, um gewagte, nur von stilistischer Meisterschaft gestützte Gedankengänge hinnehmen zu können»,[20] wie Muthesius bereits im Nachruf bemerkt hatte. Auch wenn die kulturellen Eigenheiten und Unterschiede zwischen England und Deutschland in diesen zu nationaler Bedeutung emporstilisierten Reformbemühungen eine zentrale Rolle spielten, schien der Vorwurf mangelnder Wissenschaftlichkeit etwas hoch gegriffen und in seiner Wertung von Chauvinismus geprägt, lag doch der Erfolg von Langbehns Schrift kaum in dieser Eigenschaft. Muthesius selbst hatte die Publikation als «krauses Buch» abgetan.

Der Vorwurf an Ruskin war noch ein anderer. England verdanke ihm zwar für seine Leistung Unendliches, dank der Verbreitung seiner Schriften die Bildung eines «modernen englischen Stils»,[21] doch gleichzeitig habe sein Einfluss innerhalb der gotischen Bewegung dazu geführt, dass man sich vom «Vaterländischen» abgewendet habe.[22] Tatsächlich hatte Ruskin mit seinen Untersuchungen zur venezianischen Gotik und seiner Vorliebe für diesen architektonischen Stil[23] in diesem präzisen Fall die nationale Frage ausgeklammert. Die daraus abgeleiteten Erkenntnisse hatten dazu geführt, wie Muthesius durchaus scharfsinnig erkannt hatte, dass das Interesse von Ruskin wie auch dasjenige von Morris[24] «mit der Gothik, und zwar in künstlerischer wie socialer Beziehung»[25] enden würde. Damit schienen die Grenzen der Bedeutung und des Einflusses des englischen Reformers abgesteckt. Tatsächlich war Muthesius' Bekenntnis zur Maschine kaum mit Ruskins Forderung nach ausschliesslicher Handwerksarbeit vereinbar. Auch war dessen Definition von Architektur – als ein «Zusatz» zum reinen Bauen[26] – nicht nur begrifflich, sondern auch inhaltlich zu Muthesius' Unterscheidung von Stilarchitektur und Baukunst im gleichnamigen Aufsatz diametral entgegengesetzt.

Trotz dieser scheinbar einschränkenden Kritikpunkte war der Verdienst, den Ruskin in *Das englische Haus* zugesprochen bekam und der als Herbeiführung einer «inneren Sammlung» präzisiert worden war, nicht zu unterschätzen. Schon der Platz, den er innerhalb der historischen Argumentation der Schrift einnahm, wies darauf hin, dass seine Leistung mehr als nur eine idealistische Reaktion auf den fortschreitenden «Industrialismus» – eine bezeichnende Wortschöpfung! – und die «Jagd nach Geld» gewesen war. Vielmehr schloss Ruskin einen Zeitraum ab, den Muthesius im vorhergehenden Kapitel als den des «Kampfes zwischen Klassizismus und Romantizismus» bezeichnet hatte. Und dieser Kampf war nicht nur derjenige zwischen Wissenschaft und Kunst, Industrie und Kunstgewerbe, der an der Werkbundtagung 1911 diskutiert worden war. Es war viel allgemeiner auch derjenige zwischen «romanischen Kunstidealen» und «germanischen Gefühlskräften»,[27] zwischen formaler Architektur, die sich durch «stattliche, theatermässige äussere Wirkung» hervortat und «gewachsenem bodenständigen Organismus».[28] Diese «Sammlung» bedeutete somit nicht nur Abschluss und Neubeginn. Dem

18 Muthesius 1908, S. 96.

19 Wenn Muthesius in der Geschichtsschreibung von «Morris bis Gropius» überhaupt erwähnt wird, dann meistens – auch in den jüngsten Publikationen – nur als «Bindeglied» (Pevsner) zwischen den englischen Reformern, Ruskin und Morris, und den Vertretern der Avantgarde in Deutschland – meistens reduziert auf Gropius und die frühe Phase des Bauhauses. Brooks 1987, S. 332, erwähnt Muthesius nur als Bindeglied zwischen Ruskin und dem Werkbund. Swenarton 1989, S. 195–196, hebt zwar die Bedeutung Muthesius' für die Ruskinrezeption in Deutschland hervor, doch auch hier wird Muthesius auf seine Aussagen im Werkbundstreit reduziert, in dem er tatsächlich im Vergleich zu van de Velde eine gegenüber Ruskin feindliche Position einzunehmen scheint. Auch hier wird eine direkte Linie – über Muthesius hinweg – von Ruskin direkt zur Bauhausgründung bevorzugt. Whiteley 1992, S. 179ff., stellt in seinem Aufsatz Swenartons Kritik an Pevsner, der Ruskin nicht gebührend als «pioneer» gewürdigt hätte, wieder in Frage. Doch auch er hält die Linie Morris (bzw. Ruskin)–Gropius aufrecht. Der Einfluss Ruskins auf die sozialen Forderungen der «Moderne» wird dort durch die «ethischen» (z.B. bei Le Corbusier) ergänzt. Bei Hubrich 1981 sind weder Ruskin noch Morris in der Literatur erwähnt. Der Einfluss der englischen Schriften ist in dieser Arbeit unverständlicherweise stark vernachlässigt. Auch Roth 2001 bringt keine neuen Erkenntnisse. In einem ausführlichen, nur kurz kommentierten Zitat (ebd., S. 44–45) versucht er die Unterschiede zwischen dem Stilbegriff Muthesius' und Ruskins aufzuzeigen. Eine gewichtige Ausnahme bildet die äusserst differenzierte Darstellung über die vielfältigen kulturellen deutsch-englischen Beziehungen von Stefan Muthesius 1974.

20 Muthesius 1900a, S. 44.

21 Muthesius 1902, S. 33.

22 Muthesius 1908, S. 90.

23 Vgl. «The lamp of obedience», in Ruskin 1849, in Cook/Wedderburn 1903–1912, VIII, S. 258–259. Neben der venezianischen Gotik nennt Ruskin das Pisanisch-romanische, das Frühgotische der westlichen italienischen Republiken sowie die früheste englische verzierte Gotik als mögliche Stile.

24 Für Muthesius scheint die Bedeutung von William Morris (1834–1896) in der Praxis, in der Umsetzung der Kunstideale von Ruskin zu liegen. Zum Verhältnis Ruskin–Morris vgl. Muthesius 1908, I, S. 97: «William Morris schlug den bedeutsamen Weg ein, die von Ruskin gepredigten Ideale im Handwerk praktisch zu versuchen». In ähnlichem Wortlaut in: Muthesius 1900, S. 12. Auch in Muthesius 1902, S. 33, wird Ruskin – auch wenn weniger deutlich – als der geistige Urheber betrachtet: «Der Vater dieser neuen Kunstausrichtung [was wir als den modernen englischen Stil zu bezeichnen gelernt haben] war William Morris, ihr Mittelpunkt die Ausstattung des englischen Hauses, ihr Leitsatz gesunde Handwerklichkeit, Vernünftigkeit und Aufrichtigkeit und ihre Triebfeder eine echte volkstümliche Begeisterung für die Kunst, die namentlich durch die weitverbreiteten Schriften Ruskins angefacht worden war. Vgl. Muthesius 1974, S. 119.

25 Muthesius 1901, S. 219. Damit war aber auch schon der Konflikt anlässlich der Werkbundtagung in Köln vorweggenommen. Vgl. van de Velde 1955, S. 71. Van de Velde hatte dort gerade das Gegenteil als erstrebenswert dargestellt: «Die Ruskins Buch 'Steine von Venedig' entnommenen Kapitel, die Morris selbst unter dem Titel 'Gotische Kunst' herausgab, sind eine würdige Beschreibung der Bedingungen, welche die Kunst und die Kunsthandwerker besitzen müssen, um solche vollendete Ausdruckskraft zu erreichen. Sie sind eine Paraphrase seiner eigenen Definition der Kunst: 'Die Kunst ist der Ausdruck der Freude, die der Künstler bei seiner Arbeit empfindet'».

26 «The Lamp of sacrifice», in Ruskin 1849, S. 28–29. «But if to the stone facing of that bastion be added an unnecessary feature, as a cable moulding, that is architecture.»

27 Muthesius 1908, I, S. 76.

28 Ebd., S. 55. Die Gegensatzpaare waren noch zahlreicher: «Etiquette, Katholizismus, formale Schönheitsziele; Absolutismus, leichtsinnige Moral und skeptische Spottsucht» versus «alte englische Bürgertugenden», «biedere Lebensauffassung der elisabethinischen Zeit», «Überträger» versus «Erzeuger», «Stuart» versus «Tudor», etc.

Kampf folgte *Die Entwicklung des modernen englischen Hauses*, dem Fortschrittsgedanken entsprach eine Rückbesinnung, ihr Urheber in England war John Ruskin. Obwohl ihm in der Stilfrage mangelnder Nationalsinn vorgeworfen worden war, konnte seine Bedeutung in der Argumentation von *Das englische Haus* gerade auf die Berücksichtigung einer eigenen kulturellen Tradition zurückgeführt werden. Diesen zentralen Platz, der Langbehn innerhalb der deutschen Entwicklung zugesprochen worden war, hatte Ruskin und allgemeiner die Zeit um 1860 im Aufbau von *Das englische Haus* inne. Doch im Gegensatz zu Langbehn war Ruskin ein ernst zu nehmender Kunstliterat.

In der ausführlichen Besprechung von Wilhelm Schoelermanns Übersetzung von *Die sieben Leuchter der Baukunst* hatte Muthesius mit Nachdruck die Behandlung des «Wesens des Hausbaues»[29] im sechsten Leuchter, «The Lamp of Memory», gelobt. Ruskin war dort explizit auf die Frage nach einer «nationalen» Architektur eingegangen und hatte zwei Bedingungen an sie gestellt: «The first to render the architecture of the day, historical; and the second, to preserve, as the most precious of inheritances, that of past ages».[30] Diese Würdigung einheimischer Architektur war nicht nur eine Bekenntnis an den Schutz und die Pflege alter Bauten, wie sie später durch Morris' «Gesellschaft zum Schutz alter Baudenkmäler» konsequent verfolgt werden sollte.[31] Vielmehr hatte Ruskin damit die historische Dimension der Architektur – neben der Sprache – als Erinnerungsträger unterstrichen und diese Aufgabe den Architekten als Pflicht auferlegt. Die Tradition[32] war nicht nur eine Verpflichtung gegenüber der Vergangenheit, sondern gleichzeitig eine gegenüber der Zukunft. Bemerkenswerterweise hatte Ruskin diese doppelte Aufgabe, «one of those moral duties»,[33] nicht nur an die öffentlichen Bauten delegiert, sondern zuerst für «bürgerliche Bauwerke» verlangt.[34] Diese müssten – wie er in «The Lamp of obedience» forderte – «nationalen Gesetzen» folgen, um die Verkörperung von «Polity, Life, History, and Religious Faith of nations»,[35] also Ausdruck der Eigenheiten unterschiedlicher Kulturen zu sein. Diese Erkenntnis entsprach durchaus derjenigen von Muthesius, hatte er doch *Das Englische Haus* unter diesem ganzheitlichen Anspruch untersucht und seine Mustergültigkeit in dessen «national-englischen» Charakter gesehen.[36]

Die Forderung nach einer nationalen Baukunst war nicht eine abgrenzende, sondern die Antwort auf unterschiedliche kulturelle Bedürfnisse, die im zweiten Band von *Das Englische Haus* in einer fassbaren pragmatischen Form unter «örtliche Bedingungen» – geographische, soziale, grundrechtliche und baugesetzliche – behandelt worden waren. Der Feststellung Ruskins «the form of architecture already known are good enough for us, and for far better than any of us»[37] hatte Muthesius spätestens 1911 beigepflichtet, als er auf die Verdienste des Heimatschutzes hinweisend seinen Vorbehalten gegenüber einem «Individualismus der Nichtindividuellen» das Typische gegenübergestellt und auch dort wieder auf das englische

Vorbild verwiesen hatte.[38] Nicht anders als bei Ruskin war hier die Einbindung des Einzelnen in eine bestehende Tradition und seine Umgebung gefordert worden: «The forms of architecture already known are good enough for us, and for far better than any of us; and it will be time enough to think of changing them for better when we can use them as they are». Nachdem Ruskin die historische Dimension des Typus unterstrichen und legitimiert hatte, konnte er abschliessend festhalten: «We want no new style of architecture ... But we want some style»[39] und hatte damit die Forderung Muthesius' im Werkbundstreit nach «überzeugendem Stilausdruck», als Resultat einer sich auf ihre Tradition besinnenden und als deutsch bezeichneten Bewegung um 75 Jahre vorweggenommen.[40] Mit der Frage der Dauerhaftigkeit verbunden war die Frage nach der Qualität, die bereits im zweiten Kapitel «The Lamp of Truth» in der «moralischen» Forderung nach Ehrlichkeit gestellt worden war: Wahrhaftigkeit in Konstruktion und Material sowie Verzicht auf Maschinenornament.[41] Dies waren auch die Ziele, welche die Werkbundmitglieder als Qualitätsarbeit übereinstimmend gefordert hatten.[42] Das waren aber auch die wenigen Merkmale, auf welche in der modernen Geschichtsschreibung der Einfluss Morris reduziert werden sollte.

Die Typisisierung war keineswegs nur eine Frage der Wirtschaftlichkeit, wie sie Muthesius immer wieder aufgrund seiner Werkbundthesen von 1914 bis heute noch vorgeworfen wird.[43] Gerade in seinem Vortrag «Wo stehen wir?» hatte er gleichzeitig mit dem Einstehen für den Typus als Norm architektonischen Schaffens, die Notwendigkeit unterstrichen, «der Form wieder zu ihrem Rechte zu verhelfen»[44] und ihre Voraussetzung in der lokalen Bauweise geortet. Tatsächlich war

29 Muthesius 1901, S. 220. «Welche herrlichen Worte enthält beispielweise das sechste Kapitel über häusliche Baukunst und das Wesen des Hausbaues im allgemeinen.»
30 «The Lamp of memory», in Ruskin 1849, S. 225.
31 Auch hier unterstreicht Muthesius die Vorarbeit von Ruskin: vgl. «Die 'Wiederherstellung' unserer alten Bauten», in Muthesius 1909, S. 146.
32 Zum Begriff der Tradition bei Ruskin vgl. Wheeler 1992, «Introduction», S. 1ff. Wheeler unterscheidet zwischen «the term 'tradition'», den Ruskin selber selten verwendet und «the concept of tradition».
33 «The Lamp of memory», in Ruskin 1849, S. 227.
34 Schoelermann verwendet in seiner Übersetzung von 1900 für «domestic buildings» den Begriff «bürgerlich», der auch dem Verständnis von Muthesius entsprechen dürfte: Ruskin 1900, S. 335.
35 «The Lamp of obedience», in Ruskin 1849, S. 248.
36 Muthesius 1908, I, Einleitung, S. 10.
37 «The Lamp of obedience», in Ruskin 1849, S. 255. Genau diesen Satz zitierte Muthesius in seiner Rede am Schinkelfest 1900, um auf die Gefahr vor «neuen Formen» im Kunstgewerbe hinzuweisen (Muthesius 1900b, S. 145).
38 Hermann Muthesius, «Wechselrede über ästhetische Fragen der Gegenwart», in Muthesius 1912, S. 34. Dort verweist er auf «die englischen Vorträge und Aufsätze ..., die genau dieselben Gedankengänge entwickeln, die unser heutiger Heimatschutz vertritt.»
39 «The Lamp of obedience», in Ruskin 1849, S. 252.
40 Muthesius 1914, S. 32.
41 «The Lamp of truth», in Ruskin 1849, S. 60.
42 Muthesius wird den Ausspruch «cheap and nasty», der von Carlyle stammt sowohl in *Das englische Haus* zitieren als auch in seiner Werkbundrede von 1911 in deutscher Übersetzung verwenden. Bereits 1896 hatte Richard Streiter mit diesen Worten die deutsche «Kunstindustrie» kritisiert. Vgl. Streiter 1913, S. 15. Der Aufsatz erschien zum ersten Mal 1896 in der *Beilage zur allgemeinen Zeitung* in München.
43 So reizvoll die ökonomische Argumentation sein mag, so kann sie durch ihre methodologische Einschränkung der kulturellen Debatte des Werkbunds kaum gerecht werden. Vgl. Schwartz 1996.
44 Muthesius 1912, S. 18.

der Typus zugleich das Resultat einer systematischen Auseinandersetzung mit konkreten historischen und lokalen Beispielen wie auch Grundlage für die moderne Form, Garant ihrer kulturellen Einbindung und Bedingung für die ersehnte neue «nationale Tradition».

Auch wenn Muthesius Ruskin im konkreten Fall vorwarf, sich in seinen Studien über venezianische Architektur vom «Vaterländischen» abgewandt zu haben, so waren die allgemeinen Erkenntnisse aus *The seven lamps of Architecture*, insbesondere die Forderung nach einer Rückbesinnung auf eine eigene einheimische Bauweise, wichtiger. Tatsächlich folgte in der Argumentation von *Das englische Haus* einer kurzen Würdigung von Carlyle, Ruskin und Morris die Begründung des Erfolges des modernen englischen Hauses in der Rückbesinnung auf die «anonyme» ländliche Architektur.

Ruskin hatte sich bereits 1838 in seiner ersten Schrift zur Architektur *The poetry of Architecture* mit dieser Frage auseinandergesetzt und unter zwei Aspekten untersucht, «as it is influenced by ... feelings and manners» und «as it is connected with the scenery in which it is found, and with the skies under which it is erected».[45] Seine Charakterisierung stützte sich zwar vornehmlich auf wahrnehmungsästhetische Aspekte, die seine Arbeiten zur Malerei vorwegnahmen, doch hatte er immerhin genau diejenigen «Eigentümlichkeiten des Volkes» bezeichnet – «stammliche Veranlagung» und «Klima» –, die auch Muthesius in seiner Einführung zu *Das englische Haus* angeführt hatte. Bezeichnenderweise hatte Ruskin diese Eigenschaften nur dem Cottage des «peasant» zugesprochen, von der er die Villa als Wohnhaus des «gentleman» scharf getrennt hatte, denn «the more polished the mind of its designer, the less national will be the building; for its architect will be led away by a search after a model of ideal beauty».[46] Der nationale Charakter von Architektur war somit eng mit einer anonymen, spontanen Volkskunst verbunden, mit den «prejudices and feelings inculcated and aroused in youth»,[47] ihre Wahrnehmung nur mit den beim «Rembrandt-Deutschen» heraufbeschwörten Empfindungswerten möglich. Erst viel später hatte Ruskin die Motive dieser ländlichen Architektur auch benannt und als direkte Antwort auf die Anforderungen der Konstruktion, des Materials aber auch des Klimas des Nordens bezeichnet, neben dem «honeysuckle porch and latteiced window», vor allem das Dach, als «the very soul of the cottage»,[48] – Motive, die sich in noch unveränderter Form bei William Morris' und Philip Webbs Red House wiederfanden und die Muthesius an unterschiedlicher Stelle übernommen hatte. Im Aufsatz «Über häusliche Baukunst» waren «die einfachen Motive des breiten Daches und des Schornsteins», die vom Innern erzählten oder die «Hecke, das Gartentor», die «ästhetische und gemütliche Wirkungen schon in ihrem Wesen» bergen würden, genannt worden.[49] In *Das englische Haus* hatte Muthesius dem Dach nicht nur die Eigenschaft als Wetterschutz zugesprochen, sondern auch dessen «Ausdruck des Schützenden» als «eines der sprechendsten Motive des Hausbaues» beschrieben.[50] Die geforderte Reform stand unter präzisen Bedingungen, bei denen die Frage der Form nicht nur von konstruktiven oder funktionalen Aspekten abhängig war, sondern vielmehr als Teil einer gewachsenen kulturellen Tradition verstanden wurde.

Damit waren die Eigenschaften der «neuen handwerklichen Kunstbewegung» benannt, die Muthesius auf Ruskin zurückgeführt hatte: «Einfachheit und Natürlichkeit im Bilden und Empfinden, Aufrichtigkeit in der tektonischen Gestaltung, für die im Zweck, im Material und in der Konstruktion die Bedingungen zu suchen sind, Betonung des Werkmässigen, Charakteristischen, Bodenwüchsigen, Zusammenfassen von Kunstschaffen und Naturbeobachtung».[51] Die beinahe gleichen Worte hatte er benutzt, um die Eigenschaften der alten englischen Landbauten zu bezeichnen, die als Wurzeln des «modernen englischen Hauses» beschrieben worden waren und auf die sich die führenden Architekten Philip Webb, Eden Nesfield, Norman Shaw berufen hätten: «Einfachheit der Empfindung, angemessene Konstruktion, natürliche statt zurechtgemachte Architekturformen, vernunftgemässe, sachliche Gestaltung, Gemütlichkeit der Raumbildung, Farbe und schliesslich jene harmonische Wirkung, die sich in alter Zeit aus der organischen Entwicklung auf der Grundlage der örtlichen Bedingungen von selbst ergeben hatte».[52] Zwar war die Frage der konkreten Formfindung ausgeklammert worden, aber deren Bedingungen genannt, ihre Wirkung beschrieben, Beispiele gezeigt und vor allem die intime Verwandtschaft zwischen moderner und historisch überlieferter Architektur dargestellt worden.

In der Begrifflichkeit zwar ungenau, in der allgemeinen Umschreibung hingegen sehr präzis, war das Verständnis von Architektur nicht nur auf die Forderungen nach einer ehrlichen und materialgerechten Konstruktion reduziert, sondern vielmehr als kulturelle 'Synthese' angedeutet worden, die sich sowohl in eine historische und lokale Tradition einordnete, wie auch ihr zeitgenössischer Ausdruck war. Im Gegensatz zu Morris, der diesem Programm konkrete Formen verliehen hatte, eignete sich der Kunstliterat Ruskin besser für die unbestimmte, aber einflussreiche Rolle als 'Prophet'. Somit war auch erklärbar, warum William Morris in *Das englische Haus* und in den anderen Schriften Muthesius' nur in der Nachfolge von Ruskin erwähnt wurde. Doch auch Ruskin wurde in Deutschland zugunsten einer Rückbesinnung auf eine 'nationale Tradition' durch den 'Einiger' Bismarck, den 'Prediger' Langbehn oder den 'Lehrer' Schäfer verdrängt. Mit der

45 Ruskin 1837–1838, Introduction, S. 9.
46 Ebd., S. 75.
47 Ebd., S. 74.
48 Ruskin 1854, S. 33. Im Gegensatz zu den anderen Schriften finden sich keine nachweisbaren Belege, dass Muthesius *The Poetry of Architecture* und die *Lectures* gekannt hat.
49 «Über häusliche Baukunst» (1904), in Muthesius 1909, S. 98.
50 «Bedingungen, Anlage, gärtnerische Umgebung, Aufbau und gesundheitliche Einrichtungen des englischen Hauses» (1905), in Muthesius 1910, S. 165.
51 Muthesius 1908, S. 96.
52 Muthesius 1908, S. 102.

Gründung des Deutschen Werkbunds im Jahre 1907, mit dem auch der letzte publizistische Höhepunkt der Ruskin-Übersetzungen zusammenfiel, wurde die Forderung nach der 'deutschen Form' endgültig offizielles und unter den Werkbundmitgliedern einstimmig anerkanntes Programm, ihr internationaler Charakter in der unheimlichen, aber unaufhaltsamen Propaganda der Vorkriegsjahre in der 'Weltform' gar vorweggenommen.[53]

53 Vgl. u.a. Muthesius 1914 und ders. 1915.

Hermann Muthesius, «John Ruskin †», in *Centralblatt der Bauverwaltung*, Nr. 7, 27. Januar 1900, S. 43–44.

Der am verflossenen Sonnabend, den 20. d. M., erfolgte Tod des 81 jährigen John Ruskin hat ein Leben abgeschlossen, dessen bahnbrechende Thätigkeit bereits so weit zurück liegt, daß viele erst jetzt erfahren werden, daß sich sein Ende bis in unsere Tage herein erstreckte. Ruskin, der künstlerische Apostel Englands, der Mann, dem England in erster Linie den Aufschwung verdankt, den die englische Kunst in der zweiten Hälfte des letzten Jahrhunderts genommen hat, schied auf seinem Landsitze Brantwood in Lancashire dahin, nachdem er sich schon vor fünfzehn Jahren vollständig aus der Öffentlichkeit zurückgezogen hatte. Als Sohn eines wohlhabenden Kaufmanns und einer streng und energisch-religiösen Mutter genoß er eine Erziehung, die sich zwischen Bibel und Naturstudium bewegte; die erstere hatte er auswendig zu lernen, die Natur lernte er als steter Begleiter seines Vaters auf dessen Geschäftsreisen kennen und lieben. Während seiner Studienzeit in Oxford führte er ein zurückgezogenes, den Wissenschaften gewidmetes Leben, nicht ohne sich dabei in weitgehendem Maße künstlerisch zu bethätigen, eine Beschäftigung, die er auch nach Verlassen der Universität zunächst ganz aufnahm. Bei dieser Thätigkeit lernte er sehr bald sich selbst finden: die damaligen Kunstbesprechungen in den Zeitungen, die er verfolgte, erregten seinen Widerspruch in dem Maße, daß er den unwiderstehlichen Drang in sich verspürte, die seiner Ansicht nach irrige Art der Kunstauffassung seiner Zeit zu widerlegen. Als Vierundzwanzigjähriger veröffentlichte er sein erstes Buch: «Modern Painters». Er hatte vorgehabt, ein Heftchen zu schreiben, und brachte einen umfänglichen Band heraus, ein Werk zudem, das die öffentliche Aufmerksamkeit sogleich in einer noch nie dagewesenen Weise erregte. Das Buch enthielt in Bezug auf Kunst völlig umstürzende Gedanken. Dabei war sein Inhalt vorgetragen in einem berückenden Stile, getragen von dem Feuereifer eines Propheten, im ganzen von einer hinreißenden Gewalt und überwältigender Kraft. Mit dem Erscheinen dieses Buches war Ruskins Lebensaufgabe vorgezeichnet: sein Volk zum Verständnis der Kunst zu erziehen. Ihr hat er sich von da an mit seiner ganzen Persönlichkeit hingegeben und hat einen Erfolg erzielt, der von den Thaten des scheidenden Jahrhunderts nur mit dem politischen Erfolge Bismarcks zu vergleichen ist: er hat in England, dessen künstlerischer Boden lange hoffnungslos unfruchtbar zu sein schien, eine Bewegung hervorgerufen, die dieses Land auf Jahrzehnte an die Spitze des künstlerischen Interesses stellte. In seinem ersten Buche legte er bereits die Grundfesten derjenigen Lehren nieder, die ihm in seinem späteren Lebenswerke aufzubauen vorbehalten waren: daß die Wahrheit der Inbegriff der künstlerischen Vollendung ist, daß die Natur der Ausgangspunkt jeder großen und guten Kunst ist, daß die Virtuosität kein erstrebenswerthes Ziel, aber Ernst, Eigenart und Aufrichtigkeit die Prüfsteine reinen Schaffens zu sein haben. Dem ersten Band der «Modernen Maler» folgten noch vier andere, von denen der letzte erst 1860 erschien. Inzwischen waren die Präraffaeliten emporgewachsen, die von Anfang an Ruskins thatkräftigste Unterstützung fanden und ohne ihn schwerlich ihre heutige Volksthümlichkeit in England erreicht hätten. Ihren Zielen war das Werk «Pre-Raphaelitism» gewidmet. Auch der Architektur hat Ruskin die größte Aufmerksamkeit zugewandt, ja es gehörte zu seinen Leitsätzen, daß sie die Chorführerin aller menschlichen Künste sei und wieder werden müsse. Sein merkwürdiges Buch «The seven lamps of Architecture» und nicht minder sein einflußreiches Werk «The stones of Venice» sind in England von unendlichem Nutzen gewesen. In dem ersteren suchte er die für die Malerei aufgestellten Grundsätze der Aufrichtigkeit und Wahrheit auch auf die Architektur zu übertragen, in dem letzteren brachte er seine Begeisterung für die phantastische mittelalterliche Kunst Venedigs zum Ausdruck. Der Reiz dieser Bücher wird nicht wenig erhöht durch die ganz vorzüglichen Abbildungen, die er ihnen von eigner Hand beigab. Schon früh wurde Ruskin neben seinen künstlerischen Idealen auf sociale Umgestaltungsgedanken geführt. Sie nahmen mit der Zeit immer mehr von seinem Wesen ein, ja beherrschten ihn schließlich ganz und gar. Eine ganze Reihe seiner Bücher sind socialen Fragen gewidmet, unter ihnen «Fors Clavigera», «Munera Pulveris» und andere. Wie

Morris, so hatte auch er auf diesem Gebiete weniger Erfolg als auf dem künstlerischen, was ihn nicht verhinderte, mit verdoppelter Arbeit seinem Ziele nachzustreben, ja vielleicht war es gerade die so in ihm entstandene Spannung, welche ihn 1878 an einem Nervenleiden daniederwarf, von dem er zwar in der Folge wieder genas, aber nie seine volle Kraft wiedererlangte. Die ihm in jungen Jahren zugefallene väterliche Erbschaft von vier Millionen Mark hat Ruskin, den der Erfolg seiner Bücher allein hätte zum reichen Mann machen können, im Verlauf seines Lebens fast ganz dem Allgemeinwohle in Form von Geschenken, Stiftungen, Begründung von socialistischen Gesellschaften usw. gewidmet. Er selbst lebte außerordentlich anspruchslos und zurückgezogen.

Wenn man das englische Geistesleben der letzten sechzig Jahre betrachtet, so spielt Ruskin geradezu eine der hervorragendsten Rollen darin. Es hat wohl überhaupt wenige Schriftsteller gegeben, die so auf ihre Zeit einzuwirken vermocht hätten wie er. Seine Bücher schlugen ein wie die Blitze. Sie sind weit davon entfernt, wissenschaftlich zu sein oder auch nur wissenschaftlich etwas zu bieten. Die Philosophie, die Archäologie, die Volkswirthschaftslehre, die Wissenschaft überhaupt wird über sie hinwegschreiten. Aber sie sind deshalb von nicht geringerem Nutzen gewesen. Sie haben ein ganzes Volk für das Schöne, Wahre und Gute begeistert, sie haben in der Zeit der geldgierigsten Selbstsucht, die gerade in dem englischen Boden zuerst ihre Wurzeln ausgebreitet hatte, wieder das Banner der Kunst emporgehoben und um dieses ganze Bruchtheile des Volles geschart. Sie haben eine Kunst erzeugt und zur Anerkennung gebracht, die, von allen ihren sonstigen Eigenschaften abgesehen, das innerste Bestreben verkörpert, aufrichtig, wahr, sachlich, gediegen zu sein, sie haben die Kunst und vor allem die gewerblichen Künste in einer Weise volksthümlich gemacht, mit der England heute völlig einzig dasteht. Alle Theilnahme an der Kunst kann man in England auf die Anregung zurückführen, die jeder Einzelne aus den Schriften Ruskins gesogen hat. Denn diese genießen eine Verbreitung und werden mit einer Hingabe gelesen, die bei Büchern, die über Kunst handeln, überhaupt noch nicht dagewesen sein dürfte. In Deutschland ließen sich am Einfluß auf ihre Zeit nur die Schriften Winckelmanns und, aus neuester Zeit, etwa das Buch Rembrandt als Erzieher zum spärlichen Vergleich heranziehen. Das letztere Buch giebt in seiner Buntheit des Inhalts auch ungefähr einen Begriff von der Art der Stoffanordnung der Ruskinschen Bücher. Sie halten zwar eine anscheinende Eintheilung inne, der Inhalt der Einzeltheile sprudelt aber überall über die Grenzen der Eintheilung hinweg. Der Verfasser streift fortwährend in allen möglichen menschlich-geistigen Gebieten herum, verknüpft wissenschaftliche mit künstlerischen, diese mit ethischen, moralischen und socialen Fragen, stellt kühne Behauptungen, treffende Gegensätze, schlagende Bilder auf, verurtheilt und preist im Übermaß und haucht dabei doch seinen glänzenden Satzfolgen eine Überzeugungsfähigkeit ein, die völlig hinreissend wirkt. Er hat die Macht über seine Leser, die einzelne berühmte Redner über ihre Hörer ihr eigen nannten. Dabei ist es denn nicht zu verwundern, daß die Begeisterung des Augenblicks zu Behauptungen verleitet, die in kühleren Augenblicken nicht aufrecht zu erhalten sind. In Ruskins Schriften finden sich Widersprüche geradezu in Massen. Auch steht er selbst unter dem Banne von Vorurtheilen: die ganze Renaissance war für ihn ein einziger großer Verfall, vor der Maschinenarbeit in jeder Form bekreuzte er sich dreimal. Sein Enthusiasmus war zurückblickend, sein Ideal, wie das Morris', das Mittelalter, seine Lebensauffassung das Gegentheil von praktisch. Trotz alledem hat er in England eine künstlerische Aufgabe erfüllt, wie sie nicht leicht in der Welt jemals erfüllt worden ist. Die heutige englische Kunstbewegung ist sein Werk.

Es ist eine der eigenthümlichsten Erscheinungen, daß wir in Deutschland, die wir alles studiren, alles lesen und gerade mit englischer Kunst und Literatur in der letzten Zeit reichlich überschüttet worden sind, von Ruskin noch so gut wie nichts wissen. Wer den Einfluß Ruskins in England kennt, muß sich erstaunt fragen, wie es möglich ist, daß seine Werke noch nicht in einer deutschen Übersetzung vorliegen. Es scheint indes bei näherem Zusehen, daß eine solche manche Enttäuschung mit sich bringen würde. Die Wegnahme des englischen Sprachkleides würde diese Capitel ihres besten Theiles berauben. Die kahlen, vielfach gewagten, immer launen- und nicht selten schrullenhaften Gedanken würden allein stehen bleiben, und kein Übersetzer würde es übernehmen wollen oder können, sie mit der Begeisterung zu überdecken, die sie im Englischen überzeugungsfähig macht. Die schon im Englischen häufig zum Widerspruch reizende Gedankenfolge würde hier und da strotzend unlogisch werden. Und alles in allem steckt in uns zu viel wissenschaftlicher Geist, zu viel Denkklarheit, um gewagte, nur von stilistischer Meisterschaft gestützte Gedankengänge hinnehmen zu können. Wer daher Ruskin schätzen und genießen will, der greife zum Original und nicht zur Übersetzung. Er wird dann die zauberische Macht dieses Schriftstellers verspüren; er wird ihm gern in das große Reich seines Geistesgebiets folgen und die tausendfältigen Anregungen, die er giebt, hinnehmen, er wird vor allem begreifen, wie er wirkte und zu wirken vermochte: durch ein reiches glühendes Herz, das er ganz ausschüttete, und durch die vollendete Form, in die er dessen Inhalt goß.

London. Muthesius.

«Capital from the Lower Arcade of the Doge's Palace, Venice», Taf. V in:
John Ruskin, *The Seven Lamps of Architecture*, London 1849

Carlpeter Braegger

Ruskin, dithyrambisch. Zur Ruskin-Rezeption bei Hugo von Hofmannsthal (1874–1929)

Für Michael Hamburger

Einleitend

Hugo von Hofmannsthal (1874–1929) verstand sich, als Künstler, als Ausdruck einer in weite Vergangenheit zurückführenden Pluralität. «Es ist das wahrhaft Großartige an der Gegenwart», notiert er Anfang der zwanziger Jahre, «daß so viele Vergangenheiten in ihr als magische Existenzen drinliegen». Und in Aufzeichnung aus dem Jahre 1922 formuliert er sein – im wörtlichen Sinne – konservatives Konzept einer traditionsgebundenen und zugleich traditionsbildenden Kunstpraxis: «Jeder schafft sich das Instrument seiner Kunst selbst, indem er von Eindrücken und Halluzinationen ausgeht, die dem Eros unterstehen, und damit das von Überliefertem verbindet, was er erfassen kann. Es schafft immer eine Pluralität: Landschaft, Zeitgeist, Volksgeist». Als Mary Gilbert über Hofmannsthal und England schrieb, fand sie es überraschend, dass dieser Autor, dessen «Europa das katholische Europa der Barockzeit war», selbst so grosse Betonung auf das gelegt habe, was er dem nordischen und protestantischen England verdankte. «Er benahm sich wie ein Engländer», schreibt Mary Gilbert, «und das im frankophilen Wien. Er betonte die Tatsache, daß er Mitglieder der britischen Botschaft in Wien kannte; er spielte mit großem Nachdruck Tennis zu einer Zeit, als dieses Spiel noch nicht Mode auf dem Kontinent geworden war. Er kannte die Bräuche in England so genau, daß er seinem Freund Hermann Bahr englische Rezepte versprechen konnte. Er erwähnte die Sitte, Weihnachtskarten zu versenden, er imitierte die englische Art, den Absender auf den Briefkopf zu schreiben, und er streute englische Worte in seine Briefe ... Er wurde von der Idee des *gentleman* angezogen, in dem er sein eigenes Ideal eines kultivierten Lebens personifiziert sah». Mary Gilbert führt den *Brief* des Lord Chandos und die *Briefe eines Zurückgekehrten* als Beweise dafür an, wie dieser Begriff des *gentleman* in Hofmannsthals dichterische Werke eindrang.

London nehme in seinem Vorstellungsleben einen «ungeheuren Raum» ein, schreibt Hofmannsthal 1899 an Baron Oppenheimer, «mehr Fäden, als mir aufzuzählen möglich wäre, laufen von dort aus, und die wichtigsten Einflüsse für mein inneres Leben lassen sich mehr oder weniger auf englische Kunst, englische Weltanschauung und das intensive und weltumspannende Gegenwartsleben, das sich dort konzentriert, zurückführen». Hofmannsthal betrachtete noch am Ende seines Lebens seine ersten Gedichte als einen Versuch, «den großen Engländern von Keats an» gleichzukommen, und er sah dies nicht – so Michael Hamburger – «als Gegensatz zu dem Einfluss der romanischen Literatur und Kultur auf seine Entwicklung an, weil diese, ihrerseits, die englischen Dichter des 19. Jahrhunderts so sehr bestimmt hatte».

Von daher erklärt sich Hofmannsthals frühe Faszination für die Kunst der Präraffaeliten, die er als «durch und durch englisch» empfand; eine Kunst, welche alt und neu zugleich ist und – darin seinem Schaffen zutiefst verwandt, eine mehr nachschaffende, interpretierende oder spiegelnde Kunst – an Dante, Botticelli und Lionardo heraufgewachsen «wie junge Rebe an alten Stöcken». Und es sei charakteristisch, schreibt er im *Swinburne-Essay* (1893), dass der erste, um den sich diese Gruppe von englischen Künstlern sammelte, ein Kritiker war: John Ruskin. Ruskin ist im Denken und im Werk Hofmannsthals vielfach präsent; als grosser Ästhetiker, hellsichtiger Kritiker, als «Poet der Architektur» (Werner Oechslin) und als moralischer, ja geistlich agitatorischer Denker.

I. «Ein Kritiker aus dem Willen der Natur»

Obwohl Hofmannsthal wusste, dass Reden Menschheit ist (*Der Turm*, 1925/1927),[1] dass durchs Reden alles auf der Welt zustande kommt (*Der Schwierige*, 1920),[2] hat er schon früh eine «verzweifelte Liebe zu allen Künsten» bezeugt, «die schweigend ausgeübt werden»,[3] und er hat später den stummen Künsten ganz den Vorzug gegeben: dem Mimus, dem Tanz, den Bildern, die lautlos die Welt reflektieren und die «stumm (sind) wie Träume»[4] – «Die Leute sind es nämlich müde, reden zu hören», sagt er im Mitterwurzer Essay aus dem Jahr 1895:

«Sie (die Leute) haben einen tiefen Ekel vor den Worten: Denn die Worte haben sich vor die Dinge gestellt. Das Hörensagen hat die Welt verschluckt. Die unendlich komplexen Lügen der Zeit, die dumpfen Lügen der Tradition, die Lügen der Ämter, die Lügen der einzelnen, die Lügen der Wissenschaften, alles das sitzt wie Myriaden tödlicher Fliegen auf unserem armen Leben».[5]

Am gleichen Ort spricht er von einem «entsetzlichen Verfahren, das Denken völlig unter den Begriffen zu ersticken» und warnt davor, auch aus der Malerei «durch eine Hintertüre ... einen Augiasstall des begrifflichen Denkens»[6] zu machen, und er polemisiert – ganz 'ungentlemanlike' – in der Nachfolge Nietzsches gegen das Zwitschern über Kunstwerke, «als ob sie ganz eigentlich zum Zer-redet-Werden geschaffen wären» (Nietzsche). Die ganze «ästhetische Schreib- und Schwatzseligkeit»[7] der Deutschen hat der neunzehnjährige Kritiker im Visier:

«Es gibt sehr viele Königliche und sonstige Museen, sehr viele Königliche und sonstige Kustoden, und diese gelehrten und ehrenhaften Menschen schreiben unendlich viele gescheite und gewissenhafte Bücher über lebendige und tote Maler. Aber es ist kein Vergnügen, diese Bücher zu lesen. Es ist eigentümlich, die jüngsten lebendigen und die ältesten toten Maler bekommen in diesen Büchern etwas Gemeinsames: sie interessieren einen genau gleich wenig. Es ist alles mit einer gleichförmigen Kruste akademischer Leblosigkeit überzogen, gleichsam eingewickelt in selbstverständliche Bewunderung und gedankenlose Kritik. Es ist, wie wenn Schatten zu Schatten über Schatten redeten. In der Erzeugung dieser Kruste, in dem Hervorbringen dieses schattenhaften Tones haben die Ästhetiker mit ihren ausgezeichneten Kollegen, den Philologen, eine Ähnlichkeit, die beide Teile ehrt. Auch die Philologen verstehen es, Heinrich Heine genau so langweilig zu machen wie den vortrefflichen Johann Elias Schlegel».[8]

Aus dem Gesagten wird verständlich, weshalb der junge Kritiker Ruskin wie eine Offenbarung erlebt. Er rückt den englischen Kritiker in die Nähe Nietzsches: Ruskin, «dessen Kritik ein Nachleben, ein dithyrambisches und hellsichtiges Auflösen und Wiedererschaffen ist»,[9] ist im Denken und in den Schriften des jungen Hofmannsthal ebenso gegenwärtig wie Nietzsche, von dem er, siebzehnjährig, sagt, er sei die «Temperatur, in der meine Gedanken kristallisieren».[10]

«Ruskin ... ein genialer Mensch, der malen gelernt hat, um zu verstehen, wie man Leben in farbige Flecke und verschwimmende Tinten übersetzt, um dann mit berauschender Beredsamkeit aus Bildern die lebendigen Seelen der Künstler und der Dinge herauszudeuten ...».[11]

1 Hofmannsthal 1946–1965, Bd. IV, 1958, «Dramen», S. 83.
2 Hofmannsthal 1946–1965, 1965, «Lustspiele I», S. 285.
3 Hofmannsthal 1979, «Reden und Aufsätze I 1891–1913», S. 479.
4 Hofmannsthal 1946–1965, Bd. IV, 1958, «Prosa», S. 45.
5 Hofmannsthal 1979, S. 479.
6 Ebd.
7 Nietzsche 1954, Bd. I, S. 407.
8 Hofmannsthal 1979, S. 519 f.
9 Hofmannsthal 1979, S. 144.
10 Hofmannsthal 1979, «Reden und Aufsätze III 1925–1929 / Buch der Freunde / Aufzeichnungen 1889–1929», S. 335.
11 Hofmannsthal 1979, S. 144.

Im gleichen Jahr – 1893 – erinnert Hofmannsthal in einem Essay *Die Malerei in Wien* die Leute daran,

«daß die Malerei eine Zauberschrift ist, die, mit farbigen Klecksen statt der Worte, eine innere Vision der Welt, der rätselhaften, wesenlosen, wundervollen Welt um uns übermittelt, daß Malen etwas mit Denken, Träumen und Dichten zu tun hat ...».[12]

Ruskin ist die «Atmosphäre, in welcher das (intermediale) Denken des Künstler-Kritikers Hofmannsthal, des *poète critique* (Baudelaire)[13] kristallisiert». In Ruskin erkannte er jenen «geborenen Versteher des Künstlers», einen Kritiker, «notwendigerweise aus dem Willen der Natur» (wie er von Walter Pater sagen wird).[14] Ein Kritiker, der in «die Aneignung des Sinnlichen seine ganzen Kräfte hineingab»;[15] ein Kritiker und Interpret, der das Sprechen über Kunst kunstvoll und leidenschaftlich betrieb,[16] der, um das Sehen zu lehren, «die Technik der sprachlichen Darstellung visueller Tatbestände»[17] bedeutend erweitert hatte. Am 20.3.1894 notiert Hofmannsthal: «Vor dem Schlafengehen Ruskin gelesen». Und bereits im Januar 1894: «Ruskin Modern Painters (1843–1856) / Stones of Venice 1851–53 / Preraphaelism / Giotto and his works Sesame and the lilies 1865».[18] Ende der neunziger Jahre plante Hofmannsthal einen Essay über Ruskin.[19]

II. Ruskin als Vorbild

«Loris», das Pseudonym des jungen Hofmannsthal, steht in der Literaturgeschichte nicht für Kunst- und Zivilisationskritik, sondern für «seltsam prächtige Verse» (Rilke),[20] für ein «betäubendes Ereignis» (Benn).[21] Man sprach vom «Wunderknaben» des Fin-de-siècle.[22] Es hiess auch, Loris tauche seine Hände in eine Schale mit Edelsteinen, wenn er seine juwelengleichen Verse schrieb.[23] Missgünstige Zeitgenossen sprachen von einem Infantentypus mit offenbaren Verfallszeichen.[24] Als im Dezember 1891 der knapp dreiundzwanzigjährige Stefan George auszog, einen Kreis um sich zu versammeln – «eine Vereinigung derer, welche ahnten, was das Dichterische sei»[25] – war der knapp achtzehnjährige Loris-Hofmannsthal der erste, den George zu gewinnen trachtete.[26] Hofmannsthal erinnert sich 1929, in seinem Todesjahr, an die erste folgenschwere Begegnung mit George:

«... als ich ziemlich spät in der Nacht in einer englischen Revue lesend in dem Café saß, trat ein Mensch von sehr merkwürdigem Aussehen, mit einem hochmütigen leidenschaftlichen Ausdruck im Gesicht ... auf mich zu, fragte mich, ob ich der und der wäre – sagte mir, er habe einen Aufsatz von mir gelesen, und auch was man ihm sonst über mich berichtet habe, deute darauf hin, daß ich unter den wenigen in Europa sei (und hier in Österreich der einzige), mit denen er Verbindung zu suchen habe ... die Namen Verlaine, Baudelaire, Swinburne, Rossetti, Shelley wurden dabei in einer gewissen Weise genannt ...».[27]

Hofmannsthal, dem es darauf ankommt, «daß die Kunst vom Standpunkt des Lebens betrachtet»[28] wird, war offensichtlich nicht bereit, Georges literarisches Programm voll und ganz zu akzeptieren – ein Programm, «welches praktisch jeden Kontakt mit dem profanum vulgus ausschloss».[29] Hofmannsthal wollte keinen Kreis und keine literarische Herrschaft. Ihm ging es vielmehr darum – und hier wurde er durch Ruskins Schriften bestärkt – lebendiges Interesse an der Kunst in sehr weiten Kreisen zu verbreiten. So wird er später zusammen mit Max Reinhardt und Edward Gordon Craig das Konzept für ein neues «Theater für die Menge» entwickeln – ein Konzept, für das ihn nicht zuletzt die Präraffaeliten sensibilisiert hatten.[30] Hofmannsthal entzieht sich, wie es bei Wolters heisst, «geschickt dem liebenden Zugriff des Freundes»[31] und provoziert damit fast ein Duell. Er überlässt es dem Vater, den aufgebrachten George zu beruhigen. Eine spätere Begegnung in einem Café wurde von Hofmannsthal abrupt abgebrochen unter dem Vorwand, daß George einen Hund getreten und beschimpft habe.[32] – «Ich war des festen glaubens», beklagt sich George 1902 in einem Brief an den Abtrünnigen, «daß wir – Sie und ich – durch jahre in unserm Schrifttum eine sehr heilsame diktatur hätten üben können, daß es dazu nicht kam dafür mache ich Sie allein verantwortlich».[33] In Hofmannsthals journalistischen Veröffentlichungen in Tagesblättern und verschiedenen Revuen witterte George Verrat[34] – «Bündnisse mit dem Nichtigen oder Schlechten».[35] Deshalb versucht Hofmannsthal in einem Brief an George

12 Hofmannsthal 1979, S. 526.
13 Zu Hofmannsthal und Ruskin vgl. neuerdings auch: Renner 2000; zu Ruskin: ebd., S. 177 ff. – Ferner: Stamm 1979.
14 Vgl. Stamm 1979.
15 Hofmannsthal 1979, S. 585.
16 Vgl. Renner 2000, S. 178.
17 Vgl. Kemp 1983, S. 434.
18 Hier zit. nach Renner 2000, S. 196 und S. 197.
19 Ebd., S. 197.
20 Hofmannsthal/Rilke 1978, S. 9. Im Prager Vortrag «Moderne Lyrik» (März 1898) sagt Rilke von Hofmannsthal: «daß der Name Loris immer noch wie ein Märchen klingt; nur wenig Eingeweihte finden die seltsam prächtigen Verse des Loris oder Hugo von Hofmannsthal, wie er eigentlich heißt, in den kaum zugänglichen 'Blättern für die Kunst' ... oder auf den Seiten des 'Pan', wo sie wie in Marmor gegraben, mit stillen, stolzen Lettern prangen».
21 Vgl. Benn 1965, Bd. I, S. 561 f.
22 Vgl. Hamburger 1964, S. 12.
23 Ebd., S. 12 f.
24 Vgl. Loris 1930, S. 272.
25 Hofmannsthal/George 1953, S. 235.
26 Vgl. Schirrmacher 1996, S. 101 ff.
27 Hofmannsthal/George 1953, S. 235.
28 Hofmannsthal 1946–1965, Bd. IV, 1958, «Dramen», S. 103.
29 Vgl. Hamburger 1964, S. 20.
30 Vgl. Hofmannsthal 1937, S. 71. – Vgl. ferner Renner 2000, S. 195.
31 Vgl. Lorenz 2000.
32 Vgl. Hamburger 1964, S. 19.
33 Hofmannsthal-George 1953, S. 150.
34 Vgl. Schirrmacher 1996, S. 101.
35 Hofmannsthal/George 1953, S. 155.

eine Deutung der Personaleinheit von Dichter und Kritiker, und er nennt Ruskin als das mögliche Vorbild:

«In mir ist vielleicht die Dichterkraft mit anderen geistigen Drängen dumpfer vermischt als bei Ihnen. Ich hatte von der Kindheit an ein fieberhaftes Bestreben, dem Geist unserer verworrenen Epoche auf den verschiedensten Wegen, in den verschiedensten Verkleidungen beizukommen. Und die Verkleidung eines gewissen Journalismus – in einem so anständigen Sinn genommen, daß allenfalls jemand wie Ruskin, bei uns dagegen niemand als Vertreter anzusehen wäre – hat mich öfters mächtig angezogen».[36]

Stefan George, dem rigorosen Verfechter einer 'poésie pure', stellt Hofmannsthal Ruskin entgegen, dessen Habitus, die Suche nach dem Schönen mit sozialem Bewusstsein und moralischer Leidenschaft zu verbinden,[37] ihm näher steht. – «War George stärker als ich?» überlegt Hofmannsthal 1919 in einem Brief an Rudolf Pannwitz. «Ich weiß es nicht, es ist zu viel künstliches an ihm und *er lässt zu viel aus*. ... mit der Stellung eines *coadjutor sine jure succedendi*, die er mir pantomimisch anbot, wußte ich nichts anzufangen, das war mir alles zu deutsch-phantastisch und trotz allem in der letzten Tiefe zu bürgerlich».[38]

So lehnt Hofmannsthal auch den sonst hochverehrten Walter Pater dort ab, wo er sich zu sehr vom Publikum entfernt. An *Marius der Epikuräer* verstimmt ihn das «Bewusst-Einseitige, Systematische», das ihm «beinahe unmoralisch» vorkommt, und wo er schon «*morbide* Ausschreitung der Kritik» zu erkennen glaubt:[39] «das Leben ist doch viel gewaltiger, größer und unsäglicher».[40] Im Mai 1894 schickt Hofmannsthal Elsa Bruckmann-Cantacuzene seinen Aufsatz über die englischen Präraffaeliten,

«wo Sie spüren werden, wie ich von dem etwas leeren Ästhetizismus ins Menschlich-Sittliche hinüberzulenken suche. Denn es scheint mir sehr darauf anzukommen, daß die Kunst vom Standpunkt des Lebens betrachtet werde».[41]

Hermann Bahr war einer der ersten, der in Loris, dem «geistesprinziplichen Knaben» (George über Loris),[42] mehr als nur den lebensfernen Ästheten gesehen hat, wenn er 1894 konstatiert:

«Bei uns ist Loris der Einzige, der immer von moralischen Fragen handelt. Er sucht die Stellung des Menschen zur Welt, sucht Sinn und Bedeutung der Dinge, sucht Gewissheit für den Gang des Lebens. Er will Erweckung und Erbauung. Er hat das Wilhelm-Meisterliche».[43]

III. Hellsichtig und dithyrambisch – Der Sturm Ruskin

Hofmannsthal hatte sich seinen Dichternamen «Loris» nicht auf mystische Art zusammengezaubert, wie Richard Dehmel vermutet.[44] Der junge Dichter drapierte sich mit dem Namen eines russischen Generals, eines martialischen Leiters und Opfers der grossen Politik: General Michail Tariélovic Loris-Mélikov.[45] Und er verstand sich als Mann des «Kampfes ... ringend nach neuen, lebensvollen Formen, dem lebensquellenden Ausdruck, der ungeschminkten subjektiven Wahrheit, der Befreiung von konventioneller Lüge in ihren tausend tödlichen Formen ...».[46] Von daher wird verständlich, dass er in seinem Essay über die Präraffaeliten (1894) auch auf das zu sprechen kommt, was man die «zweite Phase in Ruskins geistigem Leben» zu bezeichnen pflegt:

«die Abwendung des großen Ästhetikers von Problemen der Kunst und sein Aufgehen in moralischen, ja geistlich agitatorischen Gedanken. Der Übergang von intensiver Beschäftigung mit der Kunst zu irgendwelchem anderen hohen und priesterlichen Beruf sollte doch niemals wundernehmen».[47]

Ruskin: Das heisst für den zwanzigjährigen Hofmannsthal Kräftezuwachs, Steigerung des kritischen und des dichterischen Vermögens, «geistige Elektrizität».[48] Die Epitheta «hellsichtig» und «dithyrambisch» deuten darauf hin: Der Sturm Ruskin[49] stiess auf den Sturm Loris; und das zu einem Zeitpunkt, da der Zwanzigjährige «von einer dilettantenhaften Beschäftigung mit Kunst», wie er dem Freund Edgar Karg schreibt, «zu einer gründlichen Zurechtsetzung mit dem Leben»[50] zu kommen wünscht. Und dazu gehört eine besondere Art von Lesen:

«Das ist auch meine Art, Bücher ... zu lesen: ich meine, indem ich versuche, hinter dem Buch so einen Menschen zu spüren, der mit dem Leben fertig werden will und

36 Ebd., S. 154 f.
37 Vgl. Hamburger 1966, S. 102–120.
38 Hier zitiert nach Hamburger 1964, S. 21.
39 Hofmannsthal 1979, S. 404.
40 Hofmannsthal 1979, S. 196.
41 Hofmannsthal 1946–1965, Bd. IV, 1958, «Dramen», S. 103.
42 Zitiert nach Hofmannsthal/Rilke 1978, S. 9.
43 Bahr 1968, S. 151 ff.
44 Hofmannsthal/Dehmel 1979, S. 12.
45 Vgl. Stern 1971, S. 181–182. – Vgl. dazu ferner: Braegger 1995, S. 320.
46 Vgl. Braegger 1995, S. 320, S. 322.
47 Hofmannsthal 1979, S. 551.
48 In seiner Zürcher Beethoven-Rede (1920) spricht Hofmannsthal vom «Sturm Rousseau» und vom «Sturm Schiller», in: Hofmannsthal 1946–1965, Bd. IV, 1958, S. 20. – Vgl. ferner: «Der Sturm Elektra» im Brief von G. Eysoldt an Hofmannsthal: « ... so wie in jener Nacht, als ich Electra las, die wie ein Sturm über mich hinwegging», in: Eysoldt/Hofmannsthal 1996, S. 85.
49 Zu: «geistige Elektrizität» vgl. Beethoven-Rede (Hofmannsthal 1946–1965, Bd. IV, 1958, S. 20).
50 Hofmannsthal/Karg von Bebenburg 1966, S. 54.

sich's zu deuten, zurechtzulegen sucht. *Dichtkunst heißt doch, glaub ich, Deutekunst*».[51] (Hervorhebung CPB)

In einer erst 1997 aus dem Nachlass veröffentlichten Notiz vom Juni 1894 stellt Hofmannsthal Ruskin in eine Reihe mit Schiller, Rousseau und Goethe. Unter dem Stichwort «Cultur auf ästhetischer Grundlage» heisst es da:

«Schiller, Pater Marius the Epicurean Ruskin Rousseau Confessions VI[tes] Buch Erwachen des litterarischen Sinnes; ebenso Dichtung und Wahrheit Schöngeistige Tradition in Deutschland / meine: Dialoge über Kunst / sensitive Erziehung in der «Idylle» / Caricatur davon: Wilde Epicureismus».[52]

Die Notiz lässt erkennen, dass Hofmannsthal einen Teil seines eigenen Werkes als eine Weiterführung jenes im Werk dieser Vorgänger zum Ausdruck kommenden Bemühens um eine Kultur auf ästhetischer Grundlage versteht.[53] Das wird bestätigt durch eine andere Aufzeichnung aus dem Nachlass vom Juni 1894:

«Englischer Ästhetismus als Element unserer Kultur. I. Erstes Entgegentreten: als Sonderbarkeit, wohl etwa Affektation, Kostümtragen etc. II. Oscar Wilde 'Intentions': starker narkotischer Zauber, sophistisch verführerisch, unelegant paradoxal, Reaktion gegen englischen Utilitarismus. III. Ruskin, Pater, Madox Brown, Rossetti, Burne-Jones – die tiefen Zusammenhänge mit Seelenleben; das Ganze als Versuch einer inneren Kultur».[54]

IV. «Englische Dinge» – Tennisrackets und Kate Greenaway ...

1896 beschäftigt sich Hofmannsthal mit einer ganz bestimmten Seite von englischem Stil, und er tut es ganz im Sinne Ruskins, indem er die künstlerische und die allgemeine Produktion nicht trennt, sondern diese als Manifestation einer Kultur als Ganzheit beurteilt.[55] Die Rede ist von den «Dingen», die England seit etwa 1890 «herüberstreut»:

«café-concert Mädeln wie die Barrisons, Bilderbücher für kleine Kinder wie die von Walter Crane, Vorlagen für Tennisanzüge, und Chippendale-Möbel. Alle diese Dinge sind sehr englisch und sehr 1890. Alle sehen sie sehr einfach und kindlich aus. Und in alle sind Motive von ziemlich verschiedenen und ziemlich fernliegenden Kulturen mitverwebt und erhöhen durch ihr inkongruentes Dabeisein den komplizierten Reiz dieser merkwürdigen Kindlichkeit».[56]

Im weiteren spricht Hofmannsthal von den englischen Möbeln, die auch «sehr einfach und kindlich» aussehen, deren Form ihn vage an jene stilisierten altertümlichen Musikinstrumente 'lute' und 'harpsichord' erinnern.

«Aber sie erinnern andererseits an die Ruder, an die Tennisrackets; sie haben eine Anmut, die mit dem Ernstnehmen der Spiele und der Anbetung der Jugend im engsten Zusammenhang steht. Ihre wenig komplizierten Formen sind fast das einzige, was dem konfusen Leben von heute mit einer Art von griechischer Naivität gegenübersteht».[57]

Und schliesslich: es sei der Geist des englischen Lebens, der dem englischen Möbel die Schwere genommen und die Gestalt gegeben habe:

«es ist für die kleinen zeitähnlichen Räume der Landhäuser und für die Kabinen der Schiffe bestimmt. Das hat diese Schlankheit und Leichtigkeit der Formen hervorgebracht. Sie fassen gerade das Nötige: ein paar ernste und schöne Bücher, oder ein paar Krüge».[58]

Die gleiche *merkwürdige Kindlichkeit* findet Hofmannsthal auch in den Werken der Präraffaeliten – zumal bei Edward Burne-Jones, von denen er anlässlich der internationalen Ausstellung in Wien 1894 Reproduktionen sieht.

«Man sah eine Welt, die gleichzeitig antik, ja mythisch und durch und durch christlich, ja englisch anmutete, Gestalten mit einer fast *mystischen Traurigkeit* in den *sehnsüchtigen Augen*, mit den naiven *puppenhaften Gebärden* kindlicher Kunstepochen und dabei in allegorischem Handeln und Leiden von unendlicher Tragweite befangen. Man erblickte da Wesen, deren *schlanke*, dann und wann *hermaphroditische Anmut* für den ersten Blick nichts Unirdisches hatte, und man erblickte sie mit den Geräten und Symbolen weltlicher Eitelkeit zierlich beschäftigt: begriffen, ihre lichte Schönheit in lebendigen Wassern zu spiegeln ...».[59] (Hervorhebung CPB)

51 Ebd.
52 Zitiert nach Stamm 1997, S. 54.
53 Vgl. Stamm 1997, S. 54 f.
54 Hofmannsthal 1979, S. 386.
55 In einer Notiz zu Puvis de Chavannes heisst es: «sein Thema: la Manifestation d'âme d'une collectivité wie unser Begriff: englisches Wesen, ital. Wesen», in: Hofmannsthal 1979, S. 573.
56 Hofmannsthal 1979, S. 565.
57 Ebd., S. 571.
58 Ebd.
59 Ebd., S. 546.

Es ist unschwer zu erkennen, dass die englischen Stilisten – «eine merkwürdige Art zeichnender Dichter»[60] – Hofmannsthals assimilierende und reproduzierende (und auch dramaturgische) Phantasie stimuliert haben. Was er von diesen zeichnenden Dichtern sagt, gilt auch für sein eigenes im Visuellen wurzelnden lyrischen Frühwerk:

«Wir stehen einer raffiniert geistreichen Malerei gegenüber, einer Beherrschung der Ausdrucksmittel, die an Manier grenzt. Das Ganze hat etwas Künstliches, zumindest Gehegtes, nicht ganz Wildgewachsenes. In der Tat ist diese Malerschule ... eine von grossen und fruchtbaren Kritikern durch die verführerischste und geistreichste Interpretation vergangener italienischer Kunst zu einer künstlichen Wiederholung der Renaissance herauferzogene. An Dante, Botticelli und Lionardo ist diese ganze Kunst heraufgewachsen wie junge Rebe an alten Stöcken».[61]

Auch beim frühen Hofmannsthal findet sich eine stupende Beherrschung der Ausdrucksmittel, die an Manier grenzt. In einem Brief an Leopold von Andrian gesteht er, er habe in seiner «Stilverdrehungsmanie» die Nausikaageschichte «ganz trecentistisch, gobelinmäßig im Kopf», und die Sängerin Yvette Guilbert denkt er sich «halb Trecento, halb voyou, Botticelli-madonna am Brettl».[62] Und auch ihm wird das Leben erst lebendig, wenn es durch eine Kunst hindurchgegangen ist: «Das hat mich wohl auch zum 'Dichter' gemacht, dieses Bedürfnis nach dem künstlichen Leben, nach Verzierung und poetischer Interpretation des gemeinen und farblosen».[63]

Es sei charakteristisch, schreibt er im *Swinburne-Essay* (1893), dass der erste, um den sich diese Gruppe von englischen Künstlern sammelte, ein Kritiker war: «John Ruskin, dessen Kritik ein Nachleben, ein dithyrambisches und hellsichtiges Auflösen und Wiederschaffen ist».[64] Loris-Hofmannsthal nennt seine eigene Kunst «eine nachschaffende» und der Gymnasiast verstand einen guten Teil seiner poetischen Arbeit als «Kritikerarbeit», sie sei «Auflösung erstarrter Mythen, vermenschlichter Natursymbole in ihre Bestandteile, eigentliche Analyse, also Kritikerarbeit».[65] An Stefan George schreibt er, das Betrachten von Reproduktionen der «großen englischen Künstler» habe ihn in Zeiten der dichterischen Stagnation weiter gebracht.[66] Präraffaelitische Inspiration ist in zahlreichen frühen Werken Hofmannsthals auszumachen: *Terzinen*, *Ein Traum von großer Magie*, *Das kleine Welttheater*, *Der Jüngling und die Spinne*, *Die Frau im Fenster*, *Psyche*, um nur einige zu nennen.[67] Nicht selten finden sich in den genannten Werken Gestalten von hermaphroditischer Schönheit – «jung, schön und sanft»[68] – schlanke «Pagen Gottes» oder Kinder mit großen und/oder tiefen Augen.

«Wir sind aus solchem Zeug wie das zu Träumen,
Und Träume schlagen so die Augen auf
Wie kleine Kinder unter Kirschenbäumen,

Aus deren Krone den blassgoldnen Lauf
Der Vollmond anhebt durch die große Nacht».[69]

Aus der frühen autobiographischen Skizze *Age of Innocence*[70] (1891) erfahren wir, dass Hofmannsthal als Kind Bilderbücher von Kate Greenaway besass, und im Essay *Englischer Stil* (1896) zeigt er eine Faszination für englische junge Mädchen, als Produkt halb englischen Lebens, halb der poetischen Tradition, mit einem «starken Einschlag von Knabenhaftem ... wie die ganz jungen Herren in den Stücken von Shakespeare, die im Ton von ihren Zwillingsschwestern»[71] kaum zu unterscheiden seien.

«Wenn die Barrisons auftreten, erwartet man, daß auf der staubigen Tingeltangel-Bühne hinter ihren gelben Haaren und kindischen Schultern auch einmal der Mond aufgehen wird, der übergroße japanische Vollmond, so wie in den Bilderbüchern von Kate Greenaway hinter den fünf Schulmädeln mit gelben Haaren, Baby-Hüten und rosa Kleidern».[72]

Durch solche «kaleidoskopische Verschiebungen» (Ernst Robert Curtius)[73] schafft Hofmannsthal Figuren wie das junge Mädchen in *Das kleine Welttheater* (1897), das sich in so vielen Teichen gespiegelt hat (Shakespeare, Burne-Jones, Kate Greenaway), das es schon ganz «schläfrig» ist.[74]

«Die Nacht ist von Sternen und Wolken schwer,
Käm jetzt nur irgendeiner daher
Und säng recht etwas Trauriges,
Indes ich hier im Dunkeln säß!
...

60 Ebd., S. 536.
61 Ebd., S. 548.
62 Hofmannsthal 1946–1965, Bd. IV, 1958, S. 99 und S. 93.
63 Hofmannsthal/Karg von Bebenburg 1966, S. 19.
64 Hofmannsthal 1979, S. 144.
65 Hofmannsthal 1946–1965, S. 17.
66 Hofmannsthal/George 1953, S. 78.
67 Vgl. Braegger 1979, S. 49–56.
68 Hofmannsthal 1979, «Gedichte/Dramen I 1891–1898», S. 380.
69 Hofmannsthal 1979, «Gedichte und Dramen I 1891–1898», S. 21.
70 Hofmannsthal 1979, «Erzählungen, Erfundene Gespräche und Briefe, Reisen», S. 19 ff.
71 Hofmannsthal 1979, S. 565.
72 Ebd., S. 565.
73 Vgl. Curtius 1968, S. 14.
74 Hofmannsthal 1979, S. 566 f.

Schlaftrunken bin ich. Mir scheint, dort fällt
Ein Stern. Wie groß ist doch die Welt!
So viele Sachen sind darin.
Mir käm jetzt manches in den Sinn,
Wenn ich nur nicht so schläfrig wär ...»[75]

Hier ist jene Alchemie des Geistes am Werk, von der Ernst Robert Curtius mit Blick auf Hofmannsthals Calderon-Schöpfungen spricht:[76]: ererbte Kunstformen und Kulturgüter werden eingeschmolzen, umgewandelt und zu neuem Leben emporgeführt.[77] Das kann ein Vers von Shakespeare sein oder eben auch eine Märchenprinzessin mit der altklugen Grazie der Kate Greenaway, die «eine Gestalterin von Glückwunschkarten gewesen und als Künstlerin geblieben war»[78] und deren Bilder Hofmannsthal gewiss nicht zu den «elementaren Offenbarungen des Genius» rechnete «die da sind Landschaften von Whistler, Menschenköpfe von Rembrandt»[79] (im Unterschied zu Ruskin, der Kate Greenaway öffentlich in einer Oxforder Vorlesung in die Reihe der bedeutendsten Künstler der Gegenwart und Vergangenheit hob und ihr privat versicherte, eine handgemalte Weihnachtskarte von ihr sei eine «größere Sache als Raffaels hl. Cäcilie»).[80] Dass die Präraffaeliten Hofmannsthals dramaturgische Phantasie auch nach der Jahrhundertwende weiter beschäftigten,[81] dokumentiert unter anderem ein Brief an Clemens Freiherr zu Franckenstein vom 23. April 1902, in dem er sich für die Übersendung von *Everyman* bedankt:

«Die Engländer sind sehr glücklich, sich hier (betreffend Szenenangaben und Bühnenbild) nicht an sehr Fernes, sondern an die Belebung des Altchristlichen durch die modernen Präraffaeliten anlehnen zu können, sozusagen eine aufgegossene Form des Stilisierten zu besitzen. Ich glaube, daß unser Theater nach Ähnlichem drängt: eine Bühne, die nicht zu *sein* prätendiert, sondern sich begnügt, zu bedeuten, synthetische, sparsame Gebärden usf.».[82]

V. «Zauber der Allegorie» – Die Präraffaeliten

Was Hofmannsthal an dem grossen englischen Stilisten Burne-Jones besonders bewunderte ist, «daß seine raffiniert geistreiche(n) Malerei»[83] Phantasie und Verstand in gleichem Masse anspreche:

«so völlig waren Phantasie und Verstand mit der Aufnahme dieser wundervoll geistreichen Linien, dieser archaischen und doch raffiniert suggestiven Mimik, dieser gedankenvollen Symbolik beschäftigt und eingenommen».[84]

Nirgends sei der «Zauber der Allegorie» weiter getrieben als im Werk des Burne-Jones. Und Hofmannsthal zitiert Ruskin: «Seine (d.i. Burne-Jones) wesentliche Veranlagung und Denkart drängt zur Personifikation. ... das erste Kapitel der Genesis zu illustrieren, würde ein anderer Adam und Eva malen, er sicherlich die Allegorie eines Tages der Schöpfung».[85] Der Kühnheit des Burne-Jones liege es nicht fern,

«Geradezu den malerischen Niederschlag einer platonischen Idee zu suchen, etwa den sechs Schöpfungstagen ein durchsichtiges Becken in die Hände zu geben, angefüllt mit solchem Farbenzauber, als geeignet ist, die Vorstellung des Tages der Blumen und Bäume, des Tages der Vögel und Fische, des Tages der Wasser und Winde hervorzurufen ...».[86]

Auch Ruskin fordert in *Modern Painters* eine «Wahrheit» der Kunst, die Verstand *und* Phantasie erfasse. Im Abschnitt «Die Definition der Größe der Kunst» wendet er sich gegen eine rein unterhaltende, auf oberflächliche Schönheit abzielende – eine in seinen Augen unwahre – Kunst.[87] Seine eigenen Prosagedichte verstand Hofmannsthal als «Darstellungen der Seelenverfassungen». Und die Bewunderung für Gedichte von Rilke fasst er einmal so zusammen: «diese einzigartigen, im Visuellen wurzelnden, ins Seelische hinübergreifenden Evocationen».[88] Die Malerei der Präraffaeliten, sagt er in *Über moderne englische Malerei* (1894) sei eine «Kunst der psychisch-leiblichen Schönheit», und sie sei «durch und durch ethisch»:

75 Hofmansthal 1979, «Gedichte und Dramen I 1891–1898», S. 380.
76 Hofmannsthal 1979, S. 566.
77 Curtius 1968, S. 14 ff.
78 Kemp 1983, S. 380 f.
79 Hofmannsthal 1979, «Reden und Aufsätze I 1891–1913», S. 552.
80 Kemp 1983, S. 380 f.
81 Renner 2000, S. 195 ff.
82 Hofmannsthal 1937, II, S. 71.
83 Hofmannsthal 1979, «Reden und Aufsätze I 1891–1913», S. 548.
84 Ebd., S. 546.
85 Ebd., S. 548. S. 547 f.
86 Ebd., S. 548.
87 Renner 2000, S. 181.
88 Hofmannsthal/Rilke 1978, S. 144.

«Diese Kunstwerke reden eine veredelnde Sprache direkt, viel direkter als edle Musik oder tiefsinnig gemalte Landschaft. Diese gemalten Menschen erziehen die Seele durch das Beispiel ihres edlen Betragens».[89]

Um das Gesagte zu verdeutlichen, kommt Hofmannsthal auf Dante zu reden, denn das Versenken in Dantes «Kunstgeheimnis» bilde den Kern der Tradition dieser englischen Künstler. Die tiefe sittliche Wirkung der Mimik Dantescher Gestalten beruhe auf dem, was man «im höchsten Sinne '*Takt*'» nenne: «Sie verrät ein Seelenleben, darin die geistreichste energievollste Begabung im Dienste der intensivsten *moralischen Wachheit* und des unnachgiebigsten *Strebens nach Wahrheit*» steht.[90] (Hervorhebung CPB).

«... in den zahllosen Gesprächen Dantes mit Verdammten, Büßenden und Seligen findet sich auffallend oft die Erwähnung eines Traurigwerdens, verlegenen Lächelns, flüchtigen Erblassens oder Erzürnens bei den redenden Männern oder Frauen; und nicht selten wissen wir uns nicht sofort Rechenschaft über den Grund dieser Emotionen zu geben. Nach einigem Nachdenken wird es uns *blitzartig* klar, und wir *schauern* zusammen vor ehrfurchtsvollem *Staunen* über das subtile und unerbittlich wahrhaftige Eigenleben dieser kleinen Gestalten; die Ursache ihrer Emotion war in den meisten Fällen die, daß sie in einem Wort, einem Eigennamen, der etwa im Gespräch unterlief, einer Sentenz, die zufällig fiel, mit der Luzidität hochbegabter überlegener Menschen eine Anspielung erkannten, oder die Analogie mit einem solchen Ereignisse spürten, das in ihrem vergangenen sittlichen Leben verhängnisvoll war».[91]

In diesem Passus, der die sublime Konversation im Lustspiel *Der Schwierige* (1920/1921) ahnen lässt, ist die Rede von dem mystischen Akt des Erkennens (Plotin),[92] von jener im Werk Hofmannsthals mehrfach belegten blitzartigen Offenbarung[93] – «im Tiefsten schaudernd vor unendlichem Staunen», – dem plötzlichen Draufkommen aufs Eigentliche.[94] Es handelt sich um Momente der Erhöhung, in denen «Verhältnisse mit Zauberblick» erfasst werden. Es sind imaginäre Momente, in denen die durch «seelenlose Vielwisserei»[95] verstellte Welt transparent wird auf ihren tiefsten Sinn. Auslöser kann ein Blick, eine Gebärde, eine ganze Gestalt – «ein Block aus Gebärden, die dicht übereinander liegen» sein oder auch die «konzentrierte, in ein einziges nie auszusprechendes Wort zusammengepresste Ausdrucksfähigkeit» eines stumm dastehenden Bauwerks. «Im Gleichnis», sagt Hofmannsthal einmal, «wird ein Teil von dem Raub, den das Sprache gewordene Denken am Leben begeht, diesem zurückerstattet».[96] Und über seine *Elektra* sagt er:

«In ihr ist zum ersten Mal der Versuch gemacht, *in einen tragischen Moment* eine *ganze* menschliche Psyche zusammenzupressen, sozusagen einen Querschnitt durch die Seele zu geben *auch mit allen physiologischen Untergründen*».[97]

Dass der Dichter, für den es nicht denkbar ist, «je aus seinem Beruf Worte zu machen»,[98] herausgehen zu können, hier an Grenzen stösst, ist offensichtlich. So kann er sich «die auf Sieg und Reinigung hinauslaufende, aufwärtsstürmende Motivenfolge, die sich auf Orest und seine Tat bezieht in der Musik (d.i. Richard Strauß) ungleich gewaltiger vorstellen ... als in der Dichtung»,[99] und zur Realisierung seiner *Bühne als Traumbild*[100] ist ihm der englische stage designer Edward Gordon Craig die «wichtigste Sache der Welt». An Graf Kessler schreibt er:

«Sie überschätzen ... ein wenig die ressourcen meiner Phantasie. Sie hat ihre ganz bestimmten Grenzen: und das Realisieren des Traumes, das wahre, geniale Regieführen liegt jenseits dieser Grenzen. ... Darum werde ich ohne den stage designer nicht arbeiten, und wenn ich einem Menschen an der Nase absehen kann, daß er diesen stage-designer *nicht* ersetzen kann, so ist es Ludwig von Hofmann. Vielleicht thue ich ihm unrecht, aber er kommt mir recht vor wie der 'deutsche Künstler', träumt und kann keine Lampe anzünden».[101]

«Wer die Bühne aufbaut», heisst es in *Die Bühne als Traumbild* (1903), müsse ein Dichter unter den Dichtern sein:

«Sein Auge muss schöpferisch sein, wie das Auge des Träumenden, der nichts erblickt, was ohne Bedeutung wäre. Ein Bild schaffen, auf dem nicht Fußbreit ohne Bedeutung ist, das ist alles. ... Wer die Bühne aufbauen wird, muss durchs Auge gelebt und gelitten haben».[102]

89 Hofmannsthal 1979, «Reden und Aufsätze I 1891–1913», S. 551.
90 Ebd., S. 552.
91 Ebd., S. 551.
92 Hofmannsthal 1979, «Reden und Aufsätze I 1891–1913», S. 191. Vgl. zu Plotin hier Anm. 118. Vgl. ferner: Braegger 1979, S. 56.
93 Renner 2000, S. 221.
94 Vgl. dazu auch Stern 1974, S. 15 f.
95 Vgl. Hofmannsthal/Karg von Bebenburg 1966, S. 57 f. 1895 steht in den Aufzeichnungen: «Lebensweg; führt zu immer stärkerer Magie, Fähigkeit, Verhältnisse mit Zauberblick zu ergreifen», in: Hofmannsthal 1979, «Reden und Aufsätze III 1925–1929 / Buch der Freunde / Aufzeichnungen 1889–1929», S. 405.
96 Braegger 1982, S. 49–78.
97 Renner 2000, S. 205.
98 Hofmannsthal 1979, «Reden und Aufsätze I 1891–1913», S. 232.
99 Vgl. Hofmannsthal/Strauß 1964, S. 19.
100 Hofmannsthal 1979, «Reden und Aufsätze I 1891–1913», S. 409–493.
101 Hofmannsthal/Kessler 1966, S. 56. – Zu: «deutscher Künstler» vgl. weiter oben.
102 Hofmannsthal 1979, «Reden und Aufsätze I 1891–1913», S. 490.

Da die bildende Kunst Seele durch Körper bildet, also – mit Johann Gottfried Herder – eine «beständige Allegorie» ist[103], erstaunt es nicht, wenn Hofmannsthals Ausstellungsbesprechung moderner englischer Malerei in einer «Reflexion über das Verfahren von Allegorisierung und über Kunst als Repräsentation von Seelischem» kulminiert:[104]

«Psyche, unsere Seele. Selbstvorstellung, ahnend träumen, wie die eigene Seele unbegreiflich einsam die unsäglich schauerlichen Gefilde des Daseins durchwandelt, unwissend, von wo sie komme und wohin sie gehe, im Tiefsten *schaudernd* vor unendlichem *Staunen*, vor Sehnsucht und Traurigkeit, das ist die *tiefste Funktion aller Phantasie*. Diese *primitive Anschauung des Daseins*, in welcher *Staunen* das erste und größte Element ist, redete aus allen Bildern».[105] (Hervorhebung CPB)

VI. Die Kunstsprache und die Sprache der Wissenschaft: Leonardo, Goethe, Ruskin, Hofmannsthal

Von Ruskin sagt Hofmannsthal, er habe «mit berauschender Beredsamkeit aus Bildern die lebendigen Seelen der Künstler und der Dinge»[106] herausgedeutet. Berauschend hat hier nichts mit der «ästhetischen Schwatzseligkeit» (Nietzsche)[107] zu tun, sondern viel mehr mit der Trunkenheit des Magiers – «Festordners des Daseins»[108] – wie dieser in der Figur des Wahnsinnigen in Hofmannsthals lyrischem Drama *Das kleine Welttheater* (1897) verkörpert ist, den man sich durchaus präraffaelitisch vorstellen darf; er ist «jung schön und sanft» und von «unbeschreiblicher Anmut».[109] Von ihm sagt ein Diener:

> «... funkelnde Erfahrung legte
> Sich um seiner Augen innre Kerne.
> Wo er auftritt, bringen kluge Künstler
> Ihm herbei ihr lieblichstes Gebilde;
> Mit den Augen, den beseelten Fingern
> Rührt ers an und nimmt sich sein Geheimnis,
> Das der Künstler selbst nur dunkel ahnte,
> Nimmt es atmend mit auf seinem Wege.
> ...
> Seine Augen ruhen auf der Landschaft,
> Die noch nie ein solcher Blick getroffen:
> Zu den schönsten Hügeln, die mit Reben
> An die dunklen, walderfüllten Berge

Angebunden sind, zu schönen Bäumen,
Redet er: er will von ihnen Lächeln,
Von den Felsen will sein starker Wille
Eine atmend wärmere Verkündung,
Alle stummen Wesen will er, flehend,
Reden machen, in die trunkne Seele ...».[110]

Solchen «entbundenen ins Wesen schauenden Augen»[111] ist für Hofmannsthal gegeben, «naiv zu sehen», zu staunen, den «Banden des Hörensagens»[112] zu entspringen. Solchem sinnlich-erkennenden, ursprünglichen Sehen zeigt sich das, was dem durch Vielwisserei diskursiv verbauten Blick versagt ist. «... du vermagst nicht zu schauen, weil deine Augen vermauert sind mit dem was nicht ist», sagt Sigismund in *Der Turm* zu Olivier.[113] An Edgar Karg schreibt Hofmannsthal 1894:

«... das allein Wissenswerte, der Sinn des Daseins, ist aus jeder einzelnen tiefsinnig erfassten Erscheinung des Lebens ganz ebenso zu verstehen, d.h. in einer *blitzartigen Offenbarung* für den Moment zu erhaschen und mit *den eigenen tiefen Ahnungen* und *dumpfen Vermutungen der Seele* in Beziehung zu setzen, als wie aus einem ganzen großen System von wissenschaftlich analysierten Erscheinungen».[114] (Hervorhebung CPB)

Ein solches primitives Anschauen des Daseins, in dem Erschaudern und Staunen das erste Element ist, diese frühe Form der unverbildeten Wahrnehmung, die «am Ende des Jahrhunderts positivistischer Tatsacheneuphorie»[115] verloren zu gehen drohte, fand Hofmannsthal bei Ruskin, der – wie Leonardo und Goethe – zu den «wenigen Sterblichen» gehört, die – nach Carlyle – «dauerhaft mit dem Glück gesegnet sind, kein System zu haben».[116] Aus der folgenden Bemerkung über Pherekydes von Syros geht hervor, dass Hofmannsthal in Ruskin einen Autor sah, der den Betrachter für die ästhetischen Qualitäten des Normalen sensibilisieren wollte:[117]

103 Vgl. dazu Braegger 1979, S. 51. Dort auch mehr über die Bedeutung Herders für Hugo von Hofmannsthal.
104 Renner 2000, S. 211.
105 Hofmannsthal 1979, «Reden und Aufsätze I 1891–1913», S. 547.
106 Ebd., S. 144.
107 Vgl. Nietzsche 1954, S. 407.
108 Renner 2000, S. 332.
109 Hofmannsthal 1979, «Gedichte / Dramen I 1891–1898», S. 380.
110 Ebd., S. 382–383.
111 Hofmannsthal 1979, «Reden und Aufsätze I 1891–1913», S. 530.
112 Ebd.
113 Hofmannsthal 1946–1965, «Dramen IV», S. 455.
114 Hofmannsthal/Karg von Bebenburg 1966, S. 58.
115 Renner 2000, S. 211.
116 Kemp 1983, S. 76.
117 Ebd., S. 74.

«er (Pherekydes) scheint erhabene unsägliche Dinge in sehr schönen feinen malerischen Metaphern ausgedrückt zu haben; er wußte vielleicht über den Sinn einer geknüpften Schnur und die Philosophie eines Henkelkruges Tieferes als wir alle, wenn wir nicht zufällig John Ruskin oder Gottfried Semper heißen».[118]

In einer der unter dem Titel *Rodauner Anfänge* zusammengefassten Notizen aus dem Jahr 1906 beschäftigt sich Hofmannsthal, «anknüpfend an Nietzsche»,[119] mit der Kunstsprache von Leonardo und Goethe – beide sind «Naturforscher ohne System, Erforscher einer Natur ohne System»:[120]

«Wissenschaftlern ist alles darum zu thun: das ausrechenbare zu finden – Künstler ist sich des variablen klar und hat Seelenstärke genug doch zum Ausdruck zu streben und zwar ein bildlicher (welcher Erfahrung voraussetzt): Künst.(lerische) Erfahrung giebt Möglichkeit sich dem Wesen der Dinge anzufühlen: Wissenschaftler Opfer des mechanischen Gebrauchs ihrer Termini: dagegen Behandlung der Farbenlehre durch Goethe: hier wie bei Lionardo ist der Punkt wo eine solche Frage in der Welt steht, gesucht, das Gefühl der Würdigkeit begleitet ihn durchaus».[121]

Hierher gehört ohne Zweifel auch Ruskins «Wissenschaft von den Erscheinungen», die er «science of aspects» nannte.[122] «... es gibt genausogut eine Wissenschaft von den Erscheinungen der Dinge, wie eine 'Natur'-Wissenschaft existiert. Und es ist genauso wichtig, herauszuarbeiten, welche Wirkungen die Dinge auf das Auge oder das Herz machen, wie festzustellen, aus welchen Atomen oder Schwingungen der Materie sie bestehen».[123] In Goethes wissenschaftlichen Bestrebungen will Hofmannsthal nicht ein Hinausgehen aus der Kunst «Worte zu machen» sehen: vielmehr ziehe die Vorrede zur Farbenlehre mit «geheimnisvoller Kraft» den Leser in den tiefsten Kreis dichterischer Anschauung:

«Wie wird da den Leiden und Taten des Lichts mit der *einen* Absicht nachgegangen, die geheimnisvolle Sprache aufzuschließen, in der die Natur zu bekannten, zu unbekannten, zu verkannten Sinnen redet; ein stummes Mehr oder Weniger, ein Tuen, ein Leiden, ein Vordringendes und Zurückhaltendes, in dem das Dasein sich bewegt, mit einer Sprache zu beschenken, wie Shakespeare seinen Tätigen und Leidenden, seinem Lear, seiner Cordelia die flammenden und die milden Worte zuteilte».[124]

VII. «The Desire of the Eyes»

Hofmannsthal hat schon früh die Gabe eines «geheimnisvoll begünstigte(n) Auge(s)» mit dem Dichterischen «in mir».[125] In *Lucidor* sagt er: «Niemand findet leicht als erster etwas Auffälliges: denn es ist dem Menschen im allgemeinen nicht gegeben, zu sehen, was ist».[126] Und vom Dichter heisst es in *Der Dichter und diese Zeit* (1906), er sei der «Zuseher», der «versteckte Genosse, der lautlose Bruder aller Dinge»; «ist nichts als Auge und Ohr ... Es ist als hätten seine Augen keine Lider».[127] Nichts verbindet Hofmannsthal mit Ruskin so sehr als der Sehtrieb, die Lust am Schauen, das «spektatorische Verhalten».[128] Beide haben «durchs Auge gelebt und gelitten».[129] An der Wurzel von Ruskins Begabung sitzt, wie der Symbolist Arthur Symons gesagt hat, die «Religion der Augen»[130] – wie Ruskin selbst sagt: «The Desire of the Eyes».[131] Wolfgang Kemp hat die Karriere, den Weg vom *sight-seer* zum «*seer*» also zum Seher im übertragenen Sinne, als Leidensweg einer «zu großen Begabung» (Ruskin) luzid beschrieben.[132] Ruskin sah sich dazu berufen, stellvertretend und autoritativ zu sehen, wenn niemand sonst mehr sieht. «Wer aus der großen schwatzenden Menge kann mir die Formen und die Abgründe der weißen Gebirgskette beschreiben, die gestern nachmittag den Horizont umgürtete? Wer hat den feinen Sonnenstrahl erblickt, der von Süden kam und auf ihren Gipfeln brannte, bis sie im blauen Regenstaub dahinschmolz? Wer hat dem Tanz der toten Wolken zugeschaut, als das Sonnenlicht gestern abend von ihnen gewichen und der Westwind sie wie welke Blätter vor sich hertrieb? Alles zog vorüber, unbeachtet, ungesehen».[133]

Bei Hofmannsthal – auch er ein leidenschaftlicher Wolkenbeschauer – ist es der greise Tizian in dem Bruchstück *Der Tod des Tizian* (1892), dem es allein gegeben ist, die «Schönheit aller Formen» der Natur zu verstehen:

> «Er hat den Wolken, die vorüberschweben,
> Den wesenlosen, einen Sinn gegeben:
> Der blassen, weißen schleierhaftes Dehnen

118 Hofmannsthal 1979, «Reden und Aufsätze I 1891–1913», S. 191. – Anschliessend zitiert Hofmannsthal Plotin, der jedes Erkennen einer Wahrheit einen mystischen Akt nannte.
119 Hofmannsthal 1991, S. 126 ff.
120 Ebd.
121 Hofmannsthal 1991, S. 129.
122 Kemp 1983, S. 76.
123 Zitiert nach Kemp 1983, S. 76.
124 Hofmannsthal, 1979, «Reden und Aufsätze I 1891–1913», S. 232.
125 Hofmannsthal, 1979, S. 172.
126 Ebd., S. 176.
127 Hofmannsthal 1979, «Erzählungen, Erfundene Gespräche und Briefe, Reisen», S. 67.
128 Kemp 1983, S. 432.
129 Hofmannsthal 1979, «Reden und Aufsätze I 1891–1913», S. 492.
130 Zitiert nach Kemp 1983, S. 432
131 Ebd., S. 432.
132 Ebd., S. 432.
133 Zitiert nach Kemp 1983, S. 74 und S. 433.

Gedeutet in ein blasses, süßes Sehnen;
Der mächtgen goldumrandet schwarzen Wallen
Und runde, graue, die sich lachend ballen,
Und rosig silberne, die abends ziehn:
Sie haben Seele, haben Sinn durch ihn».[134]

Die Maler sind dazu da, wird Hofmannsthal später – mit Blick auf Van Gogh – sagen, der Erscheinung das Pathos zurückzugeben:

«Die Maler sind da, uns mit der Erscheinung auszusöhnen, der Erscheinung ihr *Pathos* zurückzugeben».[135]

Tizian lehrt die Menschen, die Dinge zu sehen. Durch ihn wird die Natur lesbar. Aber auch Nietzsches Vorstellung ist hier prägend, wonach die Natur des Künstlers bedarf: «nämlich zu ihrer eignen Aufklärung über sich selbst, damit ihr endlich einmal als reines und fertiges Gebilde entgegengestellt werde, was sie in der Unruhe ihres Werdens nie deutlich zu sehen bekommt – also zu ihrer Selbsterkenntnis».[136] Mit Van Gogh betreten wir zwar einen anderen zeitlichen Kontext, doch auch hier wird deutlich, dass Hofmannsthal, nicht anders als Ruskin, die ästhetische Wahrnehmungsfähigkeit des Menschen bedroht sah.[137] 1907 spricht er von «Verfassungen des ungeheuersten Zweifels in der europäischen Luft»[138] und 1906 von einem Gefühl tiefster Unsicherheit zwischen «Schauenden und Geschautem»:

«Eine furchtbar gesteigerte Dialectik gewohnt bauchrednerisch jeden Standpunkt im All einzunehmen hat uns enteignet in uns selbst: in schwankendem Ungefähr zerzittert unser Selbstgefühl. Zwischen Schauenden und Geschautes Fühlenden und Gefühltes drängt sich Gefühl tiefster Unsicherheit unsere Leidenschaften sind ein Citat, unsere Gesetze wurzeln nicht und nicht einmal unsere Vergehungen in unseren Herzen. *Wo nur der ganze Mensch auf einen Antrieb sich regen dürfte, regen sich immer nur Theile.* Alle Formen überwältigen uns, Mächte unterjochen uns: unendliche Relativitäten unterhöhlen uns und schließlich das Geld bleibt als Ende aller Reihen».[139]

Eine von Ruskins Obsessionen war, dass der Mensch durch die moderne Produktionsweise in blosse Segmente von Mensch geteilt, «in kleine Bruchstücke und Krumen von Leben»[140] gebrochen würde, und seine Zivilisationskritik reicht bis zur Befürchtung, das menschliche Organ, das geschaffen war, die Unendlichkeit der Schöpfung wahrzunehmen, könnte sich zurückentwickeln. In Band 3 der *Modern Painters* kommt er auf diese zunehmende Apperzeptionsschwäche der Zeit zu sprechen. Ausgangspunkt sind die neuen technischen Errungenschaften, deren

Auswirkung auf den Menschen er, so Wolfgang Kemp, «ganz richtig in den Rahmen einer Medientheorie einzuordnen versucht».[141]

«Daß wir hundert Meilen in der Stunde zurücklegen, tausend Ellen Stoff in der Minute fabrizieren können, wird uns nicht das geringste stärker, glücklicher oder weiser machen. Es gab immer mehr in der Welt, als Menschen sehen konnten, gingen sie auch noch so langsam. Bei schnellem Gehen werden sie es nicht besser sehen. Schließlich werden sie bald herausfinden, daß ihre großen (wie sie meinen) Raum und Zeit überwindenden Erfindungen in Wirklichkeit nichts überwinden, denn Raum und Zeit sind in sich unüberwindlich und wollen außerdem auf keine Weise überwunden, sondern *ausgenützt* sein. Der Tor will Raum und Zeit immer verkürzen; der Weise will sie erst gewinnen und sodann beleben. Wenn man sie recht versteht, ist die Eisenbahn nur ein Mittel, die Welt kleiner zu machen, und was das betrifft daß man nun imstande ist, von einem Ort zum andern zu sprechen, so ist es freilich gut und schön, aber stelle dir vor, du hättest im Grunde nichts zu sagen».[142]

Hofmannsthals Abneigung gegen das Telefon – «diese indiskrete Maschine» (*Der Schwierige*)[143] – ist berühmt. Hofmannsthal hat einmal die Zeit nach der Jahrhundertwende, in der nach Musil Traum verloren ging und Wirklichkeit gewonnen wurde,[144] als seine schwerste bezeichnet. Die quälende Krise, die sich in seinem Leben um 1900 nachweisen lässt, findet ihren Ausdruck in dem epochemachenden *Brief* (Brief des Lord Chandos) aus dem Jahre 1902. Hinter Lord Chandos, einem jungen Landedelmann der elisabethinischen Epoche, lasse sich, so Hermann Broch, unschwer der «gebildete Oxford-Graduate und Gentleman-Ästhet unserer Tage» entdecken.[145] Der *Brief* trägt das fiktive Datum 22. August 1603. Francis Bacon, Novalis, Maeterlinck, Mauthner u.a. bilden den Nährboden, auf dem er wurzelt.[146] Dass darin einem aktuellen Erlebnis, einer lebendigen Erfahrung des Dichters Ausdruck verliehen wurde, zeigt sich nicht zuletzt darin, dass Hofmannsthal den *Brief* nicht irgendwo, etwa im Feuilleton oder auf der Literaturseite, sondern auf der Seite 1 der Zeitschrift *Der Tag*, der damals grössten Tageszeitung,

134 Hofmannsthal 1979, «Erzählungen, Erfundene Gespräche und Briefe, Reisen», S. 255.
135 Hofmannsthal 1991, S. 437.
136 Nietzsche 1954, Bd. I, S. 326.
137 Zu Hofmannsthal und die Avantgarde vgl. Braegger 1995.
138 Hofmannsthal 1991, S. 438.
139 Ebd., S. 131.
140 Ruskin 1994, Bd. 2, S. 189.
141 Kemp 1983, S. 234.
142 Zitiert nach Kemp 1983, S. 234 f.
143 Hofmannsthal 1946–1965, «Lustspiele», Bd. 2, S. 195.
144 Vgl. Braegger 1980: «... ihre Bierhäuser ... ihre Hermannsdenkmäler ...», Hofmannsthals *Briefe des Zurückgekehrten* und *Der junge Menzel* von Julius Meier-Graefe. Zum Musil-Zitat: Musil 1970, S. 39.
145 Broch 1974, S. 119.
146 Hofmannsthal 1991, S. 280–281.

veröffentlichen liess.[147] Der *Brief* handelt – hier pauschal ausgedrückt – vom Zerfall der sichtbaren Welt in Teile. «Es zerfiel mir alles in Teile, die Teile wieder in Teile»[148] – und vom Verlust der Fähigkeit, das «ganze Dasein als eine große Einheit»[149] zu fassen.

«Mein Fall ist, in Kürze dieser: Es ist mir völlig die Fähigkeit abhanden zu kommen, über irgend etwas zusammenhängend zu denken oder zu sprechen. ... Es gelang mir nicht mehr, sie (die Menschen und ihre Handlungen) mit dem vereinfachenden Blick der Gewohnheit zu erfassen. Es zerfiel mir alles in Teile, die Teile wieder in Teile, und nichts mehr ließ sich mit einem Begriff umspannen».[150]

Am Schluss des Briefes wird eine Sprache heraufbeschworen, in der die Dinge selbst, unmittelbar, zur Sprache kommen, «eine Sprache, von deren Worten mir auch nicht eines bekannt ist, eine Sprache, in welcher die stummen Dinge zu mir sprechen, und in welcher ich vielleicht einst im Grabe vor einem unbekannten Richter mich verantworten werde».[151] Eine solche Sprache, in der das Wortlose, das Ungeheure sich hergibt, findet Hofmannsthal 1907 in den Farben. Die gleichnamige Prosaarbeit *Die Farben* ist eingefügt in *Die Briefe des Zurückgekehrten*, in denen Hofmannsthal den Begriff «ganz» geradezu fetischisiert.[152] Und diese erfundenen Briefe, 1907 entstanden und auf das Jahr 1901 zurückdatiert, sind im ganzen die schärfste Analyse und Kritik, die je eine seiner Figuren am Zustand *seiner* Epoche äussert. Es ist die Wilhelminische Zeit und die Gesellschaft des Deutschen Reiches, in welcher der 1883 Ausgewanderte sein damals mitgenommenes und in Erinnerung behaltenes Deutschland nicht mehr erkennt. «Was er feststellt ist das Syndrom eines angeblich alle Schichten erfassenden *Persönlichkeitszerfalls*».[153]

VIII. Kulturkritik – Ruskin, Meier-Graefe und Hofmannsthal

> «The whole man must move at once.»
> (Hofmannsthals Lieblingsspruch)[154]

In der Zahl guter und schöner Bücher, so wie er sie am Vorabend einer längeren Reise für den Bücherkoffer zusammenstellen würde, nennt Hofmannsthal im Herbst 1906 Julius Meier-Graefes eben erschienene Schrift *Der junge Menzel: ein Problem der Kunstökonomie Deutschlands*. Hofmannsthal attestiert Meier-Graefes Menzel «geistvolle Gerechtigkeit ... ein Produkt des Schwunges und scharfzüngiger Raschheit»:

«Das höchst prekäre Problem der deutschen bildenden Kunst ist allmählich ein zentrales, ein allgemein sittliches, ein politisches Problem geworden. Hier ist es an einem Individuum aufgezeigt».[155]

Was Hofmannsthal an Meier-Graefe hervorhebt, ist eine besondere Haltung der Kunst gegenüber, die er schon in den frühen neunziger Jahren an John Ruskin und Walter Pater wie eine Offenbarung erlebt hatte.[156] An Meier-Graefe gefällt ihm, dass er über «ein Waschgeschirr ebenso vernünftig» spricht wie «über einen Gobelin»,[157] und von dessen *Delacroix-Monografie* sagt Hofmannsthal, sie berühre, was sie berührt «im Lebenspunkt»: sie sei aus einer «wahrhaft produktiven Natur, aus *produktiver Leidenschaft hervorgegangen*», und wirke so auf das «Innerste des Lesers, mit einer wunderbaren Doppelkraft zugleich befeuernd und zügelnd». Und dann heisst es:

«Daß die ästhetische Belehrung ein Ingrediens der höchsten Bildung für die Elite einer Nation sein kann, und gerade der kraftvollsten Nation, ist bewiesen durch die Bedeutung, die ein Individuum wie Ruskin für die Engländer hatte. In Deutschland wüsste ich nicht, wer mehr dafür getan hätte als Meier-Graefe, *aus dem Ästhetischen* ein *wahres Schwungrad für das gesamte geistige Leben zu schaffen*».[158] (Hervorhebung CPB)

Meier-Graefe versteht wie Ruskin (und Hofmannsthal) die Kunst als Manifestation einer Kultur als Ganzheit, als sichtbares Merkmal ihrer Einheit, als sensibler Anzeiger der Zeit. Sie ist der grosse Meister der Kultur eines Volkes,[159] «seiner Seele, seines Genies»: Zur Erklärung der Dekadenz des späten Menzel gehört für Meier-Graefe die Voraussetzung eines «ungeheuerlichen Verfalls des Volkes». Denn: «so gut wie jedes Land die Fürsten, die Staatsmänner, die Gelehrten, die Frauen und die Polizisten hat, die ihm zukommen, so gut hat es die Kunst, die es verdient».[160] Menzels Kunst sei «unschädlich», was bedeutet: sie reisst nur an «epidermalen

147 Vgl. Quander 1985, Heft 8, S. 220.
148 Hofmannsthal 1991, S. 49.
149 Ebd., S. 47.
150 Ebd., S. 48.
151 Ebd., S. 54.
152 Vgl. Stern 1974, S. 17.
153 Ebd.
154 Hofmannsthal/Degenfeld 1986, S. 175. – Das Wort stammt von Richard Steele (1671–1729) und steht in der von Addison gemeinsam mit Steele gegündeten Zeitschrift *Spectator* vom 7. März 1711, wo der Satz lautet: «The whole man is to move together»: Hofmannsthal übernahm den Satz von Lichtenberg. Vgl. Hofmannsthal 1991, S. 273 (Erläuterungen).
155 Hofmannsthal 1979, «Reden und Aufsätze I 1891–1913», S. 374.
156 Hofmannsthal/Meier-Graefe 1998, S. 10.
157 Hofmannsthal über Julius Meier-Graefe, zitiert nach Stern 1974, S. 16.
158 Zitiert nach Stern 1974, S. 20.
159 Ruskin sagt: «Die Kunst eines Volkes ist der Ausdruck seiner gesellschaftlichen und politischen Tugenden ... Die Kunst, das heißt die allgemeine schöpferische und formbildende Energie eines Volkes, ist ein mathematisch genauer Exponent seiner ethischen Lebenskraft». Zitiert nach Kemp 1983, S. 323 f.
160 Meier-Graefe 1914, S. 258.

Empfindungen, weil sie selbst aus keiner Durchdringung der Erscheinung, sondern nur im wesentlichen von einer Aufnahmetätigkeit herrührt, die im besten Fall färbt, nicht dichtet». Menzels späte Malerei durchbohre nicht «unsere Physis bis zu unserer Seele».[161] Sie ist nicht Offenbarung, um mit Hofmannsthal zu reden, dem es vor einem Bild die Hauptsache ist,

«ob hier eine künstlerische Individualität die freie Kraft gehabt hat, eine neue, aus lebendigen Augen erschaute Perzeption des Weltbildes in einer Weise darzustellen, die sich der Seele des Betrachters zu übertragen geeignet ist».[162]

Meier-Graefe wirft dem späten Menzel Mutlosigkeit vor; er sei genial in seiner Art, sein Genie zu unterdrücken und habe seine Kunst dem vulgären deutschen Materialismus verschwistert, sei ein fleissiger Pflichtmensch geworden und damit eine Übertreibung einer längst vorhandenen Eigentümlichkeit dieses Landes. Ähnlich erkennt Meier-Graefe in der Liebe der Deutschen zum theatralischen Bombast des späten Böcklin das Korrelat zu den materialistischen und militaristischen Tendenzen der Wilhelminischen Ära. – «Der Fall Böcklin ist der Fall Deutschland».[163]

Im Juli 1907, auf dem Rückweg von Venedig nach Rodaun bei Wien, schreibt Hofmannsthal in Welsberg an den *Briefen des Zurückgekehrten*. Der Zustand ist «fieberhafte Heftigkeit des Arbeitenmüssens», wie er an Baron Oppenheimer schreibt.[164] Zur gleichen Zeit liest er in Van Goghs Korrespondenz und, bereits zuvor, in Venedig im Juni Meier-Graefes Buch über die Impressionisten.[165]

«PS. Der Mann heißt Vincenz (sic!) van Gogh. Nach den Jahreszahlen im Katalog, die nicht alt sind, müsste er leben. Es ist etwas in mir, das mich zwingt zu glauben, er wäre von meiner Generation, wenig älter als ich selbst».[166]

Das Postskript beschliesst den vierten der fünf (veröffentlichten) Briefe. Die Entwürfe aus dem Nachlass lassen erkennen, dass Hofmannsthal eine Art Novelle in Briefen plante, die dann dem ebenfalls Bruchstück gebliebenen Roman *Andreas* geopfert wurde. Zwei Notizen aus dem Nachlass lassen vermuten, dass dem Zurückgekehrten eine Art Wilhelm-meisterliche Sendung zugedacht war:[167]

«Was Farbe für ein Geheimnis ist. Ein rotbasaltener Bergkegel. ... Könnte ich das definieren: warum die *Farbe* aufschäumender Wellen an einem Sturm-regentag ... warum das – (gerade die Farbe davon) mir mein ganzes Leben zu enthalten schien es war ein grau, darin ein Abgrund, ein Dahinstürzen ... / Aus The life and sayings of Râmakrishna. / ... aus Van Goghs Correspondenz. / den Deutschen die hohe Geistlichkeit der Farbe aufschließen. Aus Fromentin eine Stelle ... / ferner Delacroix, Bodenhausen, Goethe Farbenlehre».[168]

Das Sendungsbewusstsein, das hier durchklingt, lässt ebenso an Ruskin denken wie die Leidenschaft, der Farbe ihr «abgrundtiefes Geheimnis» abzuringen.[169] Die Briefe eins bis drei, die dem *Erlebnis des Sehens*[170] der Van Gogh-Gemälde vorausgehen, stehen ganz im Zeichen einer Deutschlandschelte, die an die heftigen Ausbrüche gegen Deutschland in Hölderlins *Hyperion* und an die eruptive Deutschenschelte Nietzsches anknüpfen. Sie sind Dokumente einer Kulturkritik, «die so entschieden und unverhüllt bis dahin von Hofmannsthal nirgends geübt wurde».[171]

«Ich weiß nicht, auf was hin die Leute leben, das ist es, und je länger ich mich unter ihnen bewege, umso weniger weiß ich es. Sie sind ernsthaft, sie sind tüchtig, sie arbeiten, wie keine Nation auf der Welt, sie erreichen das Unglaubliche – aber es ist keine Freude, unter ihnen zu leben. Daß ich achtzehn Jahre fort war und nur zurück bin und das hinschreiben muss»![172]

Der Schreibende, ein Kaufmann, ist seit vier Monaten wieder in Deutschland; aber kein Haus, kein Fleck Erde, kein geredetes Wort hat ihm irgendwie ein Zeichen gegeben, dass er sich wieder in der Heimat befinde. Die Entfremdung bewirkt, dass ihm auch das Schauen «eine fast dauerlose Übelkeit» bereitet – «es war wie ein momentanes Schweben über dem Bodenlosen, dem Ewig-Leeren»:

«... ein paar Bäume ... ich konnte sie ansehen und wußte, daß sie mich an Bäume erinnerten – keine Bäume waren ... Dann kam es auf der Eisenbahn, öfter und öfter. Ich fuhr in diesen vier Monaten sehr viel Eisenbahn. Da konnte es sich einstellen, in der trivialsten Beleuchtung, um 3 Uhr nachmittag, wann immer: kleine Stadt links oder rechts von Gleis, oder Dorf oder Fabrik, oder die ganze Landschaft, Hügel, Felder, Apfelbäume, verstreute Häuser, alles in allem: das nahm ein Gesicht an, eine eigene zweideutige Miene so voll innerer Unsicherheit, bösartiger Unwirklichkeit: so nichtig lag es da – so gespensterhaft nichtig ...».[173]

Hofmannsthal beschreibt hier, wie Otto K. Werckmeister betont hat, als einer der ersten das Gefühl beklemmender Fremdheit bei der einfachen Wahrnehmung der Dinge wie wenig früher Kafka und später Musil.[174] Mit der Krise eines inneren

161 Ebd., S. 242.
162 Hofmannsthal 1979, «Reden und Aufsätze I 1891–1913», S. 527.
163 Meier-Graefe 1905.
164 Hofmannsthal 1937, S. 284.
165 Vgl. Braegger 1980 (wie Anm. 144).
166 Hofmannsthal 1991, S. 171.
167 Ebd., S. 416 ff. (Varianten und Erläuterungen).
168 Ebd., S. 436.
169 Vgl. ebd., S. 438.
170 Unter dem Titel «Das Erlebnis des Sehens» veröffentlichte Hofmannsthal die beiden letzten der fertigen Briefe in *Kunst und Künstler* (Februar 1908). Vgl. Hofmannsthal 1991, S. 425.
171 Vgl. Rudolf 1972, S. 48.
172 Hofmannsthal 1991, S. 157.
173 Ebd., S. 166.
174 Werckmeister 1961, S. 40–60.

Übelbefindens geht eine Erschütterung der Identität einher, die der Zurückgekehrte als Verunsicherung des praktischen Verhaltens erfährt.[175] Der Zufall führt ihn in eine Van Gogh-Ausstellung.[176]

«Mein Lieber, es gibt keine Zufälle, und ich sollte diese Bilder sehen, sollte die in dieser Stunde sehen, in dieser aufgewühlten Verfassung, in diesem Zusammenhang ... Da ist ein unglaubliches, stärkstes Blau, das kommt immer wieder, ein Grün wie von geschmolzenen Smaragden, ein Gelb bis zum Orange. ... Wie kann ich es dir nahebringen, daß hier jedes Wesen – *ein Wesen* jeder Baum, jeder Streif gelben oder grünlichen Feldes, jeder Zaun, jeder in den Steinhügel gerissene Hohlweg, ein Wesen der zinnerne Krug, die irdene Schüssel, der Tisch, der plumpe Sessel – sich mir wie neugeboren aus dem furchtbaren Chaos des Nichtlebens, aus dem Abgrund der Wesenlosigkkeit entgegenhob ... Wie kann ich es dir nur zur Hälfte nahebringen, wie mir diese Sprache in die Seele redete ...».[177]

Das Erlebnis des Sehens bewirkt eine Rückgewinnung der Identität – «und war wie doppelt, war Herr über mein Leben zugleich Herr über meine Kräfte, meinen Verstand ...».[178] Das Erlebnis des Sehens bewirkt eine «glänzende Disposition» bei einer Konferenz, in der es um die Fusion zweier Grossfirmen geht:

«Ich musste zu einer Konferenz, der entscheidenden, letzten in der Kette von Verhandlungen, die darauf abzielten, die holländische Gesellschaft, für die ich ... arbeite, mit einer schon bestehenden englisch-deutschen zu vereinigen ...».[179]

Das ästhetische Erlebnis befreit ihn von Dumpfheiten, verleiht ihm die «Gabe des Zusammensehens» und eine geheimnisvolle Kraft, für die er keinen Namen weiss:

«... konnte für meine Gesellschaft mehr erreichen, als das Direktorium mir für den denkbar günstigsten Fall aufgelegt hatte, und ich erreichte es, wie man im Traum von einer kahlen Mauer Blumen abpflückt».[180]

Das Deutschland, das der Zurückgekehrte vorfindet, ist offensichtlich auch in der Kunst nicht fähig, ein bezwingend Eigenes zu schaffen. Wo die Dichtigkeit der Verhältnisse, das Gemeinschaftsbildende, «all das Ursprüngliche davon, das, was im Herzen sitzt»,[181] fehlt, ist für Hofmannsthal – und darin ist er ein Schüler Ruskins – auch keine ehrliche Kunst möglich. So haben die Deutschen ein «Einerseits» und ein «Andrerseits»,

«ihre Geschäfte und ihr Gemüt, ihren Fortschritt und ihre Treue, ihren Idealismus und ihren Realismus, ... ihre Bierhäuser und ihre Hermannsdenkmäler ... und stören in den Kaisergrüften herum, als wären es Laden voll alten Trödels, und zerren Karl den Großen aus seinem Sarg und photographieren den Stoff, der um seine Knochen gewickelt ist, und restaurieren ihre ehrwürdigen Dome zu Bierhäusern ... Etwas Uniformes ist in dem ganzen Treiben».[182]

Es fehlt in dem Wilhelminischen Deutschland, das dem Zurückgekehrten wie in einem bösartigen Traum erscheint, der Zeugungsgrund für eine «harmonische Seele ... eine Seele wie Corots Seele»; es fehlt die scharfe und bunte Atmosphäre, aus der nach Hofmannsthals Meinung solche Künstler wie Goya, Hogarth oder Delacroix hervortreten. Oder Daumier, der mit seinem «wunderbaren Stift und seinem gleich wunderbaren Pinsel» etwas wie den «Mythos des modernen Lebens»[183] geschaffen habe. Hinter solchen Kunstleistungen liege, so betont Hofmannsthal 1919 in einer Ansprache an die Mitglieder des österreichischen Werkbundes, das «als bewegend gefühlte ...» Volks- und soziale Element. In der selben Rede preist er die Leistungen des österreichischen Kunstgewerbes – «diese schönen, qualitativ hochstehenden, mit Liebe gefertigten Waren» als ein Exponent des «österreichischen Wesens», als «Ausstrahlungen eines ganz bestimmten Kulturmediums».[184]

«Es ist ... jenes Element des emporkultivierten Bäuerlichen, das in unserem Kunstgewerbe eine so große Rolle spielt ...».[185]

Dem europäisch-deutschen Gegenwartsgefühl, das ihn unter den deutschen «Eisen- und Maschinenleuten und Bankleuten» verfolgt, setzt der Zurückgekehrte sein Erinnerungsbild der archaisch-bäuerlichen Verhältnisse, aber ebenso seine Erfahrungen unter Halbwilden, in den Tropen, Südamerika und Asien entgegen. Sie waren alle ganz:

«The whole man must move at once – und so waren sie ... In *einer* Geberde erschienen sie mir, ... in ihrer *einen* Geberde, in der sie an mich heran- und durch mich hindurchwehten, waren sie *ganz*. Sie waren nicht von denen, deren rechte Hand nicht weiß, was die linke thut. Sie waren eins in sich selber. Und das – oder es müsste mich seit vier Monaten bei offenen Augen der bösartigste, vieltheiligste,

175 Rudolf 1972, S. 49.
176 Zur frühen Van Gogh-Rezeption in Deutschland vgl. Renner 2000, S. 419 ff.
177 Hofmannsthal 1991, S. 168–170.
178 Ebd., S. 170.
179 Ebd., S. 165.
180 Ebd., S. 170.
181 Ebd., S. 161.
182 Ebd., S. 160.
183 Hofmannsthal 1979, «Reden und Aufsätze I 1891–1913», S. 587.
184 Hofmannsthal 1946–1965, Bd. III, 1953, «Prosa», S. 456.
185 Ebd., S. 457.

zäheste aller bösen Träume narren – das sind die Deutschen nicht».[186] (Hervorhebung im Original)

Nach dem verlorenen Krieg führte Hofmannsthal seine Sehnsucht nach Ganzheit schliesslich völlig hinter die Neuzeit zurück. Er sprach – und da kommt er Ruskins Konservatismus nah – vom Unglück der Renaissance und der Reformation, die sowohl den alten Einheitsgedanken des Heiligen Römischen Reiches als auch die Union von weltlicher und religiöser Macht in Europa zerstört hätten. «Alles Seitherige verfiel damit seiner Kritik, ein Zerteiltes, ja Zerstückeltes zu sein. Hofmannsthal sprach von 'schöpferischer Restauration' und von 'konservativer Revolution' als einem Prozess, der die verlorene Ganzheit der deutschen Nation wieder bringen solle – ein Programm, das, um das Geistige verkleinert, das Hofmannsthal meinte, nur verhängnisvoll wirken konnte und als solches auch problematisch war».[187]

IX. Das heilige Stück Mittelalter und das Kino

In dem Kapitel «Die Natur der Gotik» der *Stones of Venice* kritisiert Ruskin die moderne Produktionsweise:

«Wir haben in letzter Zeit die große Kulturerfindung der Arbeitsteilung sehr studiert und vervollkommnet, aber wir geben ihr einen falschen Namen. Richtig ausgedrückt ist nicht die Arbeit geteilt, sondern die Menschen. Sie sind in bloße Segmente von Menschen geteilt – in kleine Krumen – Bruchstücke und Krumen des Lebens gebrochen, so daß das kleine Stückchen Intelligenz, das einem Menschen übrig gelassen ist, nicht genügt, um eine Nadel oder einen Nagel zu verfertigen, sondern sich darin erschöpft, die Spitze einer Nadel oder den Kopf eines Nagels zu machen. ... Und der große Schrei, der sich aus allen unsern Fabrikstädten erhebt, lauter als das Gebläse ihrer Hochöfen, entsteht wahrhaftig nur, weil wir alles dort fabrizieren, nur keine Menschen».[188]

Hofmannsthal geht zwar nicht so weit wie Ruskin, der die Ingenieurleistungen seiner Epoche und «unsere Schrauben und Schleifen als Wahnsinnstaten» bezeichnet;[189] aber auch für ihn ist die unmittelbare Vereinigung von Arbeit und Genuss der Arbeit Voraussetzung für ein «Gefühl des Selbst, auf welchem, wie auf einem Smaragd, die Welt ruhen muss».[190] Jeder ordentliche Bauer, sagt er weiter, ist «bei uns noch sein eigener Zimmermeister, sein eigener Korbflechter, sein eigener Steinmetz».

«In diesem Element west und waltet jenes Element der *Freude* an der Arbeit, der unzerteilten Arbeitsweise, der unmittelbaren Vereinigung von Arbeit und Genuss der Arbeit. Und dieses Stück Mittelalter, dieses unüberwindliche und heilige Stück Mittelalter als Träger eines hohen Selbstgefühls ist Ihnen (d.i. den Mitgliedern des österreichischen Werkbundes) und Ihrer Atmosphäre nahe».[191] (Hervorhebung CPB)

Das grosse Übel «aller christlichen Leistungen der letzten Zeit» liegt nach Ruskin darin, daß die Menschen in Wahrheit gar nicht wissen, was sie liebten und was nicht. – «Glaubt man vielleicht, daß irgend ein moderner Architekt das leiden mag, was er baut, oder daß er Freude daran hat? ... daß irgend ein lebendes Wesen in London Triglyphen oder Dreischlitze liebt? – oder seine Herzensfreude an Giebelfeldern (Tympanum) hat?»[192] In der gleichen Ansprache an die Mitglieder des Werkbundes kommt Hofmannsthal auf die Architektur und städtebauliche Fragen zu sprechen und sieht, wie Ruskin, ein zweites Grundübel des Historismus darin, dass man nicht notwendige Dinge, die einem praktischen oder edlen Zweck dienen, baut; und er erkennt Anzeichen einer erschöpften Kultur dort, wo der bürokratische Baugeist «ein bloß Formales der Kultur als ein Herrschendes bewahren zu können glaubt»:

«Ihre (d.i. des Werkbundes) Gegner pflegen sich, wie um eine Fahne, um den Begriff des Historischen, der Tradition und der Pietät gegen die Vergangenheit zu gruppieren. Nun muss man sagen, das hält doch eigentlich einer etwas aufmerksamen Prüfung nicht stand. Diejenigen Menschen, die eines leeren Schlagwortes willen, wie die Verkehrsfreiheit, ganz ohne nachzuprüfen, wo ein Verkehr dringend notwendig ist, wo er auch wirklich besteht, die Innere Stadt, eines der herrlichsten Baugebilde, so zugrunde gerichtet haben ... die in Form eines Baubüros und in unwürdiger Weise, die Pläne eines genialen Menschen wie Semper weiter verwaltend und entseelend, ein so unglückliches Gebäude wie das Burgtheater ... geschaffen haben, die es für möglich gehalten haben, neben das Palais Kinsky auf der Freyung eine scheußliche Kopie zu stellen ... als ob sie eine Karikatur hätten geben wollen, dieselben Menschen, die es schließlich zuließen, daß etwas wie das Kriegsministerium hingestellt wird, von dem man wirklich sagen muss, so hässlich kann nur

186 Hofmannsthal 1991, S. 156.
187 Vgl. Stern 1974, S. 18.
188 Ruskin 1994, Bd. II, S. 189.
189 Zitiert nach Kemp 1983, S. 136 und S. 137.
190 Hofmannsthal 1979, «Erzählungen, Erfundene Gespäche und Briefe, Reisen», S. 308.
191 Hofmannsthal 1946–1965, Bd. III, 1953, «Prosa», S. 462.
192 Ruskin 1994, Bd. I, S. 55.
193 Hofmannsthal 1946–1965, Bd. III, 1953, «Prosa», S. 463.

mehr ein Staat bauen, der an sich selbst nicht mehr glaubt, dieselben Menschen haben keine Ursache, von Pietät zu sprechen».[193]

Fast im hölderlinschen Sinne – «Wo aber Gefahr ist, wächst / Das Rettende auch» (*Patmos*) – sah Hofmannsthal um 1920 im Film eine Hilfsmagie,[194] die es den dem Wurzelgrund des Lebens durch die Allmacht der Technik und «industriellen Begehrlichkeiten» sich selbst entfremdeten Menschen ermöglicht, sich als Ganzes zu empfinden. Es scheine ihm, sagt er in der kleinen Prosaarbeit *Der Ersatz für die Träume* (1921), die «Atmosphäre des Kinos» die einzige, in welcher die Menschen unserer Zeit, «zu einem ungeheuren Erbe, wenn auch sonderbar zugerichteten geistigen Erbe in ein unmittelbares, ganz hemmungsloses Verhältnis»,[195] treten könnten: Denn auf dem Film fliege

«in zerrissenen Fetzen eine ganze Literatur vorbei, nein, ein ganzes Wirrsal von Literaturen, der Gestaltenrest von Tausenden von Dramen, Romanen, Kriminalgeschichten; die historischen Anekdoten, die Halluzinationen der Geisterseher, die Berichte der Abenteurer; aber zugleich *schöne Wesen* und *durchsichtige Gebärden*; *Mienen* und *Blicke*, aus denen die *ganze Seele hervorbricht*. Sie leben und leiden, ringen und vergehen vor den Augen des Träumenden; und der Träumende weiß, daß er wach ist; er braucht nichts von sich draußen zu lassen, mit allem, was in ihm ist ... starrt er auf dieses flimmernde Lebensrad, das sich ewig dreht. Es ist der *ganze Mensch*, der sich diesem Schauspiel hingibt: nicht ein einziger Traum aus der zartesten Kindheit, der nicht mit in Schwingung geriete».[196] (Hervorhebung CPB)

So kommt für Hofmannsthal dem (Stumm-)Film eine ähnliche Rolle zu wie der Malerei der Präraffaeliten: der Film soll heilsam wirken auf den modernen zersplitterten Menschen. Er soll die Gefühle und Gedanken in Bewegung setzen, staunen und erschaudern machen unter Ausklammerung der Sprache. Denn im Tiefsten, ohne es zu wissen, sagt Hofmannsthal, fürchten diese Leute die Sprache; sie fürchten in der Sprache das Werkzeug der Gesellschaft: «... Über dem Vortragssaal steht in goldenen Buchstaben 'Wissen ist Macht', aber das Kino ist stärker: es ruft mit Bildern». Und Hofmannsthal kommt wieder, wie am Anfang der neunziger Jahre, auf die Sprache der Bildungsphilister zu sprechen, die nicht das wecke, «was in der Tiefe schlummert»:

«Es ist zuviel von der Algebra in dieser Sprache, jeder Buchstabe bedeckt wieder eine Ziffer, die Ziffer ist die Verkürzung für eine Wirklichkeit ... aber dies alles ist zu indirekt, die Verknüpfungen sind zu unsinnlich, dies hebt den Geist nicht wirklich auf, trägt ihn nicht irgendwo hin. All dies lässt eher ... dies Gefühl, der ohnmächtige Teil einer Maschine zu sein ...».[197]

Hofmannsthal spricht hier von denen, «die in den Städten oder großen zusammenhängenden Industriebezirken wohnen» und nicht von den andern, «den Bauern, den Schiffern, Waldarbeitern und Bergbewohnern».

«Ihre Köpfe sind leer, nicht von Natur aus, eher durch das Leben, das die Gesellschaft sie zu führen zwingt. Da sind Anhäufungen von kohlengeschwärzten Industrieorten, mit nichts als einem Streifchen von verdorrtem Wiesengras zwischen ihnen ... da sind unsere Städte, diese endlosen einander durchkreuzenden Häuserzeilen ..., die Fabrik, der Arbeitssaal, die Maschine ... die Routine des Fabriklebens ... die paar Handgriffe, immer die gleichen; das gleiche Hämmern und Schwingen oder Feilen und Drehen; und zuhause wieder: der Gaskocher ... und die kleinen Maschinen, von denen man abhängt, auch das durch Übung so zu bewältigen, daß schließlich der, der sie bewältigt, selber zur Maschine wird ...».[198]

Eine Obsession Ruskins, auf die wiederum Wolfgang Kemp hinweist, war, dass die Himmel immer dunkler würden: «Keine Meile Wegstrecke ohne Hochofen und Fabrik: ... Wieviele Quadratmeilen englischen Bodens sollen dann innerhalb der nächsten 50 Jahre Kohlegruben, Ziegeleien oder Steinbruch werden. ... Kein Hektar englischen Bodens ohne Schacht oder Maschine ... kein Fleck, an dem Sie nicht Gefahr laufen, im nächsten Moment in die Luft gejagt zu werden»?[199]

193 Hofmannsthal 1946–1965, Bd. III, 1953, «Prosa», S. 463.
194 Vgl. Stern 1974, S. 13.
195 Hofmannsthal 1946–1965, Bd. IV, 1955, «Prosa», S. 50.
196 Ebd., S. 48 ff.
197 Ebd., S. 45 f.
198 Ebd., S. 45.
199 Zitiert nach Kemp 1983, S. 210 f.

Signiertes Porträtfoto John Ruskin
(Stiftung Bibliothek Werner Oechslin, Einsiedeln)

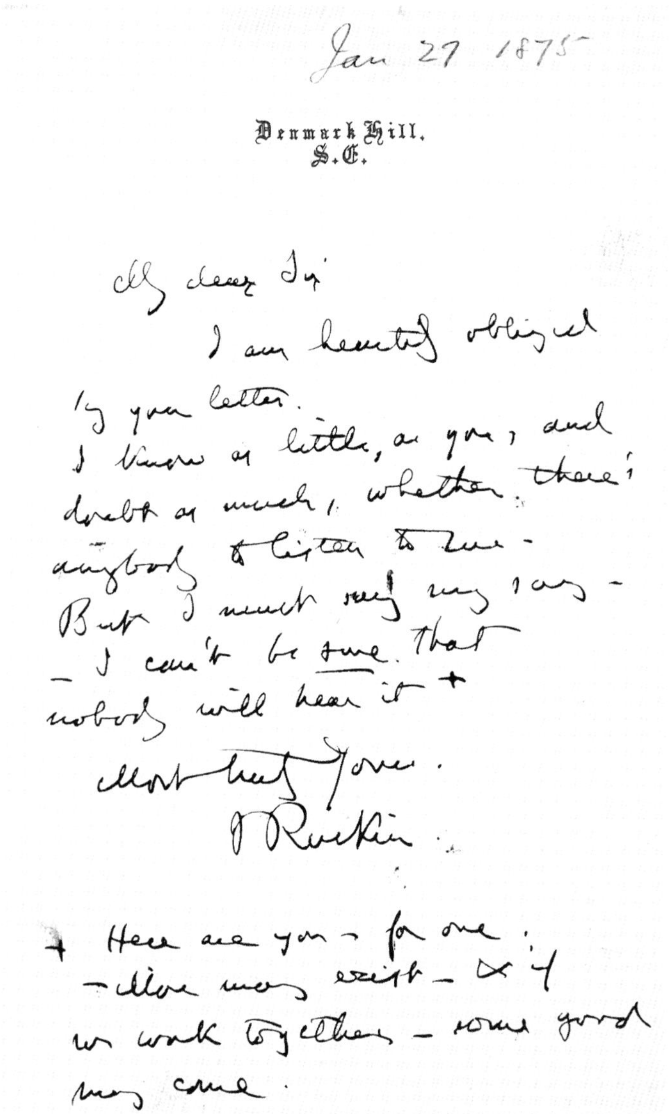
Jan 27 1875

Denmark Hill.
S.E.

My dear Sir

I am heartily obliged
by your letter.
I know as little, as you, and
doubt as much, whether there's
anybody to listen to me -
But I must say my say -
- I can't be sure that
nobody will hear it +

Most truly Yours.
J Ruskin.

+ Here are you - for one;
- More may exist - & if
we work together - some good
may come.

Handschriftlicher Brief John Ruskins vom 27. Januar 1875
(Stiftung Bibliothek Werner Oechslin, Einsiedeln)

Bibliografie

Abrams 1953: Abrams, M.H., *The Mirror and the Lamp: Romantic Theory and the Critical Tradition*, London/New York 1953 (Reprint 1974)

Ajchenval'd 1901: Ajchenval'd, Jurij, «Sesam und Lilien: Drei Vorlesungen» («Сезам и лилии: Три лекции»), in: *Vestnik vospitanija* 6 (1901), S. 37–46

Ajchenval'd 1910: Ajchenval'd, Jurij, «Notiz zu Ruskin» («Заметка о Рёскине»), in: Ajchenval'd, Jurij, *Einzelne Seiten*, Moskau 1910, Bd. 2

Altick 1974: Altick, Richard D., *Victorian People and Ideas*, London 1974

Anikin 1986: Anikin, Gennadij Viktorovič, *Die Ästhetik John Ruskins und die englische Literatur des XIX. Jahrhunderts (Эстетика Джона Рёскина и английская литература XIX века)*, Moskau 1986

Autret 1955: Autret, Jean, *L'Influence de Ruskin sur la vie, les idées et l'œuvre de Marcel Proust*, Genf 1955

Bahr 1968: Bahr, Hermann, *Zur Überwindung des Naturalismus*, Stuttgart 1968

Bakhtin 1981: Bakhtin, Michail Michajlovic, *The Dialogic Imagination: Four Essays*, Hg. Michael Holquist, Übersetzung Caryl Emerson und Michael Holquist, Austin/London 1981

Bann 1984: Bann, Stephen, *The Clothing of Clio: A Study of the Representation of History in Nineteenth-Century Britain and France*, Cambridge 1984

Bann 1988: Bann, Stephen, «Adrian Stokes. English Aesthetic Criticism under the Impact of Psychoanalysis», in: Edward Timms/Naomi Segal (Hg.), *Freud in Exile*, New Haven 1988

Barkan 1975: Barkan, Leonard, *Nature's Work of Art: The Human Body as Image of the World*, New Haven/London 1975 (Reprint 1977)

Batchelor 2000: Batchelor, John, *John Ruskin: No Wealth but Life*, London 2000

Beeching 1956: Beeching, Paul Quinn, *The eighteenth century background of Ruskin's The Poetry of Architecture*, Diss. Saint Louis University 1956

Bel'kind 1991: Bel'kind, E.L., «Blok als Leser John Ruskins» («Блок – читатель Дж. Рёскина»), in: *Alexander Blok: Untersuchungen und Materialien*, Leningrad 1991

Benn 1965: Benn, Gottfried, *Gesammelte Werke in vier Bänden*, Bd. I, Wiesbaden 1965

Benson 1906: Benson, Arthur Christopher, *Walter Pater. English Men of Letters*, London 1906

Birch 1988: Birch, Dinah, *Ruskin's Myths*, Oxford 1988

Birch 1997: Birch, Dinah, «A Life in Writing: Ruskin and the Uses of Suburbia», in: J.B. Bullen (Hg.), *Writing and Victorianism*, Harlow 1997

Birch 1999a: Birch, Dinah (Hg.), *Ruskin and the Dawn of the Modern*, Oxford 1999

Birch 1999b: Birch, Dinah, «Ruskin's Multiple Writing: *Fors Clavigera*», in: Birch 1999a

Bloom 1985: Bloom, Harald (Hg.), *Modern Critical Views: Walter Pater*, New York 1985

Bogdanovič 1900: Bogdanovič, L.A., *John Ruskin als Religions- und Schönheitsapostel (Джон Рёскин: «Апостол религии и красоты»)*, Moskau 1900

Boullée 1953: Boullée, Étienne-Louis, *Essai sur l'Art* (Hg. H. Rosenau), London 1953

Böhme 1989: Böhme, Hartmut, «Das Steinerne. Anmerkungen zur Theorie des Erhabenen aus dem Blick des 'Menschenfremdesten'», in: Christine Pries (Hg.), *Das Erhabene*, Weinheim 1989

Böhme 2000: Böhme, Hartmut, *Orientierung Kulturwissenschaft*, Reinbek 2000

Braegger 1979: Braegger, Carlpeter, *Das Visuelle und das Plastische. Hugo v. Hofmannsthal und die bildende Kunst*, Bern/München 1979

Braegger 1980: «Hofmannsthals *Briefe des Zurückgekehrten* und *Der junge Menzel*» , in: *NZZ*, «Literatur und Kunst», 15./16. März 1980

Braegger 1982: Braegger, Carlpeter, «'Die höchste Terrasse'. Baumetaphorik und Architektur-Fiktion bei Hugo von Hofmannsthal», in: ders. (Hg.), *Architektur und Sprache*, München 1982

Braegger 1995: Braegger, Carlpeter, «Dem Nichts ein Gesicht geben. Hofmannsthal und die künstlerische Avantgarde», in: Gerhard Neumann et al. (Hg.), *Hofmannsthal Jahrbuch zur europäischen Moderne* 3, Freiburg i. Brg. 1995

Brjunges 1902: Brjunges, G.J., *Ruskin und die Bibel (Рёскин и Библия: Кистории одной мысли)*, Moskau 1902

Broch 1974: Broch, Hermann, *Hofmannsthal und seine Zeit*, Frankfurt a. M. 1974

Broicher 1902: Broicher, Charlotte, *John Ruskin und sein Werk. Puritaner, Künstler, Kritiker*, Leipzig 1902

Brooks 1987: Brooks, Michael W., *John Ruskin and Victorian Architecture*, New Brunswick/London 1987

Buckley 1966: Buckley, Jerome Hamilton, *The Triumph of Time: A Study of the Victorian Concepts of Time, History, Progress, and Decadence*, Cambridge MA 1966

Bulgakov 1909: Bulgakov, S.N., «Soziale Weltanschauung John Ruskins» («Социальное мировоззрение Джона Рёскина»), in: *Woprosy filosofii i psichologii* 100 (1909), S. 395–436

Bullen 1995: Bullen, J.B., «Ruskin, Venice, and the Construction of Femininity», in: *Review of English Studies* 46 (1995), S. 502–520

Bunzen 1904: Bunzen, M.F., *Ruskin, sein Leben und seine Tätigkeit (Рёскин, его жизнь и деятельность)*, Sankt-Petersburg 1904

Burrow 1966: Burrow, J.W., *Evolution and Society: A Study in Victorian Social Theory* Cambridge 1966 (Reprint 1968)

Carlyle 1904–1905: Carlyle, Thomas, *The Standard Edition of Thomas Carlyle's Works*, 18 Bde., London 1904–1905

Carroll 1986: Carroll, David (Hg.), *The Clarendon Edition of the Novels of George Eliot*, Oxford 1986

Casillo 1986: Casillo, Robert, «The Stone Alive: Adrian Stokes and John Ruskin», in: *The Journal of Pre-Raphaelite Studies* VII (1986), S. 1ff.

Cate 1982: Cate, George Allen (Hg.), *The Correspondence of Thomas Carlyle and John Ruskin*, Stanford 1982

Chai 1990: Chai, Leon, *Aestheticism: The Religion of Art in Post-Romantic Literature*, New York 1990

Clark 1977: Clark, George Kitson (Hg.), vgl. Young 1936

Clark 1928: Clark, Kenneth, *The Gothic Revival: An Essay in the History of Taste* [1928], ³London 1962 (Reprint 1970)

Clark 1964: Clark, Kenneth (Hg.), *Ruskin Today* [1964], Harmondsworth 1967

Clemen 1900: Clemen, Paul, *John Ruskin*, Leipzig 1900 (Sonderdruck aus der *Zeitschrift für bildende Kunst*)

Collingwood 1903: Collingwood, W.G., *Ruskin Relics*, London 1903

Cook 1912: Cook, Sir Edward Tyas, *The Life of John Ruskin*, 2 Bde., ²London 1912

Cook/Wedderburn 1903–1912: Cook, Sir Edward Tyas/Wedderburn, Alexander (Hg.), *The Library Edition of the Complete Works of John Ruskin*, 39 Bde., London 1903–1912 (Erstausgabe: 1849)

Culler 1985: Culler, Dwight A., *The Victorian Mirror of History*, New Haven/London 1985

Curtius 1968: Curtius, Ernst Robert, «George, Hofmannsthal und Calderon», in: *H. v. Hofmannsthal, Wege der Forschung*, Bd. CLXXXIII, Darmstadt 1968

Dale 1977: Dale, Peter Allan, *The Victorian Critic and the Idea of History: Carlyle, Arnold, and Pater*, Cambridge MA/London 1977

Dalrymple 1823: Dalrymple, John, *An essay on landscape gardening*, Greenwich 1823

Daniels 1999: Daniels, Stephen, *Humphry Repton. Landscape gardening and the geography of Georgian England*, New Haven/London 1999

Darwin 1872: Darwin, Charles, *The Origin of Species by Means of Natural Selection* ..., ⁶London 1872 (Reprint London 1994)

Davis 1979: Davis, Fred, *Yearning for Yesterday: A Sociology of Nostalgia*, New York 1979

Dawson 1988: Dawson, John, *John Ruskin in Coniston*, Shropshire 1988

De Crescenzo 1985: De Crescenzo, Luciano, *Geschichte der griechischen Philosophie* [1983], Übersetzung Linde Birk, Zürich 1985

Dearden 1975: Dearden, James S., *John Ruskin and the Ruskin Museum at Coniston*, ²Bembridge 1975

Dearden/Thorne 1971: Dearden, James S./Thorne, K.G., *Ruskin and Coniston*, London 1971

Degen 1901a: Degen, E., «John Ruskin, Kunstvorlesungen, an der Universität Oxford im Jahre 1870 gehalten» («Лекции об искусстве, читанные в Оксфордском университете в 1870 году»), Rezension, in: *Mir božij* 2 (1901), S. 84–87

Degen 1901b: Degen, E., «John Ruskin, Moderne Maler» («Современные художники»), Rezension, in: *Mir božij* 9 (1901), S. 82–87

Degen 1904: Degen, E., «Volkskunst (J. Ruskin, L. Tolstoj, W. Morris)» («Всенародное искусство: [Дж. Рёскин, Л. Толстой, В. Моррис]»), in: *Mir božij* 3 (1904), S. 1–28; ebd., 4, S. 183–208

DeLaura 1969: DeLaura, David J., *Hebrew and Hellene in Victorian England: Newman, Arnold, and Pater*, Austin/London 1969

Demurova 1975: Demurova, N.M., *Vom literarischen Märchen im Viktorianischen England (О литературной сказке викторианской Англии)*, Moskau 1975

Dessoir/Muthesius 1912: Dessoir, Max/Muthesius, Hermann, *Das Bismarck-Nationaldenkmal. Eine Erörterung des Wettbewerbes*, Jena 1912

Dougherty 1982: Dougherty, Charles T., «A study of The Poetry of Architecture», in: Robert Rhodes/Del Ivan Janik (Hg.), *Studies in Ruskin*, Athen 1982

Dubinskij 1901: Dubinskij (Poltawskij), M.J., *Idealist des praktischen Jahrhunderts [Za druzeskoj besedoju] (Идеалист практического века)*, Sankt-Petersburg 1901

E.G. 1900a: E.G., «John Ruskin und seine Lehre» («Джон Рёскин и его учение»), in: *Russkij vestnik*, März 1900, S. 155–173; ebd., April 1900, S. 523–529

E.G. 1900b: E.G., «Ruskin über die Kunst» («Рёскин об искусстве»), in: *Živopisnoe obozrenie* 1 (1900)

Eliot 1871–1872: Eliot, George, *Middlemarch: A Study of Provincial Life*, London 1871–1872 (vgl. Carroll 1986)

Evans/Whitehouse 1953–1956: Evans, Joan/Whitehouse, John Howard (Hg.), *The Diaries of John Ruskin 1835–1847*, 3 Bde., Oxford 1953–1956

Everett 1994: Everett, Nigel, *The Tory View of Landscape*, New Haven/London 1994

Eysoldt/Hofmannsthal 1996: Eysoldt, Gertrud/Hofmannsthal, Hugo von, *Briefe*, Hg. Leonhard M. Fiedler, Salzburg/Wien 1996

Fergusson 1849: Fergusson, James, *An historical enquiry into the true principles of beauty in art, more especially with reference to architecture*, London 1849

Fergusson 1862: Fergusson, James, *A history of the modern styles in architecture*, London 1862

Finberg 1961: Finberg, Alexander Joseph, *The Life of J.M.W. Turner, R.A.*, [2]Oxford 1961

Fletcher 1985: Fletcher, Ian, «Walter Pater», in: Bloom 1985, S. 41–73

Gage 1987: Gage, John, *J.M.W. Turner: a Wonderful Range of Mind*, New Haven/London 1987

Gage 1993a: Gage, John, «Turner: the Architecture of Fancy», in: *Turner Society News* 64 (1993), August, S. 7–8

Gage 1993b: Gage, John, *Colour and Culture: Practice on Meaning from Antiquity to Abstraction*, London 1993

Gage 1994: Gage, John, «Questions of Tone: Turner's Theme and Ruskin's Exposition», in: *Harvard University Art Museums Bulletin*, Fall 1994

Gamble 1993: Gamble, Cynthia J., «Proust-Ruskin Perspectives on La Vierge Dorée at Amiens Cathedral», in: *Word and Image* 9 (1993), S. 270–286

Gamble 1997: Gamble, Cynthia J., «Proust Traducteur de *La Bible d'Amiens*», in: *Bulletin d'Informations Proustiennes* 28 (1997), S. 31–42

Garbett 1850: Garbett, Edward Lacy, *Rudimentary treatise on the principles of design in architecture as deducible from nature and exemplified in the works of the Greek and Gothic architects*, London 1850

Goreau 1974: Goreau, E.K., «Carlyle and Ruskin: The Private Side of the Public Coin», in: *Victorian Newsletter* 46 (1974), S. 15–19

Gropius 1923: Gropius, Walter, «Idee und Aufbau des staatlichen Bauhauses», in: Karl Nierendorf (Hg.), *Staatliches Bauhaus, Weimar 1919–1923*, Weimar/München 1923

Gurevič 1900: Gurevič, A., «John Ruskin als Schriftsteller, Politiker und Mensch» («Джон Рёскин как писатель, общественный деятель и человек»), in: *Žizn'* 4 (1900), S. 347–362

Gurlitt 1899: Gurlitt, Cornelius, *Die deutsche Kunst des neunzehnten Jahrhunderts. Ihre Ziele und Thaten*, Berlin 1899

Hagemann 1906: Hagemann, Carl, «Worte Ruskins», in: Carl Hagemann/Edgar Alfred Regener (Hg.), *Breviere ausländischer Denker und Dichter*, Bd. III, Minden 1906

Hamburger 1964: Hamburger, Michael, *Hugo von Hofmannsthal. Zwei Studien*, Göttingen 1964

Hamburger 1966: Hamburger, Michael, «Hofmannsthal und England», in: ders., *Zwischen den Sprachen. Essays und Gedichte*, Frankfurt a. M. 1966, S. 102–120

Handlin 1979: Handlin, Oscar, *Truth in History*, Cambridge MA/London 1979 (Reprint 1981)

Harris 1985: Harris, Anthony, *Why have our little girls large shoes? Ruskin and the Guild of St. George*, London 1985

Helsinger 1982: Helsinger, Elizabeth K., *Ruskin and the art of the beholder*, Cambridge MA 1982

Hewison 1976: Hewison, Robert, *John Ruskin: The Argument of the Eye*, London 1976

Hewison 1981: Hewison, Robert (Hg.), *New Approaches to Ruskin: Thirteen Essays*, London 1981

Hewison/Warrel/Wildman 2000: Hewison, Robert/Warrel, Ian/Wildman, Stephen, *Ruskin, Turner and the Pre-Raphaelites*, London 2000

Hilton 2000: Hilton, Tim, *John Ruskin: The Later Years*, New Haven/London 2000

Hobson 1899a: Hobson, J.A., *John Ruskin als Sozialreformer (Джон Рёскин как социальный реформатор)*, Moskau 1899

Hobson 1899b: Hobson, J.A., *Gesellschaftliche Ideale Ruskins (Общественные идеалы Рёскина)*, Sankt-Petersburg 1899

Hofmannsthal 1937: Hofmannsthal, Hugo von, *Briefe 1900–1909*, Wien 1937

Hofmannsthal 1946–1959: Hofmannsthal, Hugo von, *Gesammelte Werke in Einzelausgaben*, Frankfurt a. M. 1946–1959

Hofmannsthal 1979: Hofmannsthal, Hugo von, *Gesammelte Werke in zehn Bänden*, Frankfurt a. M. 1979

Hofmannsthal 1991: Hofmannsthal, Hugo von, «Erfundene Gespräche und Briefe», in: R. Hirsch et al. (Hg.), *Hofmannsthal, Sämtliche Werke, Kritische Ausgabe*, Frankfurt a. M. 1991

Hofmannsthal/Degenfeld 1986: Hofmannsthal, Hugo von/Degenfeld, Gräfin Ottonie, *Briefwechsel*, Hg. Marie Theres Miller-Degenfeld, Frankfurt 1986

Hofmannsthal/Dehmel 1979: Hofmannsthal, Hugo von/Dehmel, Richard, «Briefwechsel», in: Martin Stern et al. (Hg.), *Hofmannsthal-Blätter. Veröffentlichungen der Hugo von Hofmannsthal-Gesellschaft*, Heft 21/22, Frankfurt a. M./Heidelberg 1979

Hofmannsthal/George 1953: Hofmannsthal, Hugo von/George, Stefan, *Briefwechsel*, [2]München/Düsseldorf 1953

Hofmannsthal/Karg von Bebenburg 1966: Hofmannsthal, Hugo von/Karg von Bebenburg, Edgar, *Briefwechsel*, Frankfurt a. M. 1966

Hofmannsthal/Kessler 1966: Hofmannsthal, Hugo von/Kessler, Graf Harry, *Briefwechsel*, Hg. H. Burger, Frankfurt a. M. 1966

Hofmannsthal/Meier-Graefe 1998: Hofmannsthal, Hugo von, *Briefwechsel mit Julius Meier-Graefe*, Hg. Ursula Renner, Freiburg i. Brg. 1998

Hofmannsthal/Rilke 1978: Hofmannsthal, Hugo von/Rilke, Rainer Maria, *Briefwechsel*, Frankfurt a. M. 1978

Hofmannsthal/Strauß 1964: Hofmannsthal, Hugo von/Strauß, Richard, *Briefwechsel*, Hg. Willi Schuh, [3]Zürich 1964

Holloway 1953: Holloway, John, *The Victorian Sage: Studies in Argument*, London 1953 (Reprint New York 1965)

Home 1785: Home, Henry (Lord Kames), «Gardening and Architecture», in: *Elements of Criticism*, [5]Edinburgh 1785

Hough 1947: Hough, Graham, *The Last Romantics* [1947], University Paperbacks 18, London 1961

Houghton 1957: Houghton, Walter E., *The Victorian Frame of Mind 1830–1870*, New Haven/London 1957 (Reprint 1964)

Hubrich 1981: Hubrich, Hans-Joachim, *Hermann Muthesius. Die Schriften*, Berlin 1981

Hunt 1982: Hunt, John Dixon, *The Wider Sea: A Life of John Ruskin*, London/Melbourne/Toronto 1982

Hunt 1992: Hunt, John Dixon, «Sense and sensibility in the landscape design of Humphry Repton», in: *Gardens and the Picturesque. Studies in the history of landscape architecture*, Cambridge MA 1992, S. 139–169

Hunt 2000: Hunt, John Dixon, *Greater Perfections. The practice of garden theory*, London/Philadelphia 2000

Hunt 2001: Hunt, John Dixon, *The Picturesque Garden in Europe*, London 2001

Hunt/Holland 1982: Hunt, John Dixon/Holland, Faith M. (Hg.), *The Ruskin Polygon: Essays on the Imagination of John Ruskin*, Manchester 1982

Hunt/Willis 1988: Hunt, John Dixon/Willis, Peter (Hg.), *The Genius of the Place. The English Landscape Garden 1620–1820*, zweite erweiterte Auflage, Cambridge MA 1988

Istoričeskij vestnik 1900: «Der Tod Ruskins» («Смерть Рёскина»), in: *Istoričeskij vestnik*, März 1900, S. 1205 –1207

Istoričeskij vestnik 1902: «John Ruskin, Moderne Maler» («Современные художники»), Rezension, in: *Istoričeskij vestnik*, März 1902, S. 1145

I.M. 1901: I.M., «Technische Romantik als John Ruskins Utopie» («Технический романтизм, как утопия Джона Рёскина»), in: *Westnik wsemirnoj istorii* 9 (1901), S. 201–203

Jaeger 1959: Jaeger, Werner, *Paideia: Die Formung des griechischen Menschen*, 3 Bde., [4/3]Berlin 1959

Ježemesjačnye sočinenija 1901: «John Ruskin, Moderne Maler» («Современные художники»), Rezension, in: *Ježemesjačnye sočinenija* 10 (1901), S. 175

Kedenburg 1960: Kedenburg, Jürgen, *Teleologisches Geschichtsbild und theokratische Staatsauffassung im Werke Thomas Carlyles*, Heidelberg 1960

Kemp 1983: Kemp, Wolfgang, *John Ruskin 1819–1900: Leben und Werk*, München/Wien 1983

Kemp 1998: Kemp, Wolfgang, *John Ruskin. Ästhetik und Kunstphilosophie. Von der Antike bis zur Gegenwart in Einzeldarstellungen*, Stuttgart 1998

Kogan 1902: Kogan, P.S., *Philosoph des schönen Lebens [Pod znamenem nauki] (Философ красивой жизни)*, Moskau 1902

Koprоčevskij 1900: Koprоčevskij, D.A., «Der große Lehrer: Skizze des Lebens und des Werkes von John Ruskin» («Великий учитель: Очерк жизни и трудов Джона Рескина»), in: *Pedagogičeskij listok* 3 (1900), S. 330–341; ebd., 4, S. 460–475

Krasavčenko 1986: Krasavčenko, T.N., «F. Kirckhoff, *John Ruskin*, Boston 1984; und John Ruskin, *The critical heritage*, London 1984», Rezension, in: *RJ* 3 (1986), S. 108–113

Landow 1971: Landow, George P., *The Aesthetic and Critical Theories of John Ruskin*, Princeton/New York 1971

Langbehn 1890: (Langbehn, August Julius), *Rembrandt als Erzieher. Von einem Deutschen*, Leipzig 1890

Leatherbarrow 1985: Leatherbarrow, David, «Architecture and situation: a study of the architectural writings of Robert Morris», in: *JSAH* XLIV (1985), S. 48–59

Leatherbarrow 1993: Leatherbarrow, David, *The Roots of Architectural Invention*, Cambridge 1993

Leatherbarrow 2000: Leatherbarrow, David, *Uncommon Ground. Architecture, technology, and topography*, Cambridge MA 2000

Le Camus de Mézieres 1780: Le Camus de Mézieres, Nicolas, *Le Génie de l'Architecture, ou l'Analogie de cet art avec nos sensations*, Paris 1780

Lee 1981: Lee, Alan, «Ruskin and Political Economy: Unto this last», in Hewison 1981, S. 68–88

Leeds 1848: Leeds, W.H., *The orders and their aesthetic principles*, London 1848

Lerner 1972: Lerner, Laurence, *The Uses of Nostalgia: Studies in Pastoral Poetry*, London 1972

Levey 1978: Levey, Michael, *The Case of Walter Pater*, London 1978

Levin 1970: Levin, Harry, *The Myth of the Golden Age in the Renaissance*, London 1970

Lloyd 1966: Lloyd, Geoffrey Ernst Richard, *Polarity and Analogy: Two Types of Argumentation in Early Greek Thought*, Cambridge 1966 (Reprint: Bristol 1992)

Lorenz 2000: Lorenz, Dagmar, «Die gepanzerte Antimoderne. Literarische Zirkel im Zeichen der Moderne», in: *NZZ* 175 (29./30. Juli 2000), S. 67

Loris 1930: Loris (Hugo von Hofmannsthal), *Die Prosa des jungen Hofmannsthal*, Berlin 1930 (Nachwort von Max Mell)

Loudon 1837: Loudon, John Claudius (Hg.), *The Architectural Magazine*, London 1837 (Reprint London 1972)

Loudon 1840: Loudon, John Claudius (Hg.), *Humphry Repton, Sketches and Hints on Landscape Gardening*, London 1840 (Reprint: Farnborough-Hants (Hg.), London 1969)

Lovejoy 1927: Lovejoy, Arthur O., «'Nature' as Aesthetic Norm» [1927], in: *Essays in the History of Ideas*, New York 1960, S. 69–77

Lowenthal 1985: Lowenthal, David, *The Past is a Foreign Country*, Cambridge 1985 (Reprint 1988)

Macksey 1982: Macksey, Richard A., «Proust on the Margins of Ruskin», in: Hunt/Holland 1982

Maidment 1982: Maidment, Brian, «Interpreting Ruskin 1870–1914», in: Hunt/Holland 1982, S. 159–171

Mallett 1995: Mallett, Philipp, «The City and the Self», in: Michael Wheeler (Hg.), *Ruskin and Environment: The Stormcloud of the Nineteenth Century*, Manchester 1995

Mannheim 1936: Mannheim, Karl, *Ideology and Utopia: An Introduction to the Sociology of Knowledge*, Übersetzung Louis Wirth/Edward Shils, London 1936 (Reprint 1966)

Masaryk 1899: Masaryk, Tomáš Garrigue, *Die philosophischen und sociologischen Grundlagen des Marxismus. Studien zur socialen Frage*, Wien 1899

McGrath 1986: McGrath, Francis Charles, *The Sensible Spirit: Walter Pater and the Modernist Paradigm*, Tampa 1986

Meier-Graefe 1905: Meier-Graefe, Julius, *Der Fall Böcklin*, Stuttgart 1905

Meier-Graefe 1914: Meier-Graefe, Julius, *Der junge Menzel*, ²München 1914

Meynell 1940: Meynell Viola (Hg.), *Friends of a Lifetime: Letters to Sydney Carlyle Cockerell*, London 1940

Mill 1965: Mill, John Stuart, *Essays on Literature and Society*, Hg. J. Schneewind, New York 1965

Miller 1963: Miller, Hillis J., *The Disappearance of God: Five Nineteenth-Century Writers*, Cambridge Mass. 1963

Mir božij 1900: «John Ruskin. Nekrolog» («Джон Рёскин. Некролог»), in: *Mir božij* 2 (1900), S. 54

Monsman 1977: Monsman, Gerald, «Walter Pater», in: *TEAS* 207 (Boston 1977)

Mooter 1900: Mooter, P., «Ruskin», in: *Mir božij* 2 (1900), S. 55–58

Musil 1970: Musil, Robert, *Der Mann ohne Eigenschaften*, Hamburg 1970

Muthesius 1898: Muthesius, Hermann, «Italienische Reiseeindrücke», in: *Centralblatt der Bauverwaltung* 38, 17. September 1898, S. 446

Muthesius 1900: Muthesius, Hermann, *Die englische Baukunst der Gegenwart*, Leipzig/Berlin 1900

Muthesius 1900a: Muthesius, Hermann, «John Ruskin †», in: *Centralblatt der Bauverwaltung* 7, 27. Januar 1900, S. 43

Muthesius 1900b: Muthesius, Hermann, «Architektonische Zeitbetrachtungen. Ein Umblick an der Jahrhundertwende», in: *Centralblatt der Bauverwaltung*, Nr. 24, 28. März 1900, S. 145

Muthesius 1901: Muthesius, Hermann, «Ruskin in deutscher Übersetzung», in: *Centralblatt der Bauverwaltung*, Nr. 35, 4. Mai 1901

Muthesius 1902: Muthesius, Hermann, *Stilarchitektur und Baukunst. Wandlungen der Architektur im XIX. Jahrhundert und ihr heutiger Standpunkt*, Mühlheim-Ruhr 1902

Muthesius 1908: Muthesius, Hermann, *Das englische Haus. Band I. Entwicklung des Englischen Hauses*, Berlin 1908 [1904]

Muthesius 1909: Muthesius, Hermann, «Die 'Wiederherstellung' unserer alten Bauten», in: *Kultur und Kunst. Gesammelte Aufsätze*, Jena 1909 [1904]

Muthesius 1910: Muthesius, Hermann, *Das englische Haus. Band II. Bedingungen, Anlage, gärtnerische Umgebung, Aufbau und gesundheitliche Einrichtungen des englischen Hauses*, Berlin 1910 [1905]

Muthesius 1912: Muthesius, Hermann, «Wo stehen wir? Vortrag gehalten auf der Jahresversammlung des Deutschen Werkbundes in Dresden 1911», in: *Die Durchgeistigung der deutschen Arbeit. Jahrbuch des deutschen Werkbundes*, Jena 1912

Muthesius 1914: Muthesius, Hermann, «Leitsätze zum Vortrag von Hermann Muthesius», in: *Der Werkbundgedanke in den germanischen Ländern*, Jena 1914

Muthesius 1915: Muthesius, Hermann, «Die Zukunft der deutschen Form», in: *Politische Flugschriften*, fünfzigstes Heft, Hg. Ernst Jäckh, Stuttgart/Berlin 1915

Muthesius 1974: Muthesius, Stefan, *Das englische Vorbild. Eine Studie zu den deutschen Reformbewegungen in Architektur, Wohnbau und Kunstgewerbe im späten 19. Jahrhundert*, München 1974

Müsch 2000: Musch, Irmgard, *Geheiligte Naturwissenschaft. Die Kupfer-Bibel des Johann Jakob Scheuchzer*, Göttingen 2000

N.W. 1898: N.W., «Der soziale Ästhetiker» («Социальный эстетик»), in: *Knizki nedeli* 7 (1898), S. 5–28; ebd., 8, 1898, S. 45–70

Nadeždin 1900: Nadeždin, N.A., «John Ruskin und seine Theorie» («Джон Рёскин и его теория»), in: *Nowyj mir* 27 (1900), S. 51–53

Neville 1958: Neville, Sister Mary Eileen O.S.B., «The Function of the Concept of Organic Unity in the Writings of John Ruskin between 1857 and 1870», Diss. St. Louis University 1958; in: *Dissertation Abstracts* 20 (1959)

Newsome 1997: Newsome, David, *The Victorian World Picture: Perceptions and Introspections in an Age of Change*, London 1997

Nietzsche 1954: Nietzsche, Friedrich, *Werke in drei Bänden*, Bd. I, München 1954

Nikiforov 1896: Nikiforov, L.P., *John Ruskin: sein Leben, seine Ideen und seine Tätigkeit (Джон Рёскин: Его жизнь, идеи и деятельность)*, Moskau 1896

Niva 1900a: «John Ruskin. Nekrolog» («Джон Рёскин: Некролог»), in: *Niva* 5 (1900), S. 101–102

Niva 1900b: «John Ruskin, Kunstvorlesungen» («Лекции об искусстве»), Rezension, in: *Niva* 2 (1900), S. 426

Novikov 1984: Novikov, W.I., «Elizabeth K. Helsinger, Ruskin and the art of beholder, London/Cambridge 1982», Rezension, in: *RŽ* 5 (1984), S. 105–109

Novikov 1987: Novikov, W.I., «Tim Hilton, John Ruskin: The early years, New Haven/London 1985», Rezension, in: *RŽ* 2 (1987), S. 94–97

Novoe vremja 1900: F.B., «John Ruskin. Nekrolog» («Джон Рёскин: Некролог»), in: *Novoe vremja* 8575 (1900), S. 2–3

Novyj žurnal 1900a: «Aus dem Briefwechsel Ruskins und Rossettis» («Из переписки Раскина и Россетти»), in: *Novyj žurnal inostrannoj literatury* 5 (1900), S. 199–203

Novyj žurnal 1900b: «John Ruskin. Eine Biographie», in: *Novyj žurnal inostrannoj literatury*, Februar 1900, S. 330–335

Novyj žurnal 1901: «Rezension zu John Ruskin» («Джон Раскин»), in: *Novyj žurnal inostrannoj literatury* 10 (1901), S. 147–148

Oechslin 1984: Oechslin, Werner, «Natur und ihre Rückführbarkeit in Architektur», in: *Daidalos* 12 (1984), S. 44ff.

Oechslin 1999: Oechslin, Werner, «Politisches, allzu Politisches ...: 'Nietzschelinge', der 'Der Wille zur Kunst' und der Deutsche Werkbund vor 1914», in: *Moderne Entwerfen. Architektur und Kulturgeschichte*, Köln 1999

Oechslin 2002: Oechslin, Werner, «Das Ganze: Wege und Irrwege», in: *Scholion* 1 (2002), S. 19–51

O'Gorman 2000: O'Gorman, Francis, «Ruskin and the Pre-Raphaelite Imagination in the 1870s: Art, Politics and the Female Body», in: Robert Hewison (Hg.), *Ruskin's Artists: Studies in the Victorian Visual Economy*, Aldershot/Brookfield VT 2000

Ol'den-Uard 1900: Ol'den-Uard, M., *John Ruskin als Gesellschaftsreformer (Джон Рёскин как реформатор общества)*, Moskau 1900

Parchomenko 1984: Parchomenko, G.F., «R.E. Fitch, The poison sky: Mith and apocalypse in Ruskin, Athen/London 1982», Rezension, in: *RŽ* 1 (1984), S. 105–107

Pater 1910: Pater, Walter, *Appreciations: With an Essay on Style*; *The Works, New Library Edition*, 10 Bde., London 1910

Paul 1971: Paul, Jürgen, «Die Kunstanschauung John Ruskins», in: Helmut Koopmann/J. Adolf Schmoll gen. Eisenwerth (Hg.), *Beiträge zur Theorie der Künste im 19. Jahrhundert*, Frankfurt a. M. 1971

Pepper 1942: Pepper, Stephen, *World Hypotheses: A Study in Evidence*, Berkeley/Los Angeles/London 1942 (Reprint 1970)

Pevsner 1936: Pevsner, Nikolaus, *Pioneers of the modern movement. From William Morris to Walter Gropius*, London 1936

Pogodin 1898: Pogodin, A.L., «John Ruskin und der Schönheitskultus» («Джон Рёскин и культ красоты»), in: *Vestnik inostrannoj literatury* 9 (1898), S. 3–22

Polis 1966: Polis, T.W., «William Morris und John Ruskin» («Уильям Моррис и Джон Рёскин»), in: *Wissenschaftliche Abhandlungen der Aspiranten/-innen*, Bd. 5, Riga 1966, S. 105–135

Popper 1962: Popper, Karl Raimund, *The Open Society and its Enemies*, 2 Bde., 4London 1962 (Reprint 1963)

Pugin 1843: Pugin, A.W.N., *An apology for the revival of Christian architecture in England*, London 1843

Quander 1985: Quander, Georg, «Das Schweigen des Lord Chandos – eine musikdramatische Hommage à Hugo von Hofmannsthal», in: *Hofmannsthal-Forschungen*, Frankfurt a. M. 1985

Rawnsley 1901: Rawnsley H.D., *Ruskin and the English Lakes*, Glasgow 1901

Rehm 1960: Rehm, Walther, *Europäische Romdichtung*, 2München 1960

Reinhold 1801: Reinhold, C.L., «Einige Gedanken über die philosophischen Systeme überhaupt und insbesondere die Wissenschaftslehre», in: C.L. Reinhold (Hg.), *Beyträge zur leichten Übersicht des Zustandes der Philosophie beym Anfange des 19. Jahrhunderts, Zweytes Heft*, Hamburg 1801

Renner 2000: Renner, Ursula, *Die Zauberschrift der Bilder. Bildende Kunst in Hofmannsthals Texten*, Freiburg i. Brg. 2000

Repton 1795: Repton, Sir Humphry, *Sketches and Hints on Landscape Gardening*, London 1795

Riegl 1908: Riegl, Alois, *Die Entstehung der Barockkunst in Rom*, Wien 1908

Ritchy 1893: Ritchy, «Erinnerungen an Tennyson, Ruskin und Browning» («Воспоминания о Теннисоне, Рёскине и Броунинге»), in: *Mir božij* 4 (1893)

Röllin 1982: Röllin, Peter, «Steine und der Aufbau der 'Fremdenstadt'», in: *Unsere Kunstdenkmäler* XXXIII (1982)

Roque 1997: Roque, G., *Art et Science de la Couleur: Chevreuil et les Peintres, de Delacroix à l'Abstraction*, Nîmes 1997

Rosenberg 1963: Rosenberg, John D., *The Darkening Glass: A Portrait of Ruskin's Genius*, London 1963

Roth 2001: Roth, Fedor, *Hermann Muthesius und die Idee der harmonischen Kultur*, Berlin 2001

Rudolf 1972: Rudolf, Hermann, *Kulturkritik und konservative Revolution. Zum kulturell-politischen Denken Hofmannsthals und seinem problemgeschichtlichen Kontext*, Tübingen 1972

Ruskin 1837–1838: Ruskin, John (Kata Phusin), *The Poetry of architecture; or the architecture of the nations of Europe considered in its association with natural scenery and national character*, in: Cook/Wedderburn 1903–1912, I (1903)

Ruskin 1843–1860: Ruskin, John, *Modern Painters*, 5 Bde., London 1843–1860 (vol. I: 1843; vol. II: 1846; vol. III: 1856; vol. IV: 1856; vol. V: 1860)

Ruskin 1849: Ruskin, John, *The seven lamps of architecture*, London 1849

Ruskin 1851–1853: Ruskin, John, *The Stones of Venice*, Bd. 1: London 1851, Bd. 2: London 1853

Ruskin 1854: Ruskin, John, *Lectures on Architecture and Painting, delivered at Edinburgh in November 1853*, London 1854

Ruskin 1857: Ruskin, John, *The Art of Drawing; in three lectures to beginners*, London 1857

Ruskin 1886–1887: Ruskin, John, *Præterita. Outlines of Scenes and Thoughts perhaps worthy of memory in my past life*, 2 Bde., Sunnyside, Orpington, Kent 1886 (vol. I) und 1887 (vol. II)

Ruskin 1900: Ruskin, John, *Die sieben Leuchter der Baukunst*. Aus dem Englischen von Wilhelm Schoelermann, Leipzig 1900

Ruskin 1900a: Ruskin, John, *Kunst und Wirklichkeit. Ausgewählte Seiten (Искусство и действительность. Избранные страницы)*, Moskau 1900

Ruskin 1900b: Ruskin, John, *Der Kranz von Olivenzweigen. Vier Vorträge über Industrie und Krieg (Оливковый венок. Четыре лекции о промышленности)*, Moskau 1900

Ruskin 1900c: Ruskin, John, *Sesam und Lilien. Drei Vorlesungen (Сезам и лилии. Три лекции Джона Рёскина)*, Sankt-Petersburg 1900

Ruskin 1900/1905: Ruskin, John, *Vorträge über Kunst (Лекция об искусстве)*, Moskau 1900; Sankt-Petersburg 1905

Ruskin 1900–1904: *John Ruskin, Gesammelte Werke (Сочинения)*, übersetzt aus dem Englischen von D.P. Nikiforow, 1. Reihe, 10 Bde., Moskau 1900–1904

Ruskin 1902: Ruskin, John, *Florenzspaziergänge (Прогулки по Флоренции)*, Sankt-Petersburg 1902

Ruskin 1902–1912: *Ausgewählte Gedanken John Ruskins (Избранные мысли Джона Рёскина)*, Bd. 1, Moskau 1902; Bd. 2, Moskau 1912

Ruskin 1903 ff.: Ruskin, John, *Die Steine von Venedig*, übersetzt von Hedwig Jahn, Dresden 1903ff.

Ruskin 1904: Ruskin, John, *Der König des goldenen Flußes oder Die schwarzen Brüder (Король золотой реки, или Чёрные братья)*, Sankt-Petersburg 1904

Ruskin 1905a: *John Ruskin, Gesammelte Werke (Сочинения Джсона Рёскина)*, 2. Reihe, Moskau 1905

Ruskin 1905b: Ruskin, John, *Für einen Geburtstag. Gedanken für jeden Tag (На день рождения. Мысли на каждый день)*, Sankt-Petersburg 1905

Ruskin 1906a: Ruskin, John, *Pre-Raphaelitism & Other Essays & Lectures on Art* (Vorwort von L. Binyon), London 1906

Ruskin 1906b: Ruskin, John, *Diesem Letzten! Vier Abhandlungen über die ersten Grundsätze der Volkswirtschaft (Последнему, что и первому)*, Moskau 1906

Ruskin 1907: Ruskin, John, *Die Kunst zu lesen. Arbeit.* Nach dem Original übertragen von Johanna Severin, Halle a.S. 1907

Ruskin 1911: Ruskin, John, *Moderne Maler (Современные английские стилисты)*, Moskau 1911

Ruskin 1985: Ruskin, John, «Unto this Last and other Writings», in: *Penguin Classics*, Hg. Clive Wilmer, Harmondsworth 1985

Ruskin 1986: Ruskin, John, *La Bible d'Amiens*, Übersetzung, Kommentar und Vorwort von Marcel Proust, Paris 1986

Ruskin 1994: Ruskin, John, *Steine von Venedig*, Bd. 2, Dortmund 1994

Russkaja mysl' 1895: «John Ruskin, König des goldenen Flusses» («Царь золотой реки»), Rezension, in: *Russkaja mysl'* 7 (1895), S. 347–354

Russkaja mysl' 1901: «John Ruskin, Sesam und Lilien» («Сезам и лилии»), Rezension, in: *Russkaja mysl'* 7 (1901), S. 2–10

Russkaja mysl' 1905: «John Ruskin, Ausgewählte Gedanken» («Избранные мысли»), Rezension, in: *Russkaja mysl'* 3 (1905), S. 104

Russkie vedomosti 1902: «John Ruskin, Dorfblätter» («Сельские листья»), Rezension, in: *Russkie vedomosti*, 2. März 1902

Russkoe bogatstvo 1901a: «Ruskins Werke» («Сочинения»), Rezension, in: *Russkoe bogatstvo* 9 (1901), S. 45–50

Russkoe bogatstvo 1901b: «Spaziergänge in Venedig» («Прогулки по Флоренции»), Rezension, in: *Russkoe bogatstvo* 3 (1901), S. 17–19

Rybakova 1976: Rybakova, N.J., *Ruskin und D. Galsworthys Ästhetik (Д. Рёскин и эстетика Д. Голсуорси)*, Gorkij 1976

Rykačev 1903a: Rykačev, A., «John Ruskin und die politische Ökonomie» («Джон Рёскин и политическая экономия»), in: *Mir božij* 10 (1903), S. 91–109; ebd., 11, S. 82–97; ebd., 12, S. 80–102

Rykačev 1903b: Rykačev, A., «Die Freude für alle Zeiten und ihr Marktpreis oder Die politische Ökonomie der Kunst» («Радость на веки и её рыночная цена, или политическая экономия искусства»), in: *Mir božij* 2 (1903), S. 103–106

Savarenskaja 1988: Savarenskaja, T.F., «Venedig in Ruskins Augen» («Венеция глазами Рёскина»), in: *Kunst in Venedig und Venedig in der Kunst*, Moskau 1988

Sawyer 1985: Sawyer, Paul L., *Ruskin's Poetic Argument: The Design of the Major Works*, Ithaca/London 1985

Sawyer 1990: Sawyer, Paul, «Ruskin and the Matriarchal Logos», in: Thaïs E. Morgan (Hg.), *Victorian Sages and Cultural Discourse: Renegotiating Gender and Power*, New Brunswick/London 1990, S. 129–141

Schirrmacher 1996: Schirrmacher, Frank, *Die Stunde der Welt. Fünf Dichter – Ein Jahrhundert. George, Hofmannsthal, Rilke, Trakl, Benn*, Berlin 1996

Schlechta 1960: Schlechta, Karl (Hg.), *Friedrich Nietzsche, Werke*, 3 Bde., [2]München 1960

Schumacher 1902: Schumacher, Fritz, «John Ruskin, der Apostel der modernen englischen Kunstbewegung», in: *Im Kampfe um die Kunst*, Strassburg 1902 [1899]

Schwartz 1996: Schwartz, Frederic J., *The Werkbund: Design Theory and Mass Culture before the First World War*, New Haven/London 1996

Šustova 1981: Šustova, S.P., *Literarische Kritik und Publizistik J. Ruskins und das Schicksal seines Erbes in Russland (Литературнохудожественная кримика и публицистика Джона Рёскина и судьба его наследия в России)*, Diss. Moskau 1981

Selitrina 1988: Selitrina, T.L., «Von den typologischen Ähnlichkeiten der ästhetischen Anschauungen L. Tolstojs und J. Ruskins» («О типологических схождениях эстетических взглядов Л. Толстого и Д. Рёскина»), in: *Traditionen und Wechselbeziehungen in der ausländischen Literatur des XIX.–XX. Jahrhunderts*, Perm' 1988

Shapiro 1971: Shapiro, Harold I., «*The Poetry of Architecture*: Ruskin's preparation for *Modern Painters*», in: *Renaissance and Modern Studies* XV (1971), S. 70–83

Shrimpton 1999: Shrimpton, Nicholas, «Ruskin and the Aesthetes», in: Birch 1999a, S. 131–151

Sitwell 1909: Sitwell, Sir George, *On the making of gardens*, London 1909

Sizéranne: Sizéranne, Robert de la, «Ruskin et la Religion de la Beauté» («Рёскин и религия красоты»), in: *Mir božij*, 1, S. 62–86; ebd., 2, S. 91–115; ebd., 3, S. 189–216; ebd., 9, S. 164–182; ebd., 10, S. 73–96; ebd., 11, S. 54–73; ebd., 12, S. 177–195

Spear 1984: Spear, Jeffrey L., *Dreams of an English Eden: Ruskin and his Tradition in Social Criticism*, New York 1984

Spicyna 1987: Spicyna, L.W., «M. Hardman, Ruskin and Bradford: An experiment in Victorian cultural history, Manchester 1986», Rezension, in: *RŽ* 3 (1987), S. 101–103

Stamm 1997: Stamm, Ulrike, *Ein Kritiker aus dem Willen der Natur. Hugo v. Hofmannsthal und das Werk Walter Paters*, Würzburg 1997

Steffen 1902: Steffen, Gustav F., «John Ruskin. Eine biographische Skizze», in: *England als Weltmacht und Kulturstaat*, Stuttgart 1902

Stein 1975: Stein, Richard L., *The Ritual of Interpretation: The Fine Arts as Literature in Ruskin, Rossetti, and Pater*, Cambridge MA/London 1975

Stein 1985: Stein, Richard L., «Milk, Mud, and Mountain Cottages: Ruskin's Poetry of Architecture», in: *PMLA* 100 (1985), S. 328–341.

Stern 1971: Stern, Martin, «Über Hofmannsthals Pseudonym 'Loris'», in: Martin Stern et al. (Hg.), *Hofmannsthal-Blätter. Veröffentlichungen der Hugo von Hofmannsthal-Gesellschaft*, Heft 8/9, Frankfurt a. M./Heidelberg 1971

Stern 1974: Stern, Martin, «Hofmannsthals Wirklichkeit», in: *Hofmannsthal-Forschungen* II, Freiburg i. Brg. 1974

Stillinger 1971: Stillinger, Jack (Hg.), *John Stuart Mill, Autobiography*, London/Oxford 1971

Stoddart 1998: Stoddart, Judith, *Ruskin's Culture Wars: Fors Clavigera and the Crisis of Victorian Liberalism*, Charlottesville/London 1998

Stokes 1978: Stokes, Adrian, «The Stones of Rimini», in: *Critical Writings*, Bd. 1, London 1978

Streiter 1913: Streiter, Richard, «Das deutsche Kunstgewerbe und die englisch-amerikanische Bewegung», in: ders., *Ausgewählte Schriften zur Aesthetik und Kunstgeschichte*, München 1913

Super 1960–1976: Super, R.H. (Hg.), *The Complete Prose Works of Matthew Arnold*, 11 Bde., Ann Arbor 1960–1976

Svjatlovskij 1900: Svjatlovskij, W.N., «John Ruskin und seine Ideen des Humanismus in der Sphäre der wirtschaftlichen Beziehungen» («Джон Рёскин и его идеи гуманизма в сфере экономических отношений»), in: *Narodnoe chozjajstwo* 2 (1900), S. 56–69

Swenarton 1989: Swenarton, Mark, *Artisans and Architects. The Ruskinian Tradition in Architectural Thought*, London 1989

Taganov 1989: Taganov, A.N., «Proust und Ruskin» («Пруст и Рёскин»), in: *Ausländische Literatur: Methodenprobleme*, Bd. 3, Leningrad 1989

Tanner 1992: Tanner, Tony, *Venice Desired*, Oxford 1992

Taut 1919: Taut, Bruno, *Alpine Architektur*, Hagen 1919

Tavener 1898: Tavener, L., «John Ruskin: Dichter, Maler und Reformer» («Джон Рёскин: Поэт, художник и реформатор»), in: *Žurnal žurnalov* 5 (1898), S. 416–420

Tillotson 1978: Tillotson, Geoffrey, *A View of Victorian Literature*, Oxford 1978

Tišunina 1990: Tišunina, N.W., «Die Transformation der romantischen Ideen in den ästhetischen Anschauungen John Ruskins und der Präraffaeliten» («Трансформация романтических идей в эстетических взглядах Джона Рёскина и прерафаэлитов»), in: *Modifikation der Kunstsysteme im gesellschaftlich-literarischen Prozeß*, Swerdlowsk 1990

Toliver 1971: Toliver, Harold E., *Pastoral Forms and Attitudes*, Berkeley/Los Angeles/London 1971

Tolstoj 1928–1958: Tolstoj, Lew Nikolajewitsch, *Gesamtausgabe in 90 Bänden* (*Полное собрание сочинений. Юбилейное)*, Moskau/Leningrad 1928–1958

Tolstoj/Ruskin 1898: Ruskin, John, *Die Erziehung. Das Buch. Die Frau* (*Воспитание. Книга. Женщина)*, mit einem Vorwort von Lew Tolstoj, Moskau 1898

Toulmin/Goodfield 1965: Toulmin, Stephen/Goodfield, June, *The Discovery of Time* [1965], Chicago/London 1977

Tourneur 1898: Tourneur, Ch.E., «Das Leben und die Lehre John Ruskins» («Жизнь и учение Джона Раскина»), in: *Novyj žurnal inostrannoj literatury* 7 (1898), S. 1–11; ebd., 8, S. 118–130; ebd., 9, S. 210–217

Uglow 1973: Uglow, Jennifer (Hg.), *Walter Pater, Essays on Literature and Art. Everyman's University Library*, London 1973

Uhlig 1986: Uhlig, Claus, «Conceptual Architecture in Nineteenth-Century Writing», in: *Comparative Literature Studies* 23 (1986), S. 218–233

Ulke 1980: Ulke, Karl-Dieter, *Agnostisches Denken im Viktorianischen England*, Freiburg/München 1980

Umanov-Kaplunovskij 1901: Umanov-Kaplunovskij, «Kritische Betrachtungen: Von Ruskin und Repin» («Критические заметки: О Рёскине и Репине»), in: *Sever* 18 (1901), S. 567–572

Unrau 1981: Unrau, John, «Ruskin, the Workman and the Savageness of Gothic», in Hewison 1981, S. 33–50

Van de Velde 1955: van de Velde, Henry, «Ruskin und Morris. Aus einem im Januar 1898 in Brüssel gehaltenen Vortrag», in: ders., *Zum neuen Stil.* Aus seinen Schriften ausgewahlt von Hans Curjel, Munchen 1955

Vengerowa 1900: Vengerowa, Sinaida, «John Ruskin» («Джон Рёскин»), in: *Vestnik Evropy* 6 (1900), S. 674–692

Vestnik inostrannoj literatury 1898: «Ein englischer Kunsthistoriker, Moralist und Dichter: John Ruskin» («Английский художественный критик, моралист и поэт Джон Рёскин»), in: *Vestnik inostrannoj literatury* 3 (1898), S. 329–333

Vestnik inostrannoj literatury 1900: «John Ruskin» («Джон Рэскин»), in: *Vestnik inostrannoj literatury*, Februar 1900, S. 330–335

Viljoen 1971: Viljoen, Helen Gill (Hg.), *The Brantwood Diary of John Ruskin Together with Selected Related Letters and Sketches of Persons Mentioned*, New Haven/London 1971

Viollet-le-Duc 1863–1872: Viollet-le-Duc, Eugène, *Entretiens sur l'architecture*, Bd. 1: Paris 1863; Bd. 2: Paris 1872

Virchow 1858: Virchow, Rudolf, *Johannes Müller. Eine Gedächtnissrede, gehalten bei der Todtenfeier am 24. Juli 1858 in der Aula der Universität zu Berlin*, Berlin 1858

Vschody 1902: «John Ruskin, Der König des goldenen Flußes» («Царь золотой реки»), Rezension, in: *Vschody* 9 (1902)

Warrell 1995: Warrell, Ian, *Through Switzerland with Turner*, London 1995

Wedgwood 1900: Wedgwood, Julia, «Erinnerungen an John Ruskin» («Воспоминания Юлии Веджвуд о Джоне Рёскине»), in: *Mir božij* 4 (1900), S. 56–57

Weichelt 1902: Weichelt, Hans, *John Ruskin und die Freude*, Zschopau 1902

Wellek 1965: Wellek, René, *A History of Modern Criticism 1750–1950, III: The Age of Transition*, New Haven/London 1965 (Reprint 1972)

Werckmeister 1961: Werckmeister, Otto K., «Hofmannsthal über van Gogh», in: *Neue deutsche Hefte* 84 (1961), S. 40–60

Whately 1770: Whately, Thomas, *Observations on Modern Gardening*, London 1770

Wheeler 1999: Wheeler, Michael, *Ruskin's God*, Cambridge 1999

Whitehouse 1920: Whitehouse, J. Howard, *Ruskin the Prophet and other Centenary Studies*, London 1920

Whiteley 1992: Nigel Whiteley, «'Falsehood in a Ciceronian dialect'? The 'Ruskinian' tradition, Modernism, and the rise of the classical tradition in contemporary architecture», in: Michael Wheeler/Nigel Whiteley (Hg.), *The lamp of memory. Tradition and architecture*, Manchester/New York 1992

Williams 1958: Williams, Raymond, *Culture and Society, 1780–1950*, London 1958 (Reprint 1967)

Williams 1973: Williams, Raymond, *The Country and the City*, London 1973

Young 1936: Young, G.M., *Portrait of an Age: Victorian England* [1936], Hg. George Kitson Clark, London/New York 1977

The Old Dover Packet's Jib.
«In gallant trim the gilded vessel goes»,
Frontispiz von John Ruskin, *Praeterita* II, London 1887